Charged

Charged

*How the Police Try to
Suppress Protest*

Matt Foot and
Morag Livingstone

VERSO
London • New York

First published by Verso 2022
© Matt Foot and Morag Livingstone 2022
Foreword © Michael Mansfield 2022
Contains public sector
information licensed under the common open licence

1 3 5 7 9 10 8 6 4 2

Verso
UK: 6 Meard Street, London W1F 0EG
US: 388 Atlantic Avenue, Brooklyn, NY 11217
versobooks.com

Verso is the imprint of New Left Books

ISBN-13: 978-1-83976-249-9
ISBN-13: 978-1-83976-252-9 (US EBK)
ISBN-13: 978-1-83976-251-2 (UK EBK)

British Library Cataloguing in Publication Data
A catalogue record for this book is available from the British Library

Library of Congress Cataloging-in-Publication Data

Names: Foot, Matt, author. | Livingstone, Morag, author.
Title: Charged : how the police try to suppress protest / Matt Foot, Morag
  Livingstone.
Description: First hardback edition. | Brooklyn, NY : Verso Books, 2022. |
  Includes bibliographical references and index.
Identifiers: LCCN 2021060201 (print) | LCCN 2021060202 (ebook) | ISBN
  9781839762499 (hardback) | ISBN 9781839762529 (ebk)
Subjects: LCSH: Police brutality – Great Britain. | Police misconduct – Great
  Britain. | Protest movements – Great Britain.
Classification: LCC HV8195.A3 F66 2022 (print) | LCC HV8195.A3 (ebook) |
  DDC 363.20941 – dc23/eng/20220112
LC record available at https://lccn.loc.gov/2021060201
LC ebook record available at https://lccn.loc.gov/2021060202

Typeset in Fournier by MJ & N Gavan, Truro, Cornwall
Printed and bound by CPI Group (UK) Ltd, Croydon, CR0 4YY

Contents

Foreword by Michael Mansfield QC   vii

Introduction: Secrets and Lies   1

Part I. Maggie Thatcher's Boot Boys
1. The Guinea Pig: The *Messenger* Printers,
   Warrington, 1983   13
2. Maggie's UK War: The Miners, Orgreave, 1984   39
3. Boot Boys in the Beanfield: The Battle of
   Stonehenge, 1985   67
4. Murdoch's Paper Boys: Wapping, 1987   81
5. The Tinderbox: Anti–Poll Tax Protest, 1990   107

Part II. Major: Back to Basics
6. The Trap: Welling Anti-racist Protest, 1993   131
7. A Succession of Repetitive Beats: Battle of
   Park Lane, Criminal Justice Act, 1994   157

Part III. New Labour: Tough on Crime

8. The Commissioner's Kettle: May Day Protest, 2001   179
9. Barriers to Protest: G8 Summit, Gleneagles, 2005   191
10. The MP's Kettle: G20 Protest, 2009   211

Part IV. Austerity Justice

11. Charged: Student Fees Protest, 2010   233
12. State of Play   255

Acknowledgements   271
Notes   273
Index   311

Foreword

Be warned. This carefully researched book shocks and alarms. Never has such a work been more necessary. If you thought you knew, you don't. If you thought you were safe, you aren't. And if you thought you could leave it to others – you can't.

The 'it' is one of the core values of our diminishing democracy – the ability, the right, the freedom to gather together in a public space in order to express collectively a statement about issues which are of concern. This is a broader concept than the oft-cited right to peaceful protest, because it is one of the few ways in which solidarity and community can share a common purpose or cause.

Not everyone wishes to exercise this right until they realise, suddenly, it's no longer there when it matters most. It might make sense therefore to read this piece as an afterword rather than a foreword, because that is where we're at right now. This book's singular narrative unravels, step by step, the incremental erosion of freedoms, and the duplicity and determination of successive governments to suppress the perceived threat posed by public demonstration. There is but one inevitable and inescapable conclusion: that the treasured sentiments in the preceding paragraph constitute no more than lip service in the mouths of authority, and worse are at the point of extinction.

This is no vacuous hyperbole.

The British approach, at least domestically, has been a slow burn. Small, focused changes and empowerments, secreted in among a myriad of other criminal justice proposals, a bit here and a bit there. Always justified by so-called exigencies of the moment. The coronavirus legislation provides a recent fine example of how peaceful protest imperceptibly vanishes. Not far behind is the Police Crime Sentencing and Courts Bill 2021. Once again, the preface to this bill contains the routine ritual mantra:

> Protests are an important part of our vibrant and tolerant democracy. Under human rights law, we all have the right to gather and express our views.

It will surprise no one that there is a massive 'BUT' which comes after this quote, which cites the element of disruption, and then suggests that the police do not always 'strike the right balance', sometimes tipping 'too readily in favour of protesters when – as is often the case – the police do not accurately assess the level of disruption caused, or likely to be caused, by a protest'.

Such an observation is surreal – demonstrators being treated favourably!

Tell that to Alfie Meadows, the student who suffered serious head injuries in December 2010 from a police truncheon when he was on a tuition fees demonstration. Police injured dozens of others along with him with many more trapped on Westminster Bridge in dangerous and freezing night-time conditions by a deliberate police manoeuvre to humiliate and intimidate during a 'kettling' exit strategy.

Tell that to those suffering head injuries in Bristol in 2021 during a protest against the new bill.

Or the women taking part in a vigil on Clapham Common after the death of Sarah Everard.

Or those who stood in solidarity with the 2020 Black Lives Matter movement. Or the others you will meet within the pages of this book.

The rationale and justification for draconian change, therefore, is a grotesque distortion. Instead, it is entirely consistent with a general approach by government ministers who have no regard for the truth.

Once you turn your attention to the 2021 proposals themselves, seen as they now can be against the background of pre-existing powers, policies and practices clearly set out in this book, it becomes abundantly obvious that we are indeed witnessing the near extinction of the right to protest and are close to seeing the views of the protesters criminalised as well.

Put as bluntly as possible, the bill embraces a much wider ambit for the exercise of police powers to restrict processions, marches and assemblies. Failure to comply with a police order will constitute an offence, providing you knew about it or – more ominously – ought to have known, rendering you liable to imprisonment of up to ten years.

Following a series of votes in the House of Lords against sections of the bill, it was returned to the House of Commons. The government's aim has been to introduce prohibitive conditions that can be imposed where a senior officer considers that the 'noise' generated 'may' result in serious disruption to the activities of an organisation in the vicinity, and 'may' have a relevant 'significant impact on people in the vicinity'. 'Significant impact' is assessed by a senior officer in terms of whether it 'may' result in intimidation or harassment, or 'may' cause serious 'unease alarm or distress'. It does not require a rocket scientist to work out the extraordinarily subjective, discretionary predictive judgements that will be made by police in these circumstances. Are we to understand that the only acceptable demonstration is one that can barely be seen and certainly not heard!

The whole point of a public display of views is to be heard, to raise awareness, and to gather solidarity and support. It will necessarily cause some disturbance, some annoyance, some inconvenience and some unease. Change has never been effected by silence, let alone by the silent majority preferred by successive governments. Nor by the very quaint British tradition of careful containment at Speakers' Corner, Hyde Park.

The real agenda, now unashamedly writ large, is to ensure that any effective public expression is so circumscribed that not even a single voice gets much of a chance.

Fortunately, in June 2021 the Supreme Court thought differently, overturning an appeal by the director of public prosecutions, and acquitted arms fair protesters who had obstructed the highway. This finding recognised the fast-diminishing freedom of the lawful and reasonable excuse of exercising their freedom of speech and assembly under articles 10 and 11 of the European Convention on Human Rights and had a beneficial impact on a large number of other protest cases.

In 2020 an unprecedented number of Extinction Rebellion activists were arrested in relation to climate crisis protests. In the region of 600 over five days. This was complicated by the coronavirus regulations. In coordinated actions, campaigners blocked roads and glued themselves to immovable objects as had those at the arms fair. The prosecuting authorities have a discretion not to prosecute even if an evidential threshold has been crossed if prosecution is deemed not in the public interest. But in relation to the protest cases, there is a clear determination, as demonstrated in the arms fair instance, to carry on, and many more than 600 were processed for court. However, after the Supreme Court decision, a judge at the Old Bailey, HHJ Mark Dennis QC, who had overturned some convictions following a series of appeals at the beginning of August 2021, required the prosecuting authorities to review all remaining cases involving road blockages and the defence of lawful excuse. This too is a refreshing pause in the headlong onslaught by politically driven dogma.

Given that a home secretary already has the power to authorise a ban on processions anyway, this latest legislative tool just about sews things up.

In large measure that is the story of this book. A personal story for me, having had the opportunity and the privilege to represent citizens who have suffered injustice themselves, or that of others, but nevertheless have not forsaken that need to demonstrate. The first protest case I took on concerned the death of a student on an anti-fascist march on 19 June 1974. He was a student at Warwick University. Kevin Gately was killed in Red Lion Square. The march was intended to counter the National Front, who were planning to assemble in Conway Hall in the Square to object to the amnesty for illegal immigrants. He died from a brain haemorrhage caused by a heavy blow to the head. It was not established at the inquest nor by an inquiry into the event by Lord Scarman how this came about. The Square is relatively small, and Kevin had linked arms at the front of the march. There was no suggestion that he was other than peaceful. The police had drawn truncheons and deployed officers on horseback.

Five years later in April 1979 a teacher, Blair Peach, also died on an anti-fascist demonstration, also against the National Front. He died from a blow to the head. This was not admitted for many years, until the death of Ian Tomlinson, again from a blow to the head in 2009 from a member of the Territorial Support Group, which succeeded the Special Patrol Group. This led to the release of a police report into Blair's death, which had been compiled some years before. Essentially it was accepted that he had died at the hands of a member of the SPG.

Alongside these examples and almost at the same time, I became acutely aware of an even harder form of policing being practised in the North of Ireland. The Ballymurphy massacre in August 1971 resulted in the deaths of entirely innocent civilians shot by Paratroopers who were acting in support of the Royal Ulster Constabulary as a civil power. The findings by the coroner, Mrs Justice Keegan, in the recently held inquests into their deaths, were published in May 2021. Among the dead were a priest and a mother of eight children, both of whom went to the aid of the dying.

Six months later in January 1972, the Bogside massacre, better known as Bloody Sunday, resulted in another fourteen innocent deaths at the hands of British paratroopers, as the Saville inquiry (1998–2010) determined. More were shot and wounded helping others. This arose in response to a protest against the introduction of internment without trial. Fifteen thousand civilians attended a civil rights march and assembly organised by the Northern Ireland Civil Rights Association. The Stormont Government had placed a ban on such protests. The speakers at the rally, Lord Fenner Brockway and Mid Ulster MP Bernadette Devlin, also came under fire. Not a single soldier has so far been disciplined or prosecuted to conviction.

What became clear during the inquiry was that the nature of the policing and the tactics being practised upon the civilian population were derived from anti-insurgency measures which had played out in a colonial context. In Aden, Hong Kong, Kenya, Malaya, Bahrain, Cyprus, popular movements were viewed as a threat to established order. They were suppressed with paramilitary force. A key figure was Brigadier Frank Kitson, who authored 'low intensity' operations and was a brigade commander in Belfast between 1970 and 1972. According to General Mike Jackson, present on Bloody Sunday and a witness at the Bloody Sunday inquiry, as well as at Ballymurphy and the recent inquests, Kitson 'very much set the tone for the operational style in Belfast'.

The importance of these events has a bearing on the general development of paramilitary-style policing in the UK, particularly in relation to mass protests and demonstrations – notably the establishment of specialist police squads like the SPG and the TSG. The most dramatic exposé of this is the eyewitness testimony as well as the film shot and recorded by miners about events during the 1984 strike, which involved regular gatherings and rallies. I have used *The Battle for Orgreave* by Vanson Wardle Productions on talks and lectures, particularly at police colleges. People need to see the shocking scenes of mounted police charging into crowds of miners trapped in a field and the snatch squads, brutal truncheon assaults, and the aggressive use of shields, which caused many injuries, some lifelong. Margaret Thatcher would reward police for their oppression of the miners in 1984 by her support for police who traduced Liverpool fans at Hillsborough in 1989.

In London in 1986/7 similar policing was deployed against print workers protesting in Wapping about job losses. I witnessed it first-hand as I had helped establish a legal observers' group to monitor and record police activity. We were clearly visible in yellow jackets and worked in pairs – one observing and the other recording by camera and notebook. Not that the police, especially mounted, took a blind bit of notice.

Even more insidious is the Special Demonstration Squad, which existed between 1968 and 2008. An unaccountable state

within a state, undercover, using false documentation and infil-
trating perfectly lawful campaign groups and families considered
to be subversive. This is now the subject of a public judicial
inquiry (the Undercover Policing Inquiry, or the Pitchford
Inquiry). This inquiry in turn was the product of incessant pressure applied by the family of Stephen Lawrence upon the then
home secretary Theresa May, because of their belief that corruption lay at the heart of the police investigation and that there had
been police infiltration into their family associations.

At the same time and in tandem with these developments has
been the ever-increasing strictures on processions and assemblies
via enactments and regulation.

So, it cannot possibly be believed that things have steadily
been tipping in favour of the protester.

At the end of the day, it is down to us not them. I will cite
Shelley's 'The Masque of Anarchy', his response to the Peterloo massacre: 'Ye are many they are few.' It is the power of the
people not the people in power that matters most.

Michael Mansfield QC
Nexus Chambers
November 2021

Introduction: Secrets and Lies

The 2020 Black Lives Matter demonstrations brought into general consciousness the notion that history is often presented through a prism. As a result of their efforts we know the true character of statues dominating public space, representing those whom some people thought we should immortalise – slave-owners. Across the UK, school curriculums changed with a wider view of black history now incorporated in lessons.

The airbrushing of history is prevalent in other areas of our society too, not least in protest. In this book we look at how the police were empowered to deal with protesters after the Brixton riots of 1981. We selected and investigated the large-scale protests that turned violent after the introduction of a new secret police manual. During this period there were other protests that were just as important for the causes they progressed; however, they either did not turn violent or were not on the same scale. Through the mass protests selected we can see how institutions have attempted to deal with separate groups of committed people protesting against racism, job losses and draconian laws, or for environmental protection.

The records from archives and libraries, academic analysis, journalists, campaigners and authors, and the generosity of eye-witnesses, have provided a wealth of information, which we have done our best to analyse and piece together. Considering these protests collectively, rather than just as individual events, widens our understanding of public order policing to reveal the true character of the state.

The book attempts to tell the conflicted history of the relationship between the police and protesters based on the information we could gather that confirms that the public face of the state differs from its private approach to protest. Through personal accounts we can better understand the impact not just on the individual but also on the ability to freely protest.

In January 1983, Willie Whitelaw, Conservative home secretary, hosted a celebration party at the Home Office. Whitelaw was a shrewd man with 'disarming charm' who had held a number of UK government positions under prime ministers Heath and Thatcher.[1] He toasted the completion of a new secret manual for the policing of public disorder.

Invited guests numbering around two dozen included members of the Association of Chief Police Officers and Home Office staff. Many were part of a working group seconded from police forces across England and Wales who had worked privately over months to create the manual. Whitelaw congratulated everyone there. After expressing his delight at meeting them and hearing about their work, he added,

> None of us wants to see public disorder. Your aim, and my firm policy, is to see 'normal policing' as the preferred tactic. But the police have the duty to be capable, if necessary, of dealing with disorder firmly and effectively. You have made an important

contribution to this, for which I am sure the service as a whole will be grateful. And I suggest that we now return to our conversation, and our glasses.[2]

The *Public Order Manual of Tactical Options and Related Matters* covered all forms of public disorder and was considered 'outstanding' work by the Association of Chief Police Officers (ACPO). A Home Office official endorsed it with a note: 'May the force be with them.'[3] Unprecedented military-style tactics for the policing of public order were now formally available to the police. Given the manual's contents it was classified at the last minute – which meant only senior police officers of ACPO rank were ever officially allowed to see it.

The secret manual first came to light in 1985 at the trial of a number of miners arrested at a mass picket at Orgreave, South Yorkshire, during the miners' strike, when thousands of police with horses and truncheons took on nearly as many miners. Assistant Chief Constable Anthony Clement, the officer responsible on the day, stated in evidence that he was following a police manual that 'deals with all Police tactics in relation to the control of large and hostile crowds'.[4] Michael Mansfield, a barrister for the defence, immediately sought disclosure. This was resisted but the judge directed that some pages be provided. These covered public order operational tactics available to the police and included the use of arrest squads, decoys and mounted police, and the deployment of shields and truncheons.

The contents angered Tony Benn MP, who sought an immediate debate in Parliament on the manual, which had never been discussed by MPs. Benn was highlighting that potentially unlawful police tactics had been endorsed without Parliament's knowledge. He asserted that the manual was 'in clear contravention of the rules that have hitherto governed the actions of police forces ... officers had been given instructions which laid them open to charges of assault'.[5] His request was denied, but Benn won permission to place the pages in the House of Commons Library.

In the UK's devolved police structure, responsibility for operational decisions sits with individual chief constables. In the 1980s, police forces operated at the behest of their local police authority, who held the purse strings, represented their communities and expected their police force to do the same. Gareth Peirce, a human rights solicitor, who defended a number of the miners after Orgreave, wrote following the collapse of the trial that 'the testimony of all the police officers at the Orgreave trial indicated that, unilaterally, senior police officers have rewritten the law and are acting upon it.'[6]

New 'rules' on the policing of protest in the UK were seen as necessary following riots across the UK in the early 1980s. The spread of riots in St Pauls in Bristol, Toxteth in Liverpool and Brixton in London all started following incidents of oppressive policing within the black community.[7] The issue of what type of police force was required had reached a crossroads.

Two days after the rioting ended, Whitelaw commissioned Lord Scarman to carry out an inquiry. Lord Scarman had something of a liberal reputation as a chair of previous inquiries of disorder, although as a judge he upheld a blasphemy conviction against *Gay News*, and stopped the Greater London Council's 'Fares Fair' low-cost public transport policy. Scarman's report on the 1981 riots primarily encouraged greater community policing. Whitelaw, having instituted the report, publicly supported Scarman's liberal recommendations, which he described as 'a statement of philosophy and direction for the future'.[8]

Recently declassified documents reveal that, at the same time, the Home Office instigated the development of new military-style tactics assisted by a new hard-line leader of ACPO, Kenneth Oxford.[9] Privately, therefore, senior Home Office officials were collaborating with senior police officers to undermine the Scarman report. This crucial shift in public order policing redefined what amounted to reasonable force by the police. It opened the door for the police to go beyond a 'traditional method of policing'. As ACPO said, such a 'fundamental change would inevitably lead to erosion of the current image and acceptability' of the police service.[10]

Whitelaw told Parliament in 1983 that the police were 'independent officers of the Crown. That is because the powers with which we invest police officers should be exercised without fear or favour and without political interference.'[11] This was an extraordinary statement by a home secretary who had simultaneously endorsed a new secret police manual – an example of political interference that changed the landscape of how the police deal with protest. Home Office involvement in the manual has never been fully disclosed.

ACPO looked outside Great Britain for inspiration for the new public order policing methods. They found a presentation by the Royal Ulster Constabulary insufficient for the methods they sought. Instead ACPO turned to colonial practices from an officer from Hong Kong, who presented the Hong Kong manual at ACPO's annual conference, and they 'took it eagerly to heart'.

The Hong Kong method of crowd control, described by its own police commissioner as 'paramilitary', was written to cover 'the arts of suppression of public disorder'.[12] These practices provided the main inspiration for ACPO's secret police manual. The 'snatch squad' section was a direct lift of that used by the British colonial police. As Gerry Northam stated in his excellent book *Shooting in the Dark*, 'The stage was set for the most significant shift in police strategy Britain had known for a century and a half, but nothing was made public. The preparations were carried out in total secrecy.'[13]

While ACPO were looking to colonial Hong Kong, the Home Office were also reassessing how to deal with public disorder, part of which 'might be the law itself'.[14] In developing the common minimum national standards in public order training recommended by Scarman, they too embraced the opportunity to increase police powers.

Consideration of the expansion of training is set out in a recently declassified Home Office file from 1982. It confirms the state's belief that where there is a 'clash of wills or opposing interests' and where there are people with a 'cause' that is 'anti-establishment', then 'conflict, violence and force' will follow. It concludes in addition to a 'persuasive deterrent of lawful force there should also be ... additional police kept in the background to support the lawful force being used'. To develop this approach, they posed a question: 'Can these requirements be reasonably assured or improved within our accepted and traditional, if adjusted, concept of policing?'[15] The Home Office appeared to be using mandarin-type language to say, can we extend police powers dramatically while pretending to deal with civil disorder in an 'accepted and traditional' manner?

The hypocrisy of Home Secretary Whitelaw publicly welcoming the Scarman report while secretly creating brutal police methods was mirrored by the senior police. Their overriding police principle was asserted by Commissioner Sir Kenneth Newman, that every constable should 'be and be seen to be, unfettered by obligation, deciding each issue without fear or favour, malice or ill-will'.[16] This principle is incorporated in the police oath. We are constantly assured that the police are neutral and independent and that no one is above the law. However, what happened in 1983 was anything but. ACPO knew they were assisting the Conservative home secretary in a secret deal. Newman was the most senior officer in post when the new rules were instituted. In 1968 he was part of the policing of the infamous Grosvenor Square anti–Vietnam War protest and subsequently carried out a review of that police operation. By the time he became commissioner in 1982, Newman would have knowledge of another similar secret undemocratic decision taken by the most senior police and senior politicians. In 1968 a Special Demonstration Squad (SDS) was started within the Metropolitan (Met) Police comprising twelve undercover officers who embedded themselves within the anti-war movement. From these origins the SDS morphed into the spy cops scandal that became subject to the Undercover Policing Inquiry forty years later. Both the 1983 manual and the SDS were central to how protest would be policed. While we ostensibly live in a parliamentary democracy, Parliament had no knowledge of or involvement in either of these decisions.

Lord Scarman dealt with the future policing of riot by focusing on community engagement. The manual encompassed a much wider approach. From 1983 protesters were potentially subject to brutal tactics, in a manual that had been devised, developed and approved not solely by ACPO, as the general public have since been led to believe, but in conjunction with the Home Office privately. Once secretly sanctioned by the home secretary, what impact would new tactics have, not just on protest but on the UK police and the democratic governance of successive governments?

Through papers released by the National Archive, thirty years after the event, we now know that a cabal within the Home Office were aware at the time of the significance of the manual with its new 'rules'. Lord Elton, the parliamentary under-secretary of state for home affairs, was worried what would happen if 'the fact ever becomes public'.[17] He nevertheless carried on with the process and confirmed that he and the home secretary were 'content'.[18] Lord Elton had already scripted these words for his home secretary in case the manual came to light:

> The Home Secretary has very much in mind the operational independence of each chief officer of police; he notes the clear recognition given in the manual to their responsibility to take every possible step to avoid arriving at a position where any of the measures described in it have to be used and he is glad to see the way in which A.C.P.O. makes clear the extreme positions under which the more drastic measures open to them are to be used.[19]

Lord Elton appeared to be protecting the home secretary from the inevitable use of the 'drastic measures' that they had just endorsed. The protests described in this book highlight the fact that the police took their chance. Elton needed to protect the home secretary because Whitelaw had just sanctioned the Home Office and the police's creation of draconian tactics on a sliding scale that included the use of dogs, riding police horses into a static crowd, using shields and truncheons to 'incapacitate' people just for being there, using rubber baton rounds and CS gas, and driving police vehicles at a crowd. None of this had received the 'reassessment' of the law or parliamentary scrutiny that such a dramatic change to public order policing deserved.[20]

The sinister activities in the back rooms of the Home Office in 1982–3 provided the senior police with a comfort blanket. From that point forward they knew that their new powers not only had the seal of approval from the home secretary, but also had been instigated by his department, no doubt for his own political ends. The police had been given licence to prioritise these powers over Scarman's recommendations for more liberal policing. This secret collaboration raised questions for the protests that followed. Had the police been let off the leash? If so, what was left for dissent? And who did this police force serve?

Part I.
Maggie Thatcher's Boot Boys

1

The Guinea Pig

The Messenger *Printers, Warrington, 1983*

We started off with this little regional newspaper dispute and it's turned into this monster.

Alan Royston, one of the 'Stockport Six'

Undeterred, he has fought on alone.
How much the establishment voices have steered clear of him ...
though the Institute of Directors officials have been in touch.
Sunday Times on Eddy Shah, 4 December 1983

At 3:40 a.m. on 30 November 1983, the police shouted to television crews to 'turn off the lights'. They complied immediately. No lights. No filming. No television record of events. The remaining journalists then left to go home.

The police charged and everyone ran. A woman was escorted by the police and thrown into a deep ditch at the side of the road. Colin Bourne, the National Union of Journalists (NUJ) northern organiser, recalls,

The riot police then charged at least three times ... people were terrified ... screaming, people were running away ... at least a thousand people ... Some of them then ran in the fields ... the fields were in total darkness and there were large ditches ... the ground was extremely wet ... people were running away and falling over ... police were running up to them and kicking them and hitting them with their batons, even though they were already on the ground.

Two police Range Rovers drove 'at high speed into the pickets'.[1]

The 'use of vehicles to disperse a riotous crowd' was authorised by the *Public Order Manual of Tactical Options and Related Matters*.[2] It includes fifteen different tactical uses of vehicles that could be deployed with support from police on foot to use 'in close support situations or for dividing crowds there is a risk of serious injuries occurring. The option may also attract adverse criticism'.

Forty years on, Colin Bourne, now an employment barrister, recalls this event clearly: 'They turned and started driving forwards, coming towards us over the rough terrain. Their engine noise was very high.' To Bourne it felt like they were 'driving very fast in low gear, driving at us, people were running ... quite terrifying'.

Alan Royston worked at the *Stockport Messenger* as a paste-up artist/typesetter and senior shop steward. He was 'pasting up' the 11 June 1983 edition of the *Messenger* as he had done every week for years. 'There was a gap in the paper. So I asked, "Where's this advert?" I was handed it and stuck it in. I looked at it, "that's an advert for our jobs!"' He and fellow workers walked out in protest. They were promptly dismissed.

The *Messenger* was one of six free newspaper titles operated by the maverick entrepreneur Eddy Shah.[3] Educated for a time at Gordonstoun, the boarding school attended by Prince Charles, he was suspended twice.[4] He worked as a floor manager on *Coronation Street*, before he was allegedly sacked. After working on the *Manchester Evening News*, Shah identified an opportunity in the south-west of Manchester as being ripe for a new free sheet newspaper.[5] He raised the finance by selling his house and with backing from a Manchester businessman.

Considered a friendly employer, he had negotiated agreements with the National Graphical Association (NGA) print union and in the past agreed on 100 per cent trade union membership (which was known as a closed shop, a common practice at the time).

Shah asked the NGA to help him establish his new business, including sourcing suitably qualified workers. Welcoming the expanding business, the union negotiated a good agreement. However, Shah opened another typesetting plant at Bury, Greater Manchester, using non-union labour to produce the pages. Tony Burke, then president of the Stockport NGA branch, recalls, 'We went to negotiate and he flatly refused.' Shah began moving work and copy between Stockport and Bury. In the second half of 1983, Alan's life moved onto the picket line with five of his fellow workers who had all been sacked. They were dubbed the 'Stockport Six'. For months they stood on a raised roundabout across from his former place of work, often with his wife Sue and kids in support. They looked directly into the third-floor office of owner Eddy Shah, who, Alan recalls, 'used to sit in his big swivel chair and stick two fingers up and make another rude gesture'. Back at home, while Alan was on the picket line, Sue had to get up throughout the night to answer 'vile' telephone calls. As she recalls, 'most were silent, but one person claimed to be Shah himself.'

At Shah's new plant in Warrington the printing presses rolled two nights a week and the union would try and stop or delay delivery vans leaving the factory by blocking their exit with a mass of bodies. The union wanted to force Shah back to the negotiating table by disrupting his new business venture, to end the dispute and re-employ the Stockport Six. In response to the increase in numbers of pickets at Warrington, Shah sought injunctions against the NGA, and won.

Under the Conservative government's newly introduced employment laws the picket at the *Messenger* offices in Stockport was legal because it was picketing at the place of work where the dispute arose, but picketing at Shah's new plant in Warrington was not. By transferring work away from Stockport Shah effectively forced a secondary picket, which was illegal under the new employment laws.

At Warrington the numbers of pickets supporting the Stockport Six increased week on week. In mid-November, suspicious they were being spied upon by police informants, Colin Bourne briefed pickets in small groups, each of whom had to know each other. A purchase of forty lengths of rope was passed around. Pickets wrapped them over the arms, through their sleeves and round their backs to make an immovable force. That night the rope was slipped out to the pickets and Shah's vans were stopped. The pickets were happy, the police less so.

Shah continued to exploit his options in court. In parallel, negotiations continued. The union thought they had reached agreement with Shah over the weekend of 26–7 November. However, on Monday, 28 November, Shah unexpectedly withdrew the agreement, introducing a more hard-line offer. He then refused to meet in person to discuss next steps. The NGA wondered if something had gone on behind the scenes, and responded by calling for a mass demonstration on 29 November 1983, at Warrington.

Numbers were expected to be high as, the week before, a court had sequestrated 'everything of value belonging to the NGA'.[6] The dispute thus became more than getting the six their jobs back, or having a closed shop; it was about resisting unfair trade union laws and the very future of the union. The application of these new laws galvanised trade union support and escalated a local dispute into a national concern for all unions, including an immediate response from trade unions based on Fleet Street and in Manchester to down tools. No national newspapers were produced over the weekend of 26–7 November 1983.

Shah held a press conference inside the Warrington factory in front of a bank of cameras. He and about a dozen staff, six private security guards and two dogs had sufficient food, video games and beds to hold out for 'a week-long siege'.[7] He described the union's tactics as an example of 'mob rule' and said the union needed to apply the equivalent of military force to stop him distributing his papers.[8]

On Tuesday, 29 November, television and print media travelled to Warrington and stationed themselves across the road from the picket. Deputy Chief Constable Graham reported to the Home Office at 5 p.m., '40 pickets' and '60 press and TV people'. The police were ready; over 1,400 police officers were to attend.[9]

One of the industrial units had been transformed into a temporary police operational command centre. The huge, well-organised facility included catering for 2,000 officers, caged cells capable of holding thirty to forty people, a control room with three video monitors connected to rooftop night cameras, and large photographs of the Stockport Six alongside key trade union officials with a sign saying 'Do not arrest'. Two trade union stewards tried to investigate, only to be told by the police that it was a designated 'no-go area'.[10]

At 5:30 p.m. Alan returned to spend the night at Warrington. He found a mass influx of police, as forty police vans and four coachloads arrived and a few thousand pickets were all trying to keep warm on a 'bloody cold' night.[11] The NGA van, which the *Economist* described as resembling a 'travelling grocer's shop', was parked, as it had been for the last few weeks, within the picketing area.[12] Despite appearances the van was fitted with cutting-edge communications technology used for making announcements to direct pickets and coordinate with trade union officers on walkie-talkies. This was useful in an industrial estate of this kind where business units impeded the line of sight.

Reggae, Bob Dylan and other music played out of large speakers to keep up the spirits of the pickets until the distribution vans tried to leave at 5 a.m. NGA national officer George Jerrom, Colin Bourne and others stood on a makeshift stage in front of the van using a microphone, enabling running commentary mixed with humour. The pickets responded with cheers to announcements of new arrivals of trade unionists from around the country.

Tony Dubbins speaking from the NGA van at the Warrington picket, 1983.

© Stefano Cagnoni/reportdigital.co.uk

Meanwhile, lines of police, three deep, stood with their backs
to Shah's production works. As murmurs of conversation and
singing echoed off the walls; rumours of a delivery to the factory changed the mood and pickets surged against the police.
One picket, Richard Dixon-Payne, a teacher, said the 'pressure
was enormous ... pressure mounted all the time as the police
forced the picketers back and the picketers tried to stand firm'.[13]
Directed by those on the NGA microphone, they linked arms and
successfully pushed the police back against the door of Shah's
factory.[14] The door bent. People were banging on the side of the
factory, adding to the noise inside.

The police re-formed their line and pushed pickets back
towards the NGA van. In line with the new public order tactics
manual, officers formed a wedge with two or three people at the
front and increasing numbers behind. As Colin Bourne recalls,
there was 'an enormous noise as large columns of policemen
were marched in. A disciplined force, so it was easy for them to
push people out of the way using a wedge formation ... we were
never going to be as disciplined as they were.' The police easily
created a gap in the pickets, allowing other police to divide the
pickets into even smaller groups over a number of hours. There
were calls of 'We shall not be moved' and, likely for the first time,
'Maggie Thatcher's boot boys'.

BBC *Newsnight* reported live from the scene just after 11 p.m.
that despite a 'big crush of people' there was

> no particular violence ... There is a huge number of police and
> there is a limit to what they (the pickets) can do ... Someone in the
> crowd has just said they haven't resorted to any violence whatso-
> ever and I think that's true. The problem is when you have 1,000
> to 2,000 people pushing. Everyone is singing and it was like a New
> Year's Eve party and then suddenly there were some of the ugliest

scenes since Grunwick and at least two people were taken away by ambulance.[15]

The police did not let the ambulance through. They only moved to allow Shah's armoured Land Rover carrying the printing plates into the factory. This was particularly galling as, the week before, the union leaders had ensured that the pickets stepped back to allow an ambulance through for a policeman who was injured when a wall collapsed, which was accepted as an accident.

On 29 November, due to the unexpected number of pickets, the union suggested to the police that Shah delay the paper until the crowds died down. Senior police promised to put this to Shah and report back in about half an hour, but never returned. The police did relay the offer to Shah, who rejected it.[16] What the police did next was a shock to many.

They started clearing the slip road that connected the plant to the main road. NGA officials with walkie-talkies reported that police were running at the crowd, pushing people south into the area that the press had set up. Directions to stand firm came from the NGA van.

Alan Royston stood, with several thousand others, near the van. There was obvious tension. At midnight many from the Fleet Street unions arrived. The police had blocked the M62 motorway to stop them but they had walked the last stretch. As midnight passed, police numbers in the forecourt built rapidly. About twenty policemen broke away from the main line of police and descended on the NGA van with a senior officer.[17]

A policeman declared, 'That's enough, I'm having no more of this.' He grabbed the microphone and roughly manhandled a national officer of the union, Johnny Ibbotson, off the platform.

Police at the mass picket in support of
striking NGA members at Warrington, 1983.

The police managed to get control of the van. Communications
with the crowd were cut off. Loudspeakers were torn away from
their stands and thrown into a nearby skip. It was discovered
the next morning that the wires had been cut. On the other side
of the forecourt, police continued to push pickets back. Eyewit-
nesses say that from an area called 'the Kop' across the road from
the main picket a few missiles were thrown by onlookers that hit
both police and pickets, and the pickets screamed at them to stop.

Just after the van was taken over by the police, the Stockport
Six found each other nearby – someone suggested it was time
for them to go home to avoid being arrested. On the way out a
Press Association reporter stopped them for a quick chat. Alan
Royston explained, 'We'd been on the picket line at Stockport
and Warrington for 18 hours so it was time to go home. The next
day our words were misinterpreted to "we'd had enough" and
our addresses, which we did not share, appeared in a national
newspaper.'[18] As they left, there were new arrivals from around
the country with estimates of up to 4,000 pickets.

Police who were standing on the slip road leading to Shah's factory suddenly parted. Riot police with batons drawn charged towards the main road. Pickets were pushed back against the industrial unit and into the ditch beside it. They fought back, or ran. Some of the media's cameras were smashed.[19] Owen Granfield, a magistrate, had just arrived and saw people running and jumping over the cars, 'Fear in their faces from whatever they were running from.'

Richard Dixon-Payne had left the main picket as the pressure of numbers had become too much. He saw the police, 'violently tearing people from the picket and trying to force themselves through. These people then emerged after being punched and kicked through a gap at the end of the line of police next to us.'[20] Having gained the hillock for themselves, the police then stopped. They secured their victory by forming an arc of men across the T-junction, between two units.

The helmets of riot police were highlighted by the television camera lights as they marched into the main forecourt grunting in time to their steps. Then there was a stand-off, and some sporadic throwing of missiles as police snatch squads darted into the crowd to pull people out and arrest them. Owen Granfield witnessed an organised group of around fifty police officers, 'into which pickets dragged from the crowd were thrown and beaten', hidden from view.[21]

Dixon-Payne remembers, 'Suddenly the riot police were on top of us, striking out wildly in all directions. I was grabbed and snatched out of the crowd by two riot police. One said, "we've got you now."'

Robert Clay MP saw, at close quarters, 'a very large number of people who were not causing a disturbance ... I saw the police using riot shields, riot helmets and batons attempting to clear a path through those people which led to a number of them being injured ... I was not surprised to learn that some people were reported to have suffered broken ribs and broken arms. The police handling was very very rough.'[22]

Dixon-Payne was arrested for conduct likely to cause a breach of the peace. He remembers that the police said they were taking him 'away from the press and the cameras, behind the buildings away from the crowd. Glad to be still in one piece, I made no resistance. They were pushing my arms up behind my back so I couldn't move. But then of course the police officer on my right-hand side had a free arm and he was able to punch me in the face. They just punched me. They said, "Nobody's seen this. We can do what we like to you now."'

In Richard's statement for his lawyer he recorded the policeman 'hit me with great force in the face breaking my nose and causing a great cascade of blood which poured down me. I let out a scream ... Some police were walking towards us ... Their response was to jeer at me by saying in unison, "We didn't see a thing mate, we didn't see a thing."'[23]

Singing brought the crowd back from the brink of anger. The pickets were still confident they could block Shah's delivery vans from leaving. Chanting interspersed the singing. An uneasy peace with occasional crowd surges continued. With newspaper deadlines looming a number of the media left. Others repositioned themselves at the back of a raised bed that the police now occupied. From there, at 2:30 a.m., an officer announced through a handheld megaphone, 'start departing now and stop causing a breach of the peace – or suffer the consequences.'[24] Over the next hour, the snatch squads continued their work.

The media had apparently observed instructions from the police not to enter the 'no-go' area (including the temporary police headquarters) and not to be 'too overbearing' with their lights.[25]

At 3:40 a.m. a crowd with their backs to the police were
entertaining each other with a rendition of 'Auld Lang Syne'.
Suddenly, there was a cry from the police to the media to turn
out their lights. The darkness filled with the sound of boots followed by screams as riot police charged into the crowd, chasing
the pickets. Colin Bourne remembered, 'they drove at high speed
at us in Range-Rovers ... lights on full ... I ran like hell. I don't
know why you do this but when something is driving at you, you
run away from it. I twisted my ankle and veered to the right to get
back to the tarmac [forecourt] I didn't think the vehicles would
follow there. It was terrorism. It was designed to terrorise those
people who were there. It could have had no other purpose.'

In the aftermath of that night, the NGA lodged a number of
complaints against the police. After two years the reply from
the police claimed 'the order to the *Granada* Television crew
to switch off their lights was not taken to prevent them filming
the actions of the police but because they considered the lights
were dazzling and making them targets for missile throwers'.[26]
Home Office documents confirm that Deputy Chief Constable
Graham reported that television crews were *in situ* at 5 p.m. At
the end of November it would have already been dark and any
filming required lights. It was curious, therefore, that it was over
ten hours later, when most of the media had left to meet their
filing deadlines, that the police ordered television lights to be
switched off.

There were very few media reports of the period between 2:30
a.m. and 5 a.m. when the pickets had been cleared and the newspaper vans were successfully driven out of Shah's factory to their
distribution points. The *Guardian* reported, without mentioning
the time,

At one point, patrols in Land-Rovers chased pickets across a rough field at the back of the Stockport Messenger Group's works while squads wearing helmets with visors, padded jackets and leggings, and carrying batons and shields pushed groups of pickets as far back as the hard shoulder of the nearby M62 motorway.[27]

The *Financial Times* reported,

The police's physical underpinning of the law outside the Messenger plant ... was breathtaking in its efficiency and toughness. Senior officers have not been crowing in public but they were clearly pleased with the operation ... Some of the tactics [were] ... introduced after the 1981 riots ... They clearly shocked and surprised many union officials ... charges by the riot-trained police were highly effective in driving the pickets back.[28]

The police, politicians and journalists blamed the pickets for the violence. Whitelaw's successor as home secretary, Leon Brittan, described the mass picket as 'organised anarchy'.[29] In his book *Full Disclosure* Andrew Neil wrote that 'there was precious little peaceful picketing and something very close to riotous assembly'.[30] The official figures that night were eighty-six arrests, almost all for causing a breach of the peace or wilful obstruction. On the afternoon of 30 November, the home secretary reported in the House of Commons (and via Lord Elton in the House of Lords), 'Twenty-three officers were injured and three have been detained in hospital ... none appears to have been seriously injured. Thirteen pickets are recorded as having been injured, one of whom remains in hospital. Again I understand that his condition is not serious.'[31] Observers from the National Council of Civil Liberties (the forerunner to Liberty) counted over 100 civilians injured. A full inquiry was sought on the policing but refused.[32] The number of injured pickets was clearly considerably higher than the government figure given that the pickets had travelled from all over the country and returned to their localities.

In the Commons, Conservative MP Mr Fergus Montgomery asked,

> In view of the claims that the pickets are not responsible for violence, will my right hon. and learned Friend explain why so many policemen have been injured? Have they been hitting each other, or were these self-inflicted wounds? What is happening outside the printing works at Warrington is disgraceful and a breach of the law.[33]

On the final sentence, he may not have been wrong.

On the night, Owen Granfield, who had just witnessed the Range Rovers driven at pickets, was on his way home listening to a BBC Radio 4 report blaming the pickets for the violence. He called in and, as a magistrate, was given space to explain what he had seen. His local paper picked up the story, where he expanded: 'We were attacked without reason, and vehicles were driven straight at us. Many injured pickets would not go [to] hospital ... out of fear of arrest. The NGA's dispute is a civil matter. What the police were doing was criminal ... the picket itself was provoked by ... Shah.'[34]

So how did Eddy Shah gain such immense support from the police? He had made much of being a small businessman up against an all-powerful union. He claimed to be a man without friends in high places, who ran his own show and took advice from no one. The *Sunday Times* repeated this theme, 'Undeterred, he has fought on alone,' reiterating 'how much establishment voices have steered clear of him ... though the Institute of Directors officials have been in touch'.[35] Yet by the middle of December 1983 he had taken on and beaten one of the UK's strongest unions.

When Shah entered the dispute, he already had support from Fergus Montgomery MP. Montgomery had introduced Shah to the prime minister at a party on 14 October 1983, and behind the scenes Shah asked Montgomery for help with policing because of 'the danger ... faced'.[36] How long Thatcher and Shah spoke for is not known. Shah said it was a 'Hello, goodbye situation'. 'I don't even know if she really got my name ... I don't think she even knew about it [the dispute] to be honest with you.'[37] When the meeting came to light, it inspired a heated exchange in the Commons with the leader of the opposition, Neil Kinnock.

Shah was the first and only person at the time to have put Thatcher's new employment legislation to the test. The day Shah met Thatcher was the very same day that he won two injunctions under her new laws. A copy of the judgment is in the prime minister's Industrial Policy file of November 1983 marked 'Secret'.[38]

Throughout the dispute, Shah complained to a sympathetic media of the danger he and his staff were in at the factory and at home. Police reports to the Home Office, however, include no such events, attacks or break-ins. A report from the Home Office based on information from the police stated that 'the pickets' main tactic' has not been 'to use violence, but to try to stop vehicles entering or leaving the premises by sheer 'weight of numbers'.[39]

The Institute of Directors (IOD) spoke to the Home Office, repeating Shah's claim that 'petrol bombs were thrown.'[40] In response, 'the police say that reports that missiles were thrown at officers are wrong' and 'police clearly do not trust [redacted] whose reaction they regard as unpredictable.'[41]

On Friday, 25 November, in response to Shah's successful request to sequestrate NGA funds, a wildcat walkout of trade union members stopped the national newspapers and support for the local dispute spread throughout the country. Andrew Neil, the new editor of the *Sunday Times*, telephoned Shah. The call started 'Hello, Mr Shah ... You don't know me ... and thanks to you I won't have a paper this weekend.' Shah apologised, telling Neil that 'the London establishment had largely shunned him.'[42] Neil and Shah exchanged numbers and talked regularly over the next few days. Tony Burke, president of the NGA Stockport branch, recalls, 'Suddenly new harder lines were drawn' by Shah that meant the Stockport Six could not return to the *Messenger*.

On the Monday, at the Home Office morning briefing, the home secretary, Leon Brittan, reported a conversation 'with a journalist over the weekend who said he had information suggesting that there might be as many as 5,000 pickets in attendance at the plant' and raised the question of 'personal protection for [redacted] in the light of an alleged fire bomb attack on his home'.[43] No one appears to have questioned Shah, or asked the police about this claim. The home secretary said that he wished for his staff to tell the chief constable of Cheshire, George Fenn, that the rights of Shah and those who wished 'to go about their lawful business there should be maintained'. The home secretary expressed 'his complete support for the chief constable in carrying out that responsibility', including increasing logistical support that would allow the police to take 'anticipatory action to keep the area around the plant clearer'. This support was set

> against the legal background that sheer weight of [protester] numbers could itself constitute intimidation and of a recognition of past operational experience which suggested that once

pressure of numbers built up to a certain point the ability of the
police to maintain control over access to premises was inevitably
circumscribed.[44]

Was this a reminder to a chief constable (about to retire)
that the police were beaten in 1972 at Saltley coke depot near
Birmingham? Back then, 15,000 pickets overwhelmed the police
and the chief constable in charge ordered closure of the depot.

The home secretary expanded, 'if, notwithstanding this explicit
support, things went badly wrong as a result of the failure of the
Chief Constable [Fenn] to take appropriate action, he would not
then be able to support the Chief Constable publicly.' The chief
constable later that day confirmed that he 'expects to have at least
600 men available'. But he expressed doubt about his legal power
to stop coaches and pickets coming to Warrington. On Tuesday,
29 November, the morning of the mass picket, legal advice was
provided to Fenn from the Home Office that the police have the
power to stop coaches bringing pickets to the scene. Chief Constable Fenn said he did not have enough resources to do that.[45]
Within hours the number of officers at Warrington increased
from 600, to 850, then to 992 at 5 p.m. (532 from Cheshire and
460 from other forces), eventually reaching 1,450.[46]

The IOD implored the home secretary to provide enough
police to ensure the production of the *Messenger* papers. The
home secretary replied in strong terms agreeing with the IOD,
but underlining that operational issues were to be left to the chief
constable even though his private communications contradicted
this assertion.[47]

On the same day, the NGA told ACAS they would call off
the picket if talks continued. Shah refused to leave Warrington
to meet the trade union – he claimed because of the number of
pickets. However, Deputy Chief Constable Graham reported

that pickets had arrived in small numbers, with only forty pickets outside the plant by 5 p.m.[48]

Andrew Neil and Shah were in touch throughout the night of 29–30 November. Shah, who was inside his building, said, 'They've set fire to the buildings on the next block ... The mob's on the rampage – there's thousands of them. The police lines have been broken.'[49] It appears that Neil took Shah at his word and called the home secretary at home in the early hours. In his book *Full Disclosure* Neil records telling the home secretary that Eddy Shah 'thinks he and his people are going to be killed'. The home secretary reacted saying, 'I don't think it's that bad.' Andrew Neil 'angrily' told the home secretary, 'If I wake up in the morning to find that Eddy Shah is dead I'll make damn sure that the prime minister and the rest of the country is in no doubt who did nothing to stop him being killed.' Around 2 a.m. Shah told Neil, 'The Manchester riot squad has arrived.'[50] How Shah knew that the riot squad were from Manchester is anyone's guess, considering he was holed up inside the plant.

At around lunchtime the following day, Andrew Neil called the prime minister's private secretary, Richard P. Hatfield. In a 'note for the record' found in Thatcher's files marked 'Secret and Personal' the record states, 'He said that he had been in constant contact with Mr Shah throughout the night and it had been "a very close thing" in Warrington. At one point Mr Shah thought that those outside were about to break through police lines and into the factory. If that happened, someone could get killed. Mr Shah had been "very shaken" by the night's events and was "close to panicking" but would not give in.'

The *Sunday Times* editor continued,

Mr Shah had no contacts amongst influential people (apart from himself) and he had therefore wanted ... to make sure that the gravity of the situation was known ... he was worried that the Chief Constable might not have sufficient resources available to cope with the mass demonstration expected tonight (including a contingent of Welsh miners). The Editor said in his view it was essential that 'the Government win this dispute' – although he understood that the Government was not directly involved, it was essential that their legislation should not be undermined.[51]

Neil outlined Shah's plans to take the rest of his papers out at 1 p.m. and 5 p.m. on 1 December, then wait until 7 a.m. the next day for the balance, as many pickets might have left by then. A similar approach was rejected by Shah the night before when the trade union suggested it:

The Editor stressed the confidentiality of the call and of the fact that he was in touch with Mr Shah although Rupert Murdoch [proprietor of the *Sunday Times*] was in the picture and supported his approach ... (I gathered he had spoken to the Home Secretary in the night). I undertook to make sure that the information he had given me was passed on to where it might be most helpful and to do anything I could to protect its source.[52]

In *Full Disclosure*, Neil records this call, but not its contents, which have come to light through the National Archive. The notes on the call were given to the prime minister, which she read alongside confirmation that 'the gist of the conversation' with the editor had been 'passed ... over a scrambler' to the permanent under-secretary for the Home Office, Sir Brian Cubbon, who undertook to tell the home secretary, Leon Brittan.[53]

In the Houses of Parliament the home secretary, despite his earlier direction to Chief Constable Fenn, said, 'The chief constable has the responsibility for ... devising and executing the appropriate plans.'[54] Tory MPs cheered him on even after they heard from Labour MPs who were at Warrington about the violence they witnessed meted out by the police.

The expectation was that around another 2,000 to 3,000 people would turn up at Warrington on the night of 30 November. About 3,000 went to a pre-planned NGA rally in Manchester. The local authority told the NGA they were concerned on behalf of the police that if there were buses to Warrington the union could not use the hall. A decision was taken and the meeting went ahead with full capacity, but up to 2,000 of them did not go on to Warrington, although 800 pickets did.[55] Colin Bourne, the NUJ official, asked them to sit down on the road. He also urged reporters, 'Tonight, come out from behind the police line where you were last night – as you can't see what's really happening from there.'

A *News at One* report shows the pickets being lifted by arms and legs, with one policeman heard to say on camera, 'I'll smash your fucking teeth in.'[56] The names, ages, occupations and addresses of most of those arrested were printed in the *Daily Telegraph* the following day, something Richard Dixon-Payne only discovered when being interviewed for this book.[57] Shortly after this, Richard received repeated phone calls at his home, 'First of all, just ringing putting the phone down, then they started saying things like, "This is a message from your undertakers," then they'd ring back and say, "We want measurements for a coffin" and they'd be laughing at the end of the phone. I think it was the police.'

The number of police sent to Warrington was released into evidence in August 1984 when Shah sued the NGA for damages. It confirmed that, following Neil's discussions with the Home Office, police numbers increased from 1,450 officers on duty during the night of 29–30 November, when there were eighty-six arrests, to 1,849 officers on 30 November–1 December, when there were twenty-three arrests.[58] All of these arrests were for the most minor criminal offences, predominantly breach of the peace. This was to be the last mass picket of this dispute.

On 30 November, Judge Sir John Donaldson ordered the sequestration of all of the NGA's assets for continuing the picket, estimated at £11 million – effectively, the sequestrators were now the union. Donaldson had previously jailed the Pentonville Five trade unionists in 1972 for contempt of court following the introduction of new legislation. They were released after a wave of industrial action around the country. Donaldson was also the judge in the Guildford Four criminal trial in the mid-1970s, a case subsequently shown to be a devastating wrongful conviction.[59]

The Cabinet minutes on 1 December show the prime minister wanted the rule of law to prevail with the use of criminal charges and that Mr Shah and his family would be protected 'at public expense'.[60]

Shah pursued the NGA for damages for his costs relating to the dispute. An NGA report of the High Court hearing states, 'He [Shah] was challenged on a number of comments with regard to the alleged violent nature of the NGA picketing … comments that NGA members had broken into the factory and chased employees with crowbars.' Shah admitted under cross-examination 'that he had no personal knowledge of such an event'. Shah still believed himself to be and presented himself as the victim, expressing 'no knowledge' of offensive telephone calls to NGA members. The union QC's cross-examination did manage to 'draw out' of Shah that his 'motivation' was to 'get rid of the NGA or any other union'. He also highlighted 'that the publicity generated by the dispute had not been adverse for Mr. Shah which he agreed to'. Shah's manager and company director, Mr Frankland, 'was forced to admit under oath that no NGA members ever broke into the Warrington factory, or chased people with crowbars at any time'.[61] Justice Caulfield stated that he believed Shah, and dismissed all the evidence given by the NGA. He awarded financial damages including costs of around a hundred thousand pounds to Shah.

On 4 December the *Observer* revealed,

> Mr. Shah has denied consistently that any outside body has influenced his activities. But the Institute [of Directors] has been helping him ... urged him to stand firm ... use the courts and the new tough industrial relations laws ... give him the benefit of its advice during his talks ... It played a major role in the successful defeat of the mass pickets.[62]

The IOD press office provided further clarity on the level of support that Shah received from their policy unit. During the dispute they were 'working 24 hours a day for Mr. Shah', and their director-general, Walter Goldsmith, pushed the government to take action against trade unions.[63]

Andrew Neil, then the *Sunday Times* editor, apparently took Shah's version of the truth as read, without checking with other sources. Even when the home secretary advised he did not 'think it's that bad', Neil ignored him. Was Shah his guinea pig for what he had planned for his own staff?[64]

On the same day as the *Observer* article, Neil 'decided to devote most of our news analysis pages to the events surrounding the Battle of Warrington along with a damning editorial which would spare neither unions nor [Fleet Street] management ... It made Eddy Shah the hero of the hour.'[65]

Meanwhile, the Home Office received questions originating from the No. 10 private office as to whether the NGA officials 'might be prosecuted for "incitement".'[66] The home secretary asked to be kept updated, adding, 'The Prime Minister has expressed interest in this.'[67] Despite best efforts from government leading to investigations by the police, no case could be mounted.

Chief Constable George Fenn made no public statement on the police tactics at Warrington, and nor did his force. Over the coming weeks Cheshire police repeatedly reported to the home secretary that the police were not heavy-handed. In reports from the chief constable's office, the police said they made their way to the NGA van 'under assault' and that 'the action [against the van] was taken to prevent violence' after it had 'been used to broadcast abuse and messages which were leading to disorder'.[68]

The police described the event as 'an unlawful assembly ... at times it was a riotous assembly and that the Range Rovers were stoned by protesters.[69] The newly formed Police Complaints Authority investigated the Range Rover incident and responded to the NGA,

> senior officers say that they never issued instructions for such tactics to be used ... The two officers who were driving ... deny that they drove at demonstrators on the waste ground and state that it would not have been possible because the terrain was soft. One officer says he only went far enough onto the waste ground to turn his vehicle round.[70]

As complaints were made against ACPO-rank officers they were investigated by Chief Constable Frank Jordan of Kent Police. It took two years before the union were told the complaints were not upheld. The only criticism of the police was 'the lack of an operational plan in relation to the role of this van'.[71] In 1986 Chief Constable Jordan's Kent Police were investigated by Scotland Yard for fake crime figures.[72]

No one was more surprised than the Stockport Six to see thousands of police in riot gear face to face with thousands of trade unionists. Alan Royston, Tony Burke and many others suspected at the time that the police had the full weight of the state behind them; even so, Burke recalls, 'People didn't necessarily believe the police would go this far.'

The Stockport Six were unfortunate. Their dispute coming at the end of 1983 was the first big battleground for the police to test out their new powers bestowed by the Home Office earlier that year. It was never going to be an even playing field. Rather it was like a David and Goliath, with the latter having some secretly sanctioned military tactics in their back pocket. The new tactics tested on the printers included the creation of barriers formed by riot police, snatch squads and Range Rovers driven at protesters. The vast police turnout, alongside the manual, proved essential to the success of the police operation. Their approach was beyond the 'firm policy' of 'normal policing' that the home secretary aspired to in his address to ACPO at the drinks party held at the beginning of the same year.

Not expecting to be faced with police in riot gear and excessive tactics, the NGA fought a maverick employer in a traditional way. What chance did the NGA have when Shah had the support of the senior echelons of government, police, the courts and national media? The Employment Acts stripping employees of their ability to picket anywhere other than outside their workplace, even if the employer arbitrarily transferred that work to another location, gives this dispute its historical importance. These Acts had the effect of encouraging employers to use the courts rather than negotiate, to stymie a trade union's ability to operate and sap them of funds. The boundaries of lawful picketing had been redrawn. For the NGA this meant three injunctions and sequestration to tie up trade union funds and provocative policing. Arguably, the decline of trade union influence started at Warrington, which must have been a frightening prospect for all trade unions and their members.

The IOD and Andrew Neil also had a hand in influencing the police action. They appeared to believe Shah's narrative, despite his being an unknown entity. Their response enabled the government to act, even though this narrative did not reflect the police intelligence given to the Home Office.

The source for the intelligence is unclear. What has recently come to light is that on Friday, 25 November 1983, Met commissioner Sir Kenneth Newman had a secret meeting, with the Special Demonstration Squad (SDS, or 'S' Squad), a unit of undercover police officers known only to the top echelons of police and government. That meeting took place just four days before the mass picket at Warrington which the SDS's annual report described as a 'potential public order threat'.

Government interference in the policing of this dispute at Warrington echoes the way the manual came together, behind closed doors in secret. The events of 29–30 November were a police testing ground, the guinea pig for Thatcher's plans against the unions. The policing of an industrial dispute in this manner was completely unexpected for the trade unions after a period of strength that brought more equality, including the 1970 Equal Pay Act, which, following a strike of the sewing machinists at Ford Motor company, benefited all working women in the UK, as depicted in the film *Made in Dagenham*.[73] With Thatcher in power, police tactics were extended by her government in secret and beyond what the general public would consider 'normal'. It would continue for decades.

2

Maggie's UK War

The Miners, Orgreave, 1984

Violence will not succeed for the police and courts will not bow to it. They are the servants, not of government, but of the law itself. [Hear, hear and applause.]

Mrs Thatcher, Lord Mayor's Banquet speech, 12 November 1984

There is no way in which the Government or any other Department should seek to influence the police as to how they conduct their operations upon the ground.

Attorney General Sir Michael Havers,
House of Commons, 18 June 1984

On the outskirts of Sheffield at Orgreave on Monday, 18 June 1984, 6,000 police confronted 6,000 pickets. Many of the police were in riot gear, joined by fifty-eight dogs and forty-two horses. They were three months into a miners' strike that would last a year when the worst picket line violence in the strike took place. Following the Battle of Orgreave, ninety-five miners were charged with riot and unlawful assembly. Proud working men who once thought they had jobs for life found themselves facing a life sentence. What happened at Orgreave sparked controversy that continues to this day.

Gareth Peirce, a solicitor for a number of those charged, wrote an account in the *Guardian* of the events as they played out on a police film taken at Orgreave.[1] The film was apparently taken for police training purposes, to demonstrate crowd control options.[2] Shot from behind police lines, the film was not used by the prosecution when making their case against the miners, but the defence used it. As Peirce described it, you see how men arrived 'from 6am onwards being escorted by police towards an open field ... For two hours, you see only men standing in the sun, talking and laughing. And when the coking lorries arrive, you see a brief, good-humoured, and expected push against the police lines; it lasts for 38 seconds exactly.'

The police lines, made up of those in riot gear, were deployed by Assistant Chief Constable (ACC) Clement, the officer in charge of the operation. Those at the front were holding long transparent shields, six feet high and eighteen inches wide. Behind them, multiple rows of officers in ordinary uniform stood at close quarters to each other, forming a human wall.[3] Peirce continued,

> Suddenly the ranks of the long-shield officers, 13 deep, open up and horses gallop through the densely-packed crowd. This manoeuvre repeats itself. In one of those charges you see a man being trampled by a police horse and brought back through the lines as a captive, to be charged with riot. You see squadrons of officers dressed in strange medieval battle dress with helmets and visors, round shields and overalls, ensuring anonymity and invulnerability, run after the cavalry and begin truncheoning pickets who have been slow to escape.
>
> You hear on the soundtrack 'bodies not heads' shouted by one

senior officer, and then see junior officers rush out and hit heads as well as bodies.

Over the next few hours, as the police continued their rampage, occasional missiles were thrown by the miners. The police set out to 'incapacitate' miners and bystanders, as authorised by the new manual, whether or not the pickets were throwing missiles. In the early afternoon following this onslaught, the pickets started to build protective barriers against the police with anything they could find from the fields, roads and rail sidings that surrounded them. Placing this into context, Peirce refers to events which took place in court a year later:

> Another officer conceded that the purpose of the horses and the short-shield officers was to terrify; if miners did not disperse when they were ran at by the police, then they were eligible for arrest. This was the view of the law expressed by the last junior officer to give evidence before the riot trial was finally jettisoned by the prosecution.

Short shields with truncheons were a new police tactic in the 1983 manual approved by the Home Office and used for the first time on 18 June 1984, at Orgreave.[4] ACC Clement, while giving evidence at the miners' riot trial, confirmed that officers 'deployed with a round shield' were 'also instructed to draw their truncheons'.[5] Bernard Jackson, former president of a branch of the National Union of Miners at Wath Main colliery in South Yorkshire, describes the police attitude: 'As the mounted men returned … a round of applause rose from the police ranks and ran along the line from one end to the other.'[6] The riot police ran after pickets, hitting them indiscriminately – scenes that resulted in blood, tears and another miner seeing 'a man in his 50s wet himself through fear'.[7]

Jackson, one of the first to be prosecuted for riot, describes his arrest: 'An arm grabbed me around the neck from behind and I was smashed in the face with a riot shield. He encircled my neck with his other arm, took his truncheon in both hands and squeezed.' The officer threatened Jackson, 'Shut your fucking mouth or I'll break your fucking neck.'[8] In 1991, after the miners sued the police for assault, wrongful arrest, malicious prosecution and false imprisonment, the police settled. Jackson, one of thirty-nine miners who shared £425,000 of compensation from South Yorkshire Police, had been held for a week in prison after his arrest.[9] He said, 'I can't forgive the police for those things. I had respect for them before the strike, but not now.'[10]

The 1984–5 strike started after miners took national industrial action against colliery closures announced by the National Coal Board (NCB). The NCB, a nationalised industry, announced that twenty pits were to close with the loss of 20,000 jobs. The NCB called the pits uneconomic, but the National Union of Mineworkers (NUM) said otherwise, and claimed there was a wider plan against their union with many more pit closures in the offing. Industrial action in Scotland had been running for some months when, on 6 March 1984, miners across the UK voted with their feet and walked out.

The Conservative government led by Prime Minister Margaret Thatcher denied there was a plan for pit closures. However, records obtained after the strike show the NCB's plan to close seventy-five pits with the loss of nearly 70,000 jobs. Thatcher had full knowledge of the plan, having been briefed at a secret 10 Downing Street meeting in September 1983, the record of which was 'not to be photocopied or circulated outside [her] private office'.[11] During the strike, Home Secretary Leon Brittan stated that police operations were the responsibility of chief officers.[12]

His predecessor, now Lord Willie Whitelaw, said in March 1984, 'The Government's interests will continue to be best served by its policy of non-involvement in the dispute.' However, documents recently declassified at the National Archive relating to the miners' strike give the lie to these claims.

Margaret Thatcher came to power in 1979. One of her aims was to build on the Ridley plan produced by the Conservatives in opposition, after the coal strike of 1973–4 had brought down the Heath government.[13] Thatcher instructed a study on the NCB/NUM 'problem', emphasising the need for 'very tight security' and a plan for 'withstanding' a miners' strike.[14] She established the Civil Contingencies Unit (CCU), who stated that 'the effectiveness of Government intervention would ... depend on the existence of sufficient stockpiles,' and advised her to accept the 1981 NUM pay claim to 'avoid confrontation' while the coal stocks were built up.[15]

By 1984, coal stocks had been built up and pit closures were announced. Just after the start of the strike, the prime minister received a secret memo annotated 'sole copy' from her policy adviser, David Pascall. It confirmed that endurance of around eleven months could be achieved if some coal was kept moving from the central coal fields. This finding emphasised 'the importance of the police operation in Nottingham and surrounding areas'. Pascall concluded, 'The Government now has a unique opportunity to break the power of the militants in the NUM.'[16] It was unlikely the government could do this without help.

Margaret Thatcher's interference in policing operations started before she became prime minister. In 1979, while in opposition, Thatcher had a spat with the then Labour home secretary, Merlyn Rees, about the lorry drivers' strike. She suggested in the House of Commons that 'chief constables should be given advice about what they should be doing'. Three months of correspondence ensued. The home secretary said he had 'no power to give instructions to chief constables' on 'how they ... preserve public order', or how to enforce the law in an industrial dispute. Rees asserted that this approach had been taken by successive governments. Thatcher contended that it was 'proper and desirable' for a home secretary to give advice to the police on both criminal and civil matters. She received a sharp retort: 'It is fundamental to our system of Government that the home secretary does not interpret the law to the police or intervene in the operational responsibilities of Chief Officers.'[17] By the time it was decided to make pit closures in 1984, Thatcher's mind was unchanged.

Thatcher approved the appointment of the NCB chief Ian MacGregor, who had overseen large-scale closures in the American coal industry as well as mass redundancies and closures at the UK's nationalised steel industry.[18] Discussions followed a meeting between MacGregor and Thatcher on 14 March 1984, where he confirmed that he had started civil injunction proceedings against Yorkshire pickets.[19] MacGregor resiled from enforcing the injunction amid concerns that a civil action would be 'likely to have unwelcome effects ... tend to swing union support ... behind the strike leadership', as at Warrington.[20]

MacGregor also expressed his concern over the failure to apply the criminal law; the Secretary of State for Energy agreed. The prime minister was 'deeply disturbed ... The events at Saltley cokeworks were being repeated ... It was essential to stiffen the resolve of Chief Constables to ensure that they fulfilled their duty to uphold the law', particularly as the police 'were now well paid and well equipped and individual forces had good arrangements for mutual support'.[21]

Immediately following Thatcher's meeting with MacGregor on 14 March, she met with a number of her Cabinet. She complained that the police were 'not carrying out their duties fully as large pickets were being permitted and few arrests were being made'. The home secretary, Leon Brittan, responded he had already made public statements confirming that 'large numbers of pickets were intimidatory' and 'it was the duty of the Police to uphold the criminal law and prevent such intimidation.'[22] He also ensured that chief constables were aware that the government expected them to carry out their duty, having 'gone to the limit of what the home secretary could do while respecting the constitutional independence of [the] Police'.[23] But this was not enough for Thatcher. At the end of the meeting, she determined that 'the Home Secretary [was] to ensure that Chief Constables carried out their duties fully'.[24]

She and members of her Cabinet reflected on the success of preventing pickets from gathering for secondary picketing at Warrington, which was achieved via roadblocks.[25] Michael Havers, the attorney general, issued a public statement to 're-affirm the criminal law on [secondary] picketing', which led to the use of roadblocks – a tactic that was legally questionable.[26]

A police National Reporting Centre (NRC) was established to coordinate mutual aid resources, a system where chief police officers request that police from one area move to another to support their forces. During the miners' strike, mutual aid officers were used to stop mass pickets who had travelled from other pits, known as secondary picketing. The use of mutual aid – moving police from their area of work to another – could itself be seen as an act of 'secondary policing', but had been sanctioned by government.

The NRC was supposed to be only for coordinating responses to requests for mutual aid.[27] However, recently declassified files confirm it had an additional role 'co-ordinating ... intelligence and disseminating it to the Chief Constables concerned'. This intelligence was shared with the home secretary, who reported to a special cabinet with senior ministers set up by Thatcher (MISC101).[28] The MISC101 was held at least twice a week, specifically to discuss the miners' strike. The establishment of the NRC and a promise from government to cover no less than 90 per cent of additional costs of policing the strike distorted the balance of power and undermined local oversight of the police. Thatcher's government pushed yet further.

Within days of the introduction of the NRC, roadblocks were seen around the country. At the Dartford Tunnel, police turned back miners from Kent, hundreds of miles away from their destination, the coalfields of Nottinghamshire and Yorkshire. Miners were under threat of arrest for breach of the peace merely for travelling to protect their jobs, even though the courts held that that would only be justified if the police could show such a breach was imminent.

At the MISC101 on 8 May 1984, Thatcher extended her grasp by asking the Secretary of State for Scotland to 'explore and report ... about the policing of the dispute in Scotland. He should establish in particular whether the Scottish Chief Constables were willing as a matter of policy to take action similar to that taken in England to prevent pickets from going to the scene of possible disturbances.'[29] On the same day at around the same time as this meeting, a mass picket was being held at Hunterston in Ayrshire.

Patrick McCarroll, a twenty-two-year-old miner, had arrived at Hunterston coking plant at about 8 a.m. with around 700 other miners. Hunterston supplied coke to the Ravenscraig steelworks in Ayrshire. There had been clashes between miners and the police at Ravenscraig the week before when nearly 300 were arrested on one day after a fracas when lorries delivering coal failed to slow down.[30] At Hunterston, Patrick sat on one of two bankings that stretched over a few hundred metres and led down to the road where the lorries would leave from the plant, from left to right. There were only a few officers present. He remembers enjoying the sun he rarely saw as a miner when about twelve double-decker buses arrived at around noon. 'At first we thought it was more pickets arriving, but they weren't. They were police. They were marched up and lined up along the road. Over 1,000 police, some of them mingled about us on the bank.'

There was some banter between the police and miners, though Patrick thought the atmosphere was tenser than it had been on other days at Ravenscraig. The expected push of miners against police happened as the lorries left the plant around 1 p.m. Patrick recalls, 'There were hundreds of us and over 1,000 of them; we weren't going to get through. We never did, the police always held the line. We just pushed, like miners do. I was in the middle.

'I saw the horses from the corner of my eye. Six of them just standing there and I thought "they'll not come". I thought "they aren't going to move". But they did. The police charged their horses right into us; I was in the middle of that crowd. They really moved – they galloped at us. It was scary. I heard them first. The gallop, I could hear it and I ran back up the hill. I was quick, others weren't. Pandemonium. I am surprised no one died. A few were in hospital.'

Later, Ayrshire chief superintendent Harry Corrigan insisted police action had prevented possible deaths: 'If we hadn't had the horses, the pickets would certainly have broken through our lines onto the road because of the momentum and someone could have died under the wheels of a lorry.'[31]

Patrick has a different view: 'It wasn't a danger, it was a push. When the police horses got through, they went back and stood. They didn't charge again but they could have. They didn't need to. The lorries came out and we hurled abuse – it was crazy what they did. It was on the BBC that night but that showed us in a bad light. They said there were disturbances caused by the miners. What was said wasn't what happened.' It was the first time Patrick had seen anything like that on the picket line. It was 'terrifying'.

Cantering on a crowd is authorised in the manual, to disperse people rapidly by using 'fear created by the impetus of horses'.[32] However, it is 'inappropriate to use such a manoeuvre against a densely packed crowd', as at Hunterston. Following this horse charge the Secretary of State for Scotland met with a group of Labour MPs to discuss policing in Scotland and declared that the police were 'entirely impartial' and that 'Chief Constables are not subject to instructions from Ministers and none have been given'.[33]

The police in Scotland employed 'new methods', including stopping miners over forty miles from the intended picketing sites in a manner that reflected the public statements made by the home secretary and the attorney general. When eight coaches were stopped on their way to Ravenscraig, nearly 300 miners sat down in protest on the main road from Stirling to Glasgow, and were arrested.[34] The Scottish police went a step further, advising bus operators that by transporting miners 'they might be breaking the law'.[35] According to the *Glasgow Herald* it was the police, not the bus companies, who were overstretching the law.[36]

The Scottish Trades Union Congress (STUC) convened a meeting on 11 May 1984 that included Members of Parliament, regional and district councils and the NUM, where concerns were expressed about the 'extremely violent' tactics being used by the police and the 'worrying in-roads on civil liberties involving the action of the police in preventing coaches and cars travelling to Ravenscraig and Hunterston for the purposes of picketing.' The former solicitor general of Scotland, Lord McCluskey, expressed his view (as a lawyer) that while such action would have to be 'tested in a Court of Law', it was 'highly unlikely that judgement would be given in favour of the miners'.[37]

Shortly after this meeting, a deal was struck by Scottish miners' leader Mick McGahey to allow coal deliveries and normal steel production to resume at Ravenscraig. Following this agreement, British Steel wrote to the Secretary of State for Scotland in mid-May 1984 to congratulate and thank the police for their work at Ravenscraig.[38]

Confrontations between police and pickets at Orgreave in South Yorkshire started near the end of May. On 29 May, long shields were deployed for the first time during the miners' strike.[39] On the same day, three weeks after their use at Hunterston, police horses were used at Orgreave three times. According to Sheffield Police Watch, horses were sent in 'entirely without provocation' to move the crowd 'with the help of dogs'. They concluded that the use of horses three times 'prior to any disturbance' must have been a 'calculated' decision.[40] The next day, Arthur Scargill was arrested for obstruction at Orgreave, as were a number of other miners.

Shortly after Hunterston, Nottinghamshire police charged miners at Mansfield with riot. Following accusations in the press of being 'archaic', the Home Office privately sought incidences of the successful use of riot charges from 1972 to 1982.[41] Thatcher chaired the MISC101 on 30 May that discussed 'support for the police efforts to bring more serious charges where appropriate'.[42]

The next day, top civil servant Sir Brian Cubbon, the permanent under-secretary to the Home Office, called the chief constable of South Yorkshire, Peter Wright, to discuss Orgreave. Cubbon was an obvious candidate to make contact, having built a relationship with police forces across the country in the years before the strike. These meetings continued during the dispute, including a meeting with West Yorkshire CID in April 1984 and, on 21 May 1984, with the Met Police. At this meeting, Cubbon explained that it was time for the Home Office and the Met to 'reflect', to 'ensure that there was mutual understanding of the responsibilities and obligations' between the two.[43] He thought there had been 'considerable success in building up the public face of the relationship'. He was also 'certain that the private relationship necessarily had to be much closer than the public face'. Just a few weeks before Orgreave the Met and Cubbon discussed sharing best practice between the Met and other forces, on 'policy and operational matters'.

On the call to Wright, Cubbon welcomed the charges made against miners of 'affray'. His note to Home Office staff, however, raised concerns about the next stage; the impression given was that the Orgreave plant itself was vulnerable as Arthur Scargill, the miners' leader, was planning action 'which he saw as his new Saltley'. Did Cubbon up the ante?[44] At around the same time the attorney general advised that 'the government must not, in any way, seem to be interfering in the administration of justice'. He also counselled, 'As regards prosecutions policy and the handling of cases by the courts, overt intervention by central Government would be inappropriate.'[45]

A 1985 Labour Party report into the strike, led by former home secretary Merlyn Rees (who had the argument with Thatcher in 1979) and future prime minister Gordon Brown, concluded that 'charges made [by the police] could often have been of the minimum, but ... the severest charges were laid before the courts.'[46] *Guardian* journalist David Conn has commented, 'Official documents from the time reveal that Chief Constable Peter Wright himself commanded a plan in advance to charge arrested miners not with minor public order offences such as affray, but with the ancient and serious criminal offences of riot or unlawful assembly.'[47]

Civil servants and members of the Cabinet were considering charging levels at the same time as were the police. Given that coincidence it appears highly improbable that they were not in collusion.

Orgreave was a strategic location for the miners. If they could stop coke supplies, they might be able to impact steel production for manufacturing plants across the country, and increase their negotiating power. Scargill called for all striking miners to go to Orgreave on 18 June 1984. The hope for Orgreave was a repeat of the success at Saltley that Scargill had helped organise in 1972. As a result the Conservative government both respected and feared Scargill.[48]

It was the hundredth day of the strike. The terrain at Orgreave favoured the police. Bernard Jackson was ushered into a cornfield with others from his pit. At the field's bottom border, lines of police flanked the Orgreave plant. As Jackson looked towards them, the road on the left was lined with police dogs and their handlers; the thick line of trees and bushes on the other side hid a branch siding, where mounted police and dogs were deployed; and a steep embankment down to the main railway line was to his back. If anything happened, the only obvious way out for the miners was up a single-carriage road then across a narrow bridge.[49] The men in the field were surrounded.

As the lorries left the plant around 8 a.m. the miners pushed, as expected, against the police lines; the push lasted thirty-eight seconds. Shortly after, mounted police at full pelt galloped straight into the crowd of pickets, with truncheons drawn, this was repeated several times. Many officers were without identification numbers, something Assistant Chief Constable Clement

acknowledged at the subsequent Orgreave trial. There were
reports of miners' cameras being seized and film destroyed by the
police and of the police shouting 'camera' to alert colleagues.[50]

Patrick McCarroll, previously at Hunterston, was there on 18
June 1984 having travelled from Scotland to Orgreave. He recalls,
'We'd been down a week, staying at a gym hall in a college, 100
or so miners from all over, Wales, Scotland. The 18th was the
last day — we were going back that night. There was thousands
of police and banter. Then it got all serious. The lorries had left.
We were in the field, near the back. There were dogs everywhere.
I was chased all the way. The dogs were barking, I ran across the
railway line, away from them. I ran and ran, there was an Asda;
I ran through that, there were horses chasing men through the
car park. There were people hiding up trees, people trying to
hide everywhere. The dogs had big, long, 30-foot leads and were
chasing us, they were allowed to chase us then pulled back.'

The police charges, both mounted and on foot, went on for
three hours. Then after all lull, the few hundred left in the field
were charged again.

Miners run from the police, Orgreave, 18 June 1984.

© Martin Shakeshaft

'I was twenty-two then, and I'm not going to lie, it was an adventure, going round the country … at my first day of work in 1979 the older miners were saying, "She's [Thatcher] coming for us." It was pure politics. At Orgreave I was terrified. Anyone that says they weren't is a liar. On the bus back that night we laughed it off – but only later, that's when you realise it was out of order.'

The official number of pickets and police injured at Orgreave varies in government reports over the years. Statements prepared following the miners' compensation payout in 1991 inflate the number of police injured from those in 1984.[51] Police and other reports generally state that fifty-one pickets and twenty-eight police went to hospital. Some miners say they didn't go to hospital as there were reports of arrests being made there. Some of those arrested found medical attention was not provided or was inadequate. One ambulance man recounts he 'spent the day sitting around waiting to be called on if needed. I thought everything must have been orderly as I wasn't called upon. I was so angry when seeing the TV news. I saw the violence and injuries on screen.'[52]

In the 1980s the ITV and BBC evening news were 'the news'. Television coverage was often filmed from behind police lines, the effect being, as academic Len Masterman notes, that 'stones and bricks hurled at the police are also aimed at us. *We* are on the receiving end … even the leader of the Labour Party … [is] willing to accept the agenda set … and condemn "picket line violence."'[53]

After the strike a group of Labour MPs accused the government of actively campaigning to 'wholly' blame 'the striking miners for violence on the picket line'.[54] They were not wrong. The prime minister's files show that the government's aim was to wean the public away from siding with the miners.[55] The government thought they were 'successful' in this and 'very successful in keeping the dispute at an industrial rather than a political level'.[56]

There were no twenty-four-hour news channels so millions watched the ITN news in collective horror as a policeman ran up to Russell Broomhead, who tried to protect himself from a barrage of truncheon hits. He was not the only person rescued by other miners. The main BBC early evening news, however, had the backdrop of a picket attacking the police. Their eyewitness reporter, John Thorne, spoke of the 'horrific' attacks on the police that resulted from Arthur Scargill's 'military operation'.[57]

Shockingly, the BBC report reordered the film footage taken of the day, showing items being thrown at the police followed by the horse charge. By reversing the order of footage millions of viewers were led to believe that it was the miners and not the police who instigated the violence that day. Thorne made no mention of the police violence. Subsequent examination of the BBC's coverage confirmed that they had the Broomhead incident that ITN had shown but cut the footage just before the police attacked him.[58] Scargill was also knocked unconscious on the day but the BBC downplayed his injuries, creating doubt about whether a policeman hit Scargill with his shield.

The assistant director general of the BBC, in an internal meeting the following day, noted that their coverage 'might not have been wholly impartial'.[59] After many years of campaigning, the BBC finally admitted, in a letter to the NUM, that the footage of the police charge was shown in the wrong order.[60] Even then they tried to pass it off as an 'inadvertent ... mistake'. The BBC failures on 18 June 1984 at Orgreave went beyond the mere reversal of film footage, including the script narrative, John Thorne's omissions and a still selected from all the footage showing a miner attacking the police. It is implausible that the footage reversal was a single mistake and for the BBC to maintain such a position for nearly four decades reflects on their integrity.

In his excellent analysis of the BBC's and ITN's coverage of

18 June 1984, Masterman highlights 'a sanitising operation of considerable proportions' throughout the strike. This meant, 'in their eagerness to select and shape events to fit a preformulated interpretation, they missed by a mile what was to become the main story of Orgreave'.[61] Police instigated and escalated violence against UK citizens with horses, truncheons, short shields and dogs. It wasn't the last time the media misrepresented protesters.

Newspapers' weekly average circulation at the time was upwards of 15.5 million, 75 per cent of whom were editorially supportive of the Conservatives. They repeatedly reported that the miners were at fault and the police were not.[62] The day after Orgreave, the *Sun* ran their front-page headline 'CHARGE', with the article starting, 'mounted police made an amazing cavalry charge on picketing miners yesterday. The officers faced a hate barrage of bricks, bottles and spears as they broke up a bloody riot.'[63] The first group of miners facing charges of riot at Orgreave found themselves in the dock at Sheffield Crown Court.

During the Orgreave trial, defence barrister Michael Mansfield's forensic cross-examination of ACC Anthony Clement revealed for the first time the classified police manual, the secret rules on policing public order.[64] Without that court exchange the very existence of the secret manual might have remained hidden. Mansfield insisted on its disclosure and obtained some pages of the manual, which contained questionable tactics involving the use of dogs and horses and the banging of shields, and the authorisation to use truncheons to 'incapacitate' people just for being present. The use of horses without warning was accepted at the trial as being contrary to the manual.[65] The use of 'shield banging' was singled out for criticism in the Scarman report in

1981, which described their use as officers 'losing control' and called for an end to the practice. That ACPO and the Home Office disregarded Scarman's findings when they created the manual in secret in 1983 was confirmed by Clement, who said 'shield banging' was an approved tactical option for the police in a public order situation. Public outcry following Orgreave finally led to chief officers banning its use.[66]

ACC Clement also stated that the manual was not intended to cover public disorder in an industrial dispute. Home Office files released thirty years later confirm the tactics in the manual were intended for an industrial situation.[67] The prosecution and the judge shut down a question from the defence regarding Home Office involvement in the creation of the manual. This protected its origins and also the facade that government were not involved in the dispute behind the scenes. If the Home Office were not involved, then why would the prosecution raise an objection?

Recently disclosed Home Office documents provide a number of private and internal reports into policing and tactics by the Met Police and South Yorkshire Police Committee, and an ACPO report that was sent to the Home Office, none of which were made public at the time. These confirm influence from the top of government on police operations during the strike that enabled excessive policing, not just at Orgreave in June 1984 but at Hunterston in Scotland the month before and for the duration of the year-long strike in mining villages across the country.

Sheffield Police Watch, a group established during the miners' strike, questioned the use of dogs and horses, suggesting that the 'police guidelines on the use of dogs and mounted officers had deliberately been flouted ... Since then we [Sheffield Police Watch] have procured a copy of police guidelines for dog handlers ... They say that dogs should not be used against large crowds as they become "excited" and may bite people.'[68] Despite this, dogs were *in situ* at Orgreave on 18 June 1984 and were used to effect. ACC Clement said at the Orgreave trial that 'the use of dogs is a totally acceptable option ... with a situation as serious as this'.[69]

Home Office files now reveal that the Home Office Standing Advisory Committee 'rejected the use of dogs', stating, 'The only options accepted are ... to guard property and patrol areas on the periphery of a disturbance.'[70] Dogs 'confronting a crowd' attracted 'serious reservations'. A review by ACPO officers apparently dismissed such expert advice, concluding that dogs had a 'potentially greater public order use than previously envisaged'. Their use in demonstrations was approved, with a section redrafted to reflect dogs as 'a serious, but not unimaginable, tactic'.[71]

It appears, therefore, that the approved tactics were against both Scarman's recommendations and the copy of police guidelines for dog handlers. At least two people are known to have been bitten by police dogs on 18 June 1984.[72] Despite this, two police dog handlers 'received commendations' after Orgreave, 'and – according to the police – "no one" had been bitten'.[73]

ACPO justified the use of dogs and horse charges at Orgreave because of the 'potential for disorder'.[74] When a chief superintendent, and second in command at Orgreave on 18 June 1984, was asked at the trial about what happens when there is conflict between the standing orders and the manual, he replied that 'the Chief Constable ... is autonomous in [his] area'. Mansfield pressed ACC Clement about the use of mounted police against a static crowd. Clement said that he would 'not [be] the slightest' bit worried if they were trampled on by police horses:[75]

CLEMENT: The reason I used horses was to disperse the riotous crowd of people who were behaving unlawfully and were injuring my officers. They had to be cleared back. They were a riotous crowd who had come hundreds of miles to attack.

MANSFIELD: You were thinking that before they ever arrived, weren't you?

CLEMENT: Of course.[76]

In July 1985, after thirty-eight days of trial at Sheffield Crown Court, the prosecution against fifteen miners for riot at Orgreave collapsed. Thereafter, the prosecution quietly dropped the rest of the cases against all ninety-five miners arrested on 18 June 1984. The defence exposed police lies through detailed and forensic mapping of police statements and their movements that proved the policemen could not have made the arrests they said they made. According to Peirce, 'records and notebooks claimed to be contemporaneous on which officers were giving evidence in court disappeared – one at a court lunch adjournment – never to be found.'[77]

At the time, the defence team's meticulous work gave a hint of who the police in 1984 really were (long before the Hillsborough disaster inquiry, the Guildford Four acquittal or the phone hacking scandal) and what they thought they could get away with.[78] This resulted, seven years after the miners' strike, in nearly half a million pounds of compensation from taxpayers' money being paid to thirty-nine miners.[79] Tony Benn MP described the payments as 'unprecedented in the history of British law'.[80] Home Office files from 1991 include the pre-prepared response drafted for government ministers to potential questions following the miners' compensation payout. They reveal the government thinking:

'Is the Home Secretary afraid that an inquiry would uncover collusion between the Government and the police in handling the miners' strike?' A flat denial and a repeat that 'Chief Constables exercised their operational discretion as they saw fit.' 'Will the Home Secretary publish the Tactical Options Manual used by ACPO?', 'It is for ACPO to give it the circulation that seems appropriate ... I understand that over the last year it has been redrafted ... [and] is expected to receive ACPO's final approval shortly.'

And curiously, 'Has the Home Secretary approved the Tactical Operations Manual?' The response is carefully worded: 'It is not for me to approve this ACPO manual which is concerned with operational matters properly within the discretion of chief officers.'[81]

This response referenced the current home secretary (Leon Brittan), not his predecessor, who had indeed secretly approved the manual (Willie Whitelaw), shortly before receiving a hereditary peerage.

The Conservative government of 1991 seemed keen to continue the secrecy around the manual and its creation, giving further credence to the lie that the Home Office and the home secretary were not involved in police operational matters. South Yorkshire Police privately admitted to their solicitors that 'many officers did "*over re-act*" [*sic*] and that there was evidence of perjury relating to at least two arrests.' No police officer has been held to account. An officer who was on film repeatedly hitting a miner faced no disciplinary or criminal charges. In his interview under caution in June 1984, he disclosed, 'It's not a case of me going off half cock. The Senior Officers, Supers and Chief Supers were there and getting stuck in too – they were encouraging the lads and I think their attitude ... affected what we all did.'[82]

CR

In May 2015, thirty years after the Old Bailey trial collapsed, the Independent Police Complaints Commission (IPCC) published a report including an investigation into conspiracy between the police and the county prosecuting solicitor to elevate the charges against the miners to riot and unlawful assembly. It contained aspects of potential police criminality at Orgeave. In 2016, Home Secretary Amber Rudd refused an inquiry it was rumoured because she felt it would 'slur the memory of Thatcher'.[83] The IPCC investigation uncovered new evidence that confirmed the police altered evidence and likely held back documents in both the criminal and civil cases. While the IPCC confirmed that the chief constable and the prosecutor spoke, they found no direct evidence to substantiate the criminal offence of conspiracy.[84] That might be tenable on the evidence the IPCC had at the time, but big questions remain about government involvement, given what we now know. The involvement of Thatcher alone, in the policing and prosecuting of miners, should warrant a public inquiry into the policing at Orgreave. The IPCC report states that there is no time limit to bringing a prosecution for conspiracy.[85]

Throughout the strike the narrative of the government and the media countered that of the miners. In 1992 it was revealed that all the pits were to close – Scargill was proved absolutely right. There was a mass show of public support on a demonstration in London, but the pits closed anyway, devastating communities. Shopping centres now stand where coal mines once were. The local community is no longer supported by well-paid jobs, yet for many decades after the strike, the UK became a net importer of coal.

Despite the government's alleged concern about controlling public expenditure, no cost or effort was spared in the attempt to defeat the NUM. Andrew Turnbull, Thatcher's private secretary, wrote to the Home Office, 'The Prime Minister ... agrees that the Chief Constable of South Yorkshire should be given every support in his efforts to uphold the law.' A handwritten note by Margaret Thatcher reads, 'Is this enough? Can we provide the funds direct?'[86]

The Conservatives had secured power as the party of economic prudence and efficiencies, and 'law and order'. Many, including Brown and Rees, pointed out that there was excessive policing, including one pit where fifty-five police vehicles supported one man going to work.[87] The NCCL report recorded the 'first striker who had returned to work was accompanied by between 1000 and 2000 police officers.'[88] Courts and police were accused of excessive charges and bail conditions, with some miners, particularly in Scotland, being sacked even if acquitted, losing not only redundancy money but their pensions too.

The government's public statements on the autonomy of chief constables have been revealed as lies by events at Orgreave. According to Gareth Peirce, 'Events at Orgreave evidenced a turning point in British policing of lawful assembly and protest and set the scene for policing thereafter.'[89] Mutual aid policing during the strike resulted in an extra policing cost of £400 million and a substantial payout to miners in compensation, yet the president of ACPO, Chief Constable Hall, wrote that the police can be 'justifiably proud' of their actions during the miners' strike.[90]

Despite facing the full might and interference of the state, the miners showed incredible resilience to fight for a year on no pay. At its height, no less than 142,000 miners went on strike.[91] Some 11,313 miners were arrested, 10,372 were charged in England and Wales, and 5,653 cases were put on trial – 1,335 were acquitted and 200 were imprisoned.[92] In Scotland, 603 miners were convicted and 140 acquitted. Of those Scottish convictions many will be quashed as a result of a judge-led inquiry into policing during the miners' strike in Scotland that concluded in 2020 that the miners were treated in a 'grossly excessive manner'.

The total number of police injured during the strike was 1,399 in England and Wales and 110 in Scotland. The Orgreave Truth and Justice Campaign say 7,000 pickets were injured and several people died.[93]

The Home Office held back around thirty files of government papers on the miners' strike despite the thirty-year disclosure rule. Files released confirm 'appropriate steps to prepare' for and win a strike against the miners was deliberate. This included the creation of government 'endurance potential for the future' implemented three years before the strike started.[94] It has also been stated that Thatcher had a more passive role in the miners' strike, often egged on by close advisers particularly around the 'monstering' of the miners.[95] Thatcher's papers confirm the opposite.

A secret memo sent to the prime minister in August 1984 reveals how informed Thatcher was about developments. She was advised that intelligence sources against the miners ranged from the 'ordinary course of events' to 'covert operations (e.g. surveillance, agents)' to 'intelligence obtained by the Security Service from their operations against subversives'.[96] Special Branch and the security services passed intelligence to both the police and the National Reporting Centre. Publicly the NRC was for the coordination of mutual aid only, yet an officer of ACPO rank was based at the NRC, responsible for the coordination of that intelligence.[97] The miners had the upper hand as intelligence on their organisation was limited 'because it has been difficult for many years to place or acquire sources in that particular community'.[98]

After a review by Frank Taylor, assistant chief constable of Lincolnshire, on the management of information and intelligence, a National Intelligence Unit (NIU) was established in September 1984. The 'existence' of the NIU 'was known to only a few people'.[99] The deputy chief constable of Cambridgeshire, who had 'oversight of intelligence matters' in the NRC, was moved to run the NIU. The links between the units were maintained.[100] The secret services were also 'directly involved in the running of it'.[101]

Before the NIU opened, Home Secretary Leon Brittan encouraged a 'specific objective' to obtain 'information about the organisation of criminal activities with a view to prosecuting more senior people'.[102] A month later, he wrote to the prime minister 'in no doubt about the determination of the police to bring ring leaders before the courts wherever possible'.[103] Even with such reassurance, Thatcher remained 'a little disappointed' and hoped that the police and security services would 'continue to give priority to obtaining information' to prevent and punish crime.[104]

The government, the police and civil servants had a symbiotic relationship, directed by the prime minister. The bias of government was the polar opposite of the independence publicly declared. Thatcher drove the strike; she pushed the police, civil servants and her ministers to defeat the miners.

The secrets and lies of police and government during the miners' strike fundamentally changed the way Britain works and opened the door to a further increase of police powers through the Public Order Act 1986. This codified the common law charges of riot, unlawful assembly and other public order charges, making them easier for the police and courts to use.

What is obvious is the Home Office and police also wanted to keep the manual, its origins and their collusion secret. They had ample opportunity during and after the miners' strike to reveal the manual's provenance. They didn't. This meant that the police and the government could carry on with their agendas.

The miners walked back to work in March 1985 with trade union banners held high. A few days later the Home Office held another party to thank the police for all they 'did during the miners' strike'. A drinks event had been planned for the previous summer, but 'ACPO got cold feet due to fears of over close identification with the government during the miners' strike'. Around thirty guests attended, including those from the police forces most directly involved in the miners' strike, senior staff of the National Reporting Centre, ACPO, Sir Brian Cubbon and officials from the Home Office. As they celebrated the creation of the secret manual in 1983, so they celebrated its successful brutal use two years later. Also at the celebration were Chief Constable Peter Wright and Assistant Chief Constable Clement from South Yorkshire Police, who had overseen the policing at Orgreave. And Mrs Thatcher.[105]

Within a few weeks of the party, Wright met Thatcher again at the Hillsborough stadium, the day after a tragedy that would result in the deaths of ninety-seven Liverpool football fans. Thatcher unconditionally supported the police and promoted the lie that the fans were responsible for the disaster. It took twenty-three years for the Hillsborough families to expose the police cover-up and obtain justice. The behaviour of South Yorkshire Police that day cannot be disassociated from their behaviour at Orgreave.

For those miners who believe they experienced a parallel universe to what the government, police and sections of the media said, an inquiry would help right the wrongs they have faced. Arthur Critchlow, one of the men compensated for Orgreave, explains,

You don't feel fully vindicated. As far as everyone else is concerned ... They seem to have a view that we were just violent. They don't see what happened behind the scenes, the perjury, the lying, and the assaults ... Every paper I read and I have them all, there's no mention of false statements, perjury, fabrications. All that was said in the papers was just pickets cleared ... I would have rather not had the money. I would have rather there had been an inquiry and people prosecuted. If we are going to have laws they need to be for everybody. Otherwise it's not a law. Money doesn't make up for it.[106]

3
Boot Boys in the Beanfield
The Battle of Stonehenge, 1985

The battle of Stonehenge seemed to have ended yesterday in a victory for law and order. The coils of barbed wire ... glittered in the sunshine, while at a roadblock nearby young policemen basked leisurely in the afternoon heat ... 520 ... were arrested ... after violent clashes ... Twenty-four were taken to hospital with injuries.

Thomson Prentice, 'Hippie convoy limps away from Stonehenge after violent clashes with police', *The Times*, 3 June 1985

It was fortunate that the opposing sides were dressed in their respective team strip, for otherwise I would have found it difficult to distinguish between those upholding the law and those flouting it.

Pamela Storey, letter to *The Times*, 7 June 1985

On 1 June 1985, over 500 travellers, known as the Peace Convoy, wound their way to Stonehenge in Wiltshire. The line of 150 vehicles doubling as homes included many families with young babies. They comprised small groups of people who preferred to live on the road, rejecting inner city life and embracing freedom.

Many were hoping to have their newborn babies blessed at Stonehenge on 21 June, the summer solstice.

New travellers gathered at Stonehenge as the 'central event of their year' and had established a free festival in the area that attracted travellers, and city dwellers who wanted a festival break.[1] According to a police statement, '"Free Festivals" are believed to have originated as religious gatherings ... usually degenerating into wild sexual orgies.'[2] This was to be its eleventh year.

The year before, there had been accusations of damage to Stonehenge. But the travellers said 'the worst of the damage had been caused by farmers and by police trying to evict them'.[3] Nick Davies, of the *Guardian*, reported that some of the travellers vehicles were 'destroyed, and many of them were arrested. They went to the High Court and successfully challenged the eviction. The 1984 festival, which attracted some 30,000 people, then went ahead – the final straw for the Wiltshire establishment.'[4] The number of new travellers was doubling year on year.

Nick Davies discovered that in February 1985 'the whole of the Wiltshire establishment, had sat down to decide what to do about the convoy', and on taking legal advice, decided on 'civil injunctions to justify all that then happened'.[5] An injunction was secured against eighty-three people. Barbed wire was brought in to fortify Stonehenge and an extensive advertising campaign was used to keep festival goers away.[6] A known fascist, Les Vaughan, who was hired by local farmers to provide security on their land, apparently gathered the names for the injunction. Vaughan visited the convoy a number of times and in what must have been a ploy tried to sell the travellers guns.[7] They had no interest, and asked him to leave and not return.

Prior to the solstice period of 1985 the police set up roadblocks on the outskirts of Stonehenge. Assistant Chief Constable Lionel Grundy of Wiltshire Police, the man in charge of the operation, said the police were there to avoid a breach of the peace. Even though the police had no authority to enforce a civil injunction, Grundy said, 'we have a duty to enforce.'[8]

As the law stood, roadblocks were allowed in specific circumstances, none of which applied at Stonehenge.[9] There were also no provisions for roadblocks in the 1983 tactical manual; they were only added in 1987 after an ACPO review of the miners' strike. Having cancelled all police leave and called upon mutual aid from six other forces, Wiltshire's chief constable, Donald Smith, was prepared for anything that may arise. Nick Davies said that it was 'highly questionable whether what happened was really lawful'.[10]

A few miles from the start of the injunction exclusion zone an outrider spotted the first roadblock, with gravel tipped onto the road. He warned the convoy, which detoured and turned left and then right onto the A303, where it met a second roadblock near Cholderton, ten miles from Stonehenge. The police radio log at 14:31 states, 'Confrontation is imminent. Have you got any ambulances standing by?'[11]

The convoy stopped. Many travellers, unaware of the roadblock, got out of their vehicles. Alan Lodge ('Tash'), a photographer and former ambulance man, looked up and down the convoy. From both sides, police were closing in on them. Police were shouting 'get out'; their raised truncheons were then brought down, smashing the windows of vehicles while travellers were still inside.

Tash and his family tried to escape and followed some others into a field, driving through a gap in the fence. More followed. The police drove a van towards the gap to block it but instead collided with a traveller's bus. The radio log 'stressed' that the travellers should be allowed into the field, as then 'we have a suitable breach of the peace situation'.[12]

Trying to get away, some travellers drove into the next field, a beanfield. The police surrounded them on all sides. A stand-off over the next four hours saw people feeding their kids, while others, including Tash, helped the injured and tried to negotiate their way out:

> I was directed to a number of head injuries that had resulted from the initial conflict on the road. All of these injuries were truncheon wounds to the back of the head and some people were quite distressed. I was shown one man, about 20 years old, who was semi-conscious with yet another head wound. I was fearful of him dying.[13]

The police were initially amenable when the travellers offered to leave the county peacefully. Grundy, at headquarters, refused; he arrived by helicopter just after 5:30 p.m. Still he 'refused to negotiate an alternative'.[14] Tash said, 'The tone of the meeting was "do what you're told or else!" ... people should leave their vehicles or be arrested.'[15] The radio log of Grundy reads, 'My conversation with them with a view to their coming out safely was of no value, although it's quite clear that a number of people in there do not want confrontation.'[16] Reporters from ITN and the *Guardian* got themselves into the field. The rest of the media stood, 'like sheep', at the bottom of the field where the police had told them to stand.[17]

At 7 p.m., ACC Grundy gave the order 'Shields up.'[18] Kim Sabido of ITN, who had reported from Toxteth and Northern Ireland, described the approach as 'almost like a scene from *Zulu* ... a whole line of policemen banging their shields, moving slowly, progressively up the field, smashing any vehicle or anybody in their way'.[19]

The travellers revved their engines and drove around in circles. Grundy sent police in on foot to arrest everyone in the field.

First they had to stop around thirty buses, trucks and converted ambulances on the move. The police started to throw objects, including their truncheons and portable metal fire extinguishers; one was seen to throw a large stone. They shattered vehicle windows as mothers and children tried to protect themselves inside. Shields were used like 'a frisbee ... to try and hit the driver and bring the vehicles to a halt'.[20]

The police helicopter which had been following the travellers' movements all day issued a warning: '"You cannot escape. Give yourselves up." Some did.'[21]

Two coaches crashed. There was a fire. Within half an hour only one 'big bus careered on'.[22] The police commandeered other vehicles and tried to ram the last bus. A swarm of police moved in, climbed through broken windows to drag people out 'through a storm of truncheons'.[23] The ITN footage shows police running up to stationary buses and smashing windows, screaming at people to come out. People were dragged out by their hair and thumped in the face by police so their legs gave way. Those arrested were marched away with blood on their necks, police holding them by their heads. A girl's hair was pulled and then she was thrown to the ground. A man, his face in the grass, hands outstretched, sobbed. A young black teenager was led away by two officers, screaming, crying, 'Somebody help me. Help me.'[24]

Kim Sabido spoke directly to camera – in the background there were the final scenes of the battle:

> What we ... have seen in the last thirty minutes here in this field has been some of the most brutal police treatment of people that I've witnessed in my entire career as a journalist ... The number of people who have been hit by policemen, who have been clubbed whilst holding babies in their arms in coaches around this field, is

Police surround the last coach to be stopped in a
field near Stonehenge, 1 June 1985.

A bloodied teenager is led away from the Stonehenge
Peace Convoy, Nick Davies in the background.

still to be counted ... There must surely be an enquiry after what has happened here today.[25]

Nick Davies said that for the first time in his career he felt sick.[26] There were over 500 arrests, one of the largest number at any one event this century (comparable to the mass arrest of 1,314 at Trafalgar Square in London in 1961 at a protest organised by an offshoot of CND).[27] They were taken to a number of different police stations. Some were held in a cold police garage, and strip-searched before being crammed into cells with up to twelve others. They were held for many hours, with little food. Many of their children were incarcerated before social services took them away.[28] Over 240 were charged with unlawful assembly and most of the others with obstruction charges.[29]

There were many complaints of police brutality. Grundy said allegations would be investigated, adding, 'I have not seen any such incidents.'[30] A police spokesman pre-empted findings: 'Any claims of police brutality are ridiculous. Our officers did all they could in the face of the problem and we have nothing but praise for their action.'[31] So proud were Wiltshire Police that in their official history the section on 'Policing Stonehenge' fails to mention the event.[32]

Robert Key, Conservative MP for Salisbury, witnessed events, 'There is no doubt in my mind who caused the violence. The police action was carefully planned and executed by officers.'[33] Deputy Chief Constable Ian Readhead disagreed. In 1985, he was one of three Wiltshire inspectors trained to deal with public disorder and said, 'the policing operation had not been thought through very well ... [we] never had the briefing ... there couldn't have been any plan to put travellers into the Beanfield'.[34]

By the time it was broadcast, Kim Sabido's piece to camera had been replaced with a voiceover that better reflected the police statements. When he got back to London, most of the worst scenes filmed had disappeared. BBC news showed clips from the police video.[35] Nick Davies's copy was also not immune, he claimed an *Observer* newsroom executive 'tampered with the story ... adding false details which had apparently been supplied by Wiltshire police'.[36] Most journalists had compliantly watched from a spot designated by the police and filed stories of 'utmost dishonesty'.[37] One *Observer* photographer was arrested but later acquitted. His editor responded, 'I can't imagine why they would want to remove any working photographer ... unless there were some ulterior motive ... like the desire not to have their actions photographed.'[38]

Twenty-six travellers brought a civil trial for damages against the police. In court, an inspector also revealed that 'the plan was to arrest everyone "irrespective of whether they had done anything wrong, beyond being there at that time".'[39] Aided by credible witnesses and the fact that some of the footage from the missing ITN archive resurfaced, the jury found for the travellers and awarded damages. However, the main issue of whether it was reasonable for the police to arrest everybody was a decision for the judge alone, who decided against them. As a result, they received no damages.

As one traveller said, 'If you had a couple of football hooligans in a football stadium, you wouldn't arrest everybody in the stadium just to get at the hooligans.'[40] The judge disagreed: 'the police couldn't distinguish between who was peaceful and who was still wanting to make trouble, and the only way they could find out – or the only way they could prevent trouble – was to arrest everybody.'[41]

Many complaints made about excessive policing were

investigated by the Police Complaints Authority, who concluded differently from the judge: 'in the act of making the arrests some officers clearly used excessive force.' However, the PCA reported that it was not 'possible to identify them amongst the 1,363 officers involved and therefore disciplinary proceedings, which demand a clear identification of office[r]s', were 'impossible'.[42] Many officers did not have their identification numbers showing. Nick Davies found this surprising, as after the miners' strike there were 'reassurances' from the Home Office 'on the record and officially that that would never happen again'.[43] Tim Greene, a defence solicitor, said, 'the report had vindicated complaints by convoy members.'[44]

Even before the miners' strike, the government and police were looking at ways to stop travellers, driven by complaints from constituents about the 'presence of the campers'. From 1982, the Home Office examined existing laws and the possibility of using injunctions, even though, 'It had to be accepted, however, that neither the presence of the campers nor their way of life in themselves amounted to any crime.' The media piled on, making 'wild allegations' which police enquiries showed 'to be without foundation'. A policy of low-level policing was decided. However, minute-by-minute surveillance of the travellers' movements ensued and information was shared between different police forces and the Home Office.[45]

In a letter, Home Office Minister Douglas Hurd expressed his concern at the constant moving on of travellers by the police, 'as if they were a band of medieval brigands'.[46] Reacting to Hurd's views, a Home Office official wrote, 'I am sorry to see that it is now a cause for such concern to be a vaguely anarchic ageing hippie, and am duly warned.' Hurd also asked if the travellers were now 'a matter of national policing'. Was this code for ACPO, who had taken on national policing issues, to pick up the chalice?[47]

The police investigated many claims and rumours about the travellers, including ones reported in the *News of the World*, which linked them to explosions, grenades and guns.[48] All were unfounded, 'as the site was at all times supervised by the police … the noise of gunfire and the explosion of grenades could be calculated to have attracted their attention. Nothing was seen or heard.' The police also interviewed the *News of the World* journalist, who 'could only say that he had seen a bandolier of shotgun cartridges in the camp'.[49]

Rather than calling on the media to report truthfully, the Home Office focused their attention on the travellers who had returned to Wiltshire. Police and Home Office minutes confirm that 'none of the activities of the convoy … can constitute terrorism' and that there were no terrorist links.

In November 1983, they drew up a 'Home Office future action' plan on the request of Douglas Hurd, which included the feasibility of injunctions and bringing in ACPO to help. It concludes an approach of 'non-intervention' for 1984, but it was not known 'how Ministers will react to this – given their stronger feeling than their predecessors that the law should be enforced vigorously'.[50] However, despite the 'non-intervention' decision in April 1984, ACC Grundy was on the ground with 400 officers when an injunction was served on travellers evicting them from their site near Stonehenge. After this operation the National Trust looked to 'restrict or contain' the festivals.

After events at the Beanfield, senior Home Office officials, including Lord Elton and the home secretary, replied to a number of letters from MPs.[51] The home secretary, Leon Brittan, wrote in full support of the police, implying that the travellers had breached the injunction when they had not. He was 'assured … the officer in charge … only took such steps as he considered necessary [to] effectively police the situation'.[52]

Not everyone agreed with this approach. DCC Readhead reflected that

> if there had been someone ... at that time, willing to say to the travellers, 'Let's stop this now, let's ... talk this through', I think it would have got sorted out. But ... we [had] someone in authority ... it was very much along the lines of, 'There have been acts of criminal damage ... we want to apprehend the people who did that.' ... They'd gone in the field not to cause criminal damage but because ... they were confused ... frightened ... police officers in the kind of equipment we were wearing on the day are frightening.[53]

It was not the first time ACC Grundy, the officer in charge, had taken steps he 'considered necessary'. Grundy was the arresting officer for Gerry Conlon in a case later exposed as a notorious miscarriage of justice in 1989 – the Guildford Four. Accused of planting an IRA bomb, Conlon signed a false confession after he was tortured. He named Grundy as one of two officers who hit him from behind and put him in 'the search position' naked, and 'when I fell they picked me up by my testicles.'[54] Conlon's false confession led to their convictions as well as those of the Maguire Seven. They spent up to fifteen years in prison labelled terrorists before their convictions were quashed.[55]

Despite this, Grundy was promoted to deputy chief constable, receiving an OBE in 1988. Just before the court confirmed that Conlon and others were innocent, Grundy was seconded to the Home Office Police Department, and on retirement he travelled the world as inspector general for the Foreign Office, 'advising governments on police restructuring, senior management and human rights'. He became a Conservative councillor, then head of Kennet District Council and chair of the local Conservative association.[56] After he died in May 2020, his obituaries failed to mention his role in the miscarriages of the Guildford Four and Maguire Seven, or at the Beanfield.

Following the policing of the miners' strike, the rural police were empowered. They turned against alternative lifestyles, support-ing the landowners with civil injunctions. By applying violent methods in and beyond the manual at the Battle of the Beanfield, the police acted in a manner more appropriate to barbarians. Despite this brutal behaviour the government extended the law against travellers. The Public Order Act 1986 was introduced with a clause nicknamed 'the hippy clause' that stopped assem-bly on private land. Originally not intended to include Gypsies, Margaret Thatcher did 'not see why gypsies should not be caught by the new clause'.[57]

Of the charges against travellers at the Battle of the Bean-field, 119 were dropped by the Crown Prosecution Service in December 1986, for reasons of cost and length of time.[58] Before the charges were dropped, solicitor Tim Greene commented, 'I believe the whole police operation that day was illegal, that the police used excessive force and then tried to use the advantages they feel ... to provide a justification for that illegality. That has now failed.'[59] The prosecutor complained, 'The law does not at present adequately deal with those types of offences,' which is now 'recognised ... in the new Public Order Act'.[60]

The charges against travellers were dropped less than a month after the Conservative government introduced the new Public Order Act. Over the next decade this Act was used against the travellers, but to what purpose? In 1984, the damage to Stone-henge cost £50,000 to fix. The police operation of 1 June 1985 and subsequent court cases reportedly cost the taxpayer around £5 million.[61] Having fought the travellers for a decade, the local council and the police decided it would be cheaper to let the travellers, druids and others in.

It appears that in the 1980s the police were only held to account if challenged in court. Lord Tony Gifford, a barrister for the defence, said that the people in this case

> called the police to account ... They have secured a number of verdicts in their favour ... this is part of the restraining factors ... when they decide what sort of operations to mount ... you must always have ... faith in the power of people ... to restrain the powers of authority.[62]

DCC Readhead concluded that people 'were hurt ... by police officers ... and that can't be right ... If you believe in a police force operating in a democracy, they must operate within the law, otherwise you do not have policing by consent; you have a different form of policing.'[63]

Printers were about to find out how true this was in a place called Wapping, East London.

4
Murdoch's Paper Boys
Wapping, 1987

[The police] maintain the right of passage and the right to demon-strate; they were not working for Mr Murdoch.

Home Office minister Giles Shaw to Clive
Soley MP, meeting record, 20 May 1986

We have learned how the resources of the State can be deployed to crush trade unionism and drive workers onto the dole queue.

Tony Benn, *Wapping Post*, 24 January 1987

In 2011, the *Guardian* exposed a scandal.[1] The Murdoch UK newspaper empire was hacking the phones of celebrities and MPs and that of Milly Dowler, a young teenager who had been murdered. The uproar from this behaviour led to the Leveson inquiry 'into the culture, practices and ethics of the press', commissioned by then prime minister David Cameron. In his evidence to Leveson, Cameron suggested that the inquiry was a 'cathartic moment where press, politicians, police, all the relationships that haven't been right; we have a chance to reset them, and that is what we must do.' It also led media mogul Rupert

Murdoch to admit, 'I failed.'[2] The appalling behaviour by News Corporation companies, of which he was chairman, arguably had its genesis in London's Fleet Street and Wapping dispute during the 1980s.

Kelvin MacKenzie, then editor of the *Sun*, created a department dedicated to reporting celebrity gossip. Two of those who worked on the desk were Andy Coulson and Piers Morgan.[3] Coulson rose to become editor at the *News of the World* in 2003, before resigning in 2007 after one of his staff and a private detective were sent to prison for phone hacking. Despite this, David Cameron hired Coulson as director of communications at No. 10 Downing Street. According to former Conservative Justice Secretary Kenneth Clarke, this was the outcome of a deal between Cameron and Murdoch to secure his newspaper's support for the Conservatives in the 2010 election.[4]

In 1995 Piers Morgan, who had been the youngest ever editor at Murdoch's *News of the World*, became editor at the *Daily Mirror* before being sacked in 2004 for publishing fake photographs. At the Leveson inquiry Morgan tried to convince them he was ignorant about phone hacking. Leveson concluded, 'What it [the evidence] does, however, clearly prove is that he was aware that it was taking place in the press as a whole and that he was sufficiently unembarrassed by what was criminal behaviour that he was prepared to joke about it.'[5] Morgan later admitted he did know of the phone hacking practice; however, he did nothing to stop it or report it to the police.[6]

In the 1980s, the UK national newspaper industry was based in and around Fleet Street, London. It was a highly unionised industry, whose printing unions had negotiated high salaries for printers, which they believed were a reflection of their poor working conditions. Management disliked the printers. Terry Smith, a former compositor at the *Sun*, confirms why: 'We would actually in fact stop a paper if ... at times we felt that there was some reporting that was over the top and unfair.'[7] He recalls that during the 1984–5 miners' strike, 'There was the picture of Arthur Scargill waving, which they [the *Sun*] produced as if he was doing a Nazi salute. That got right up our nose, "No, we can't touch that. You want this, it's not going with that picture." So we took the picture out and we put a panel in and they agreed the panel because it said precisely "you're doing it not us".'

As John Bailey, a proofreader at the *Sun*, explained that 'cheap shots at enemies of the Thatcher government were becoming commonplace, increasingly vitriolic and lacking in any form of balance'.[8] If there was time, the unions warned the 'victims' so they could seek a right of reply. 'The *Sun* would not comply with their requests so the next step was to refuse to publish these attacks.'[9] Where production schedules did not give time for a right of reply, the unions took immediate action, as in the case of Tony Benn MP when the 1 March 1984 edition was halted due to a spurious article denouncing Benn as 'off his rocker'.[10]

When those such as the *Sun*'s editor, Kelvin Mackenzie, complained about trade unions stopping the front pages, the focus fell on trade union power. No one, except the trade unions, asked why the newspapers were regularly trying to publish photographs, headlines and articles such as those that compared Scargill to Hitler in the first place. Were such articles reporting the news, or showing a lack of neutrality and pushing a political agenda? Even with such occasional stoppages, Murdoch's UK businesses generated £45 million or 60 per cent of his worldwide profits in 1985. In America, however, the business had financial issues and had to meet interest payments of £460,000 a day on loans that followed the purchase of Fox News and Metromedia.[11]

Alongside UK employment laws, technological advances in printing newspapers afforded Murdoch an opportunity. Legal advice from his solicitors, Farrer & Co., who also advised the queen, confirmed, 'if a moment came when it was necessary to dispense with the present workforce ... the cheapest way of doing so would be to dismiss employees while participating in a strike or other industrial action.'[12] Murdoch's corporation set plans in place to use the law to get rid of his trade union workforce in Fleet Street and replace them with an entirely new and non-unionised workforce at a new location, in Wapping, East London.

Considerable effort was made to keep secret the planned move to Wapping. There were lies and subterfuge – primarily that Murdoch's new state-of-the-art plant was for a new newspaper, the *London Post*. A dummy of the *London Post* was printed at Wapping without the Fleet Street trade unions in September 1985. A strike was considered but rejected. This may have been 'a serious mistake', as a strike at that time 'would have caused Murdoch serious damage'.[13]

Contrary to popular belief, the trade unions were not resistant to new technology at Fleet Street. Negotiations around the introduction of new technology and printing at Wapping had started long before the strike and by the end of 1985 a deal was close. Near the end of that year, Murdoch's negotiators changed tack and offered the unions terms that they could not accept: an end to strike action and the autonomous and unchallengeable right of management to manage. Some in the unions had suspicions that Murdoch wanted to get rid of them altogether, but had no proof of Murdoch's real plan until it was too late.[14]

The Transport and General Workers Union (TGWU), who were also negotiating with Murdoch's company to distribute new newspapers produced at Wapping, discovered in an informal meeting that the transport company TNT had signed a contract to 'uplift any product' from Wapping.[15] Just a few days before the strike was called by the print unions, Murdoch assured the transport union that *The Times* and the *Sun* would continue to be printed at their existing locations around Fleet Street, even though a new colour section of the *Sunday Times* had already been produced at Wapping.[16]

On 19 January 1986, as this new section was being read in living rooms around the country, Murdoch had lunch at Chequers with Margaret Thatcher, her husband and Woodrow Wyatt. Wyatt was a former Labour politician, right-wing journalist and Thatcher confidant. On the way back to London, Murdoch gave Wyatt a tour of his new Wapping plant and admitted that the *London Post* was 'a ploy'. That weekend, Wyatt recorded in his diary, 'Rupert in high spirits … He said the police were ready in case there were pickets and they had riot shields stored in the warehouse nearby and every now and again a police helicopter came over to see that there was no trouble.'[17]

On 22 January 1986, as talks between the unions continued, Home Secretary Douglas Hurd 'hoped that the Metropolitan Police were fully prepared for any disorders which might follow from an industrial dispute'. A civil servant was dispatched to seek this assurance.[18] The same day, Met Police commissioner Kenneth Newman drew on legislation from 1839 to restrict the movement of vehicles and people around the Wapping area.[19] At the end of that week, the trade unions called a strike over the move of operations from Fleet Street to Wapping. In response, News International, acting on legal advice, sacked over 5,500 people without notice or redundancy pay – not just the printers but all the support and administrative staff.

Despite moving the printing of existing titles to Wapping, journalists from Murdoch's newspapers expected to remain in the offices around Fleet Street. However, over the weekend of the print union sackings, the editors of Murdoch's four papers told journalists that their jobs would also move to Wapping immediately. They were offered an ultimatum, £2,000 and private health insurance to move, or be sacked.

Many journalists who relied on being accessible baulked at the move to a location surrounded by high fences, barbed wire, floodlights and CCTV. The security measures earned the plant its nickname, 'Fortress Wapping'. Their union, the NUJ, argued that the journalists should not go. After many impassioned discussions at trade union meetings over the weekend, most of the journalists were at a desk with a new computer inputting their copy directly, at Wapping. Many said they went because they were worried about being blacklisted.[20] Around 100 who decided not to go were supported by the NUJ through the strike.

A thirteen-month dispute followed. Demonstrations outside Murdoch's plant in Wapping, though initially small, grew to 10,000 following sequestration of the trade union funds in February 1986.[21] Larger demonstrations took place on Wednesdays and Saturdays and police deployment reached over 1,000 on three days up to May.[22] The government declared 'operational independence' while concealing that the officer in overall charge at Wapping, Deputy Assistant Commissioner (DAC) Wyn Jones, had 'various meetings' with ministers.[23]

The Wapping plant was situated in the back streets of the East End of London. By mid-February 'the police began to use riot equipment and horses'.[24] At the rally on Saturday, 3 May 1986, 1,700 police were on duty. Their behaviour resulted in numerous complaints, including excessive policing, lack of identification (ID) numbers worn by police officers, failure in command and no warning before a horse charge. An ITN crew were injured and the BBC had camera lights smashed; neither reported this on the news.[25] Photographer Andrew Moore, aged twenty-three, was photographed being carried from the scene after he was struck by police batons in four separate incidents. With blood streaming from his head, an eye swollen and a suspected fractured skull, nurses described his injuries as being akin to a road accident.[26] The BBC and ITN also complained of being 'continually harassed' by police.[27] When Tony Benn MP spoke in the Houses of Parliament of excessive policing, Home Secretary Douglas Hurd laughed and walked out of the chamber.[28]

Labour MP Clive Soley obtained a meeting with Home Office minister Giles Shaw to discuss the policing at Wapping. He raised a lack of ID numbers on police uniforms. Shaw agreed it was 'unacceptable' but tried to excuse the issue by claiming numbers were only handed out on the night. On 3 May a young reporter asked two inspectors and a superintendent about the lack of ID numbers. He received three excuses, none of which matched that given by Shaw: 'They fell off'; 'we didn't have time to put numbers on'; and they were 'torn off by demonstrators'.[29]

Soley also highlighted the failure of the police to give a warning before a mounted police charge which caused 'many innocent people, including some children' to be put in danger. The minister responded that 'warnings were usually given by the police when dealing with a static demonstration.' The pages of the manual released during the Orgreave trial state, 'A warning to the crowd should always be given before adopting mounted dispersal tactics.' The revised 1987 manual that followed Wapping states the same. The Metropolitan Police replied to a question from the Home Office issued following Mr Soley's queries that the officer in charge, Mr Jones, 'was well aware of the need to issue a warning before the deployment of officers on horseback ... However, the ferocity and the suddenness of the violence on this particular occasion demanded an immediate response, which made it

impossible for such a warning to be given.'[30] This version of
events does not accord with numerous eyewitness accounts from
those who, unlike DAC Jones, were on the ground at Wapping
on 3 May.[31]

Soley argued that people should be aware that the police
were required to issue warnings during public order events. To
achieve this, he asked the minister of state to make the ACPO
manual public. In response, Mr Shaw 'emphasised' that while
accounting for 'the circumstances of any particular situation',
the manual 'provided advice on the <u>options</u> open to the police in
dealing with situations of escalating public disorder'. He would,
he said, consider the release of 'relevant standard force procedures' but not the manual itself.[32]

A further court order that limited trade union actions at Wapping
resulted in sequestration of the Society of Graphical and
Allied Trades (SOGAT) union funds and a fine for the NGA.
Instructions were issued by SOGAT to pickets listing the court's
instructions, including no more than six pickets. This ruling mirrored one issued at the end of the miners' strike where more
than six people picketing was considered intimidatory.[33] While
the courts applied the letter of the law on trade unions, the TNT
drivers who delivered the papers were not pursued. TNT lorries
drove at speed through the narrow streets of Wapping. Early in
the dispute one lorry injured two pickets after it collided with a
group of them. No action was taken against the driver due to a
lack of evidence.[34] Pickets and residents became angrier when
police continually failed to enforce speed limits on TNT lorry
drivers as they left the Wapping plant.[35]

Warnings that someone would be killed by a TNT lorry driver
were realised a few weeks before the one-year anniversary of the
start of the strike. Michael Delaney, a nineteen-year-old local on

Police confront demonstrators in Wapping, 24 January 1987.

his way back from his birthday celebrations, was hit by a lorry. A handwritten letter from Michael's sister said the driver 'seemed to be above the law and thoroughly protected by his company and the police'.[36] Little did she know of a police comment made over the radio minutes after Michael's death: 'they needn't worry, he wasn't a picket so they haven't got a martyr.'[37] A jury verdict of 'unlawful killing' was given at the coroner's court despite Judge Douglas Chambers directing they return a verdict of 'misadventure' or 'accidental death'.[38] Even so, the director of public prosecutions refused to prosecute the driver.

The anniversary of the start of the strike was marked by a march and rally on 24 January 1987. Trade unions who were liaising with police estimated that 7,000 people would march to Wapping. It was led by a jazz band, with a platform in the park given over to speakers, surrounded by tea vans and stalls. The event was promoted as a rally at which families were welcome. On the day, over 12,000 marched the two and a half miles from the Strand in solidarity with the 5,500 sacked workers in what was, initially, a 'carnival atmosphere'.[39] The pre-event police estimates were lower, ranging between 4,000 and 5,000. They 'planned accordingly' for disorder. Over 1,000 police officers were deployed in riot gear with forty-seven mounted officers available.[40]

Throughout the dispute, the police and Home Office denied they were taking sides and said the police were facilitating both 'the right of passage and the right to demonstrate; they were not working for Mr Murdoch'.[41] However, the December issue of the 1986 *Police Review* magazine describes the police briefings differently: 'The senior officer explained that the police presence was to ensure that News International employees could get in and out of the plant unimpeded. The second police job was to ensure that the distribution lorries taking the papers out of the plant are not obstructed.'[42] On the night of 24 January 1987 outside the Wapping plant there was an expectation, certainly among seasoned photojournalists, that something would kick off after a year of tensions. A trade union leader, Mike Hicks, had been arrested and jailed for what were considered political reasons. Michael Delaney's death was also fresh in the minds of many.

As the mass march of men, women and children moved towards Wapping, a small group gathered on the opposite side of the Highway from Virginia Street, one of the roads that connected the Highway with Murdoch's plant. The police cordoned off Virginia Street behind a barrier that looked more portable than the barriers police had been using for Saturday night demonstrations over the previous year.[43] The group threw stones and despite the 'hail of missiles [that] rained down' the police didn't react.[44] The police appeared to be waiting for the main march to arrive, which happened ten minutes later.

According to the Haldane Society of Socialist Lawyers, who had twenty-five observers on the night, the Highway itself 'was blocked'. Three lines of uniformed officers straddled the width of the road, behind which mounted police were visible. This prevented marchers from continuing down the Highway to try and stop TNT lorries from leaving the plant as was their normal practice. The effect of this cordon was to direct the march left into Wellclose Street up to a T-junction with Wellclose Square. The march passed the trade union support vehicles and turned right into the park, which quickly became packed.[45] Speeches from the platform in the park started just before 8 p.m.

DAC Wyn Jones released a statement on the night that the protesters' 'sole intention was to attack the police'.[46] He repeated this view in an open letter to the *Police Review* magazine two years later, adding, 'At no time was any attempt made to prevent any movement into or out of the News International Plant. The total fury and violence of the demonstrators was directed exclusively at police officers and firm action was required to stop it.'[47] What Jones failed to mention was that, to prevent the lorries from leaving the plant, the pickets would have had to fight their way through the three lines of riot police and mounted officers on the Highway to get there. Instead the protesters saw the police block and dutifully turned left.

As more of the march arrived, additional officers in riot gear moved into Virginia Street. The jazz band's lorry that headed the march was parked across Virginia Street in front of the police line. About twelve people turned the lorry over and tried to set it alight. More missiles were thrown.[48] A snatch squad was released from Virginia Street with truncheons drawn. The police tried to push back the densely packed crowd but were unable to do so because of the number of people in the streets. The police made no attempt to move the police lines blocking the Highway that would have released the pressure from within the crowd.[49] Officers randomly hit people with their truncheons. A second snatch squad increased the panic.

The police withdrew and the crowd settled down. Following an announcement, a JCB moved the overturned lorry to behind police lines. Over the next two hours the protesters and police went backwards and forwards, with the Haldane Society reporting that officers went 'in waves for approximately 45 minutes and by 8:15 p.m. there were considerably fewer demonstrators left in The Highway'. The protesters had been pushed back, and were now some distance from where the News International lorries would exit the plant. A number of innocent bystanders were caught up in the clearance and became involved in the action against the police.[50]

The protesters managed to push forward again almost to Virginia Street. At 8:45 p.m. around fifty officers with truncheons and short shields charged the crowd in Wellclose Street. People were hit at random and pushed against metal railings.[51] At the same time, an order to deploy mounted officers was withdrawn by DAC Jones, who wanted to assess the situation himself. Reminiscent of scenes at Warrington, half an hour later 'powerful police spot lamps which had been shining into the crowd were switched off'.[52] 'Immediately', thirty-five mounted officers came out of Virginia Street, crossed the Highway and cantered into the densely packed crowd followed by foot officers with long and short shields.[53]

Twice the mounted police charged. The horses went up Wellclose Street to the T-junction with Wellclose Square 'without stopping until they reached the union buses'.[54] This manoeuvre breached the manual on a number of levels, including 'halting at a predetermined' spot, a lack of warning before deployment, and that it would be 'quite inappropriate to use such a manoeuvre against a densely packed crowd' who should have space into which they could move.[55] Wellclose Street is not a wide road and at the time had metal railings along its length, one side bordering the park. The police later admitted, 'innocent people were knocked aside.'[56]

Having cleared the Highway of many of the protesters, the police went much further and pursued the protest as a whole throughout the night. Near the close of the evening they entered the park, with truncheons drawn, and all round the stalls and speakers' platform used their truncheons against the remaining protesters, including women and children.

A BBC report confirmed that there was no warning before the horse charge, which 'seriously aggravated' those who had 'previously been passive'.[57] The officer in charge of the mounted unit, Andy Petter, claimed that a warning was given. According to Petter, 'We had taken great care to act within ACPO guidelines in use of horses for crowd dispersal ... when we advanced upon the crowd we did so in a manner that met with the approval of the Association of Chief Police Officers and the Home Office.'[58] As the manual was not disclosed at the time, the public could not see the truth behind Petter's statement, that brutal tactics had been approved by the Home Office.

Two additional mounted charges followed and at one point a youth trying to stop the mounted officers stretched a wire or a rope across Wellclose Street. It was quickly taken down.[59] Others built a barricade of rubble to slow the horses.[60] Many reported mounted officers used their truncheons indiscriminately, hitting protesters. As Terry Smith recalls, 'They charged up the road. Most of our people were on each pavement as usual, minding their own business so to speak. The worst thing you can do when there's a cavalry charge ... [they] turned and ran which is the perfect position for a cavalryman to cut them down. Are they going to hit them on the arms? From up there on the horse? The nearest thing to them is their heads. They hit them.'[61]

An ITN reporter witnessed riot police running along the

Highway with other officers applauding them. Police at Orgreave had done the same.[62] *Morning Star* photographer Ernie Greenwood was trampled under a horse, breaking his arm.[63] A policeman wielding a truncheon knocked photographer Derek Hudson unconscious, earning him six stitches.[64] John Bowden, a solicitor wearing a yellow vest that identified him as a 'legal observer', was beaten in the face in what he described as an 'unprovoked and gratuitous' attack that left him suffering dizzy spells five years later.[65] Even BBC war reporter Kate Adie was not immune. She was hit in the face by a truncheon after she responded positively to an officer who said, 'It's Kate Adie, isn't it?'[66] Terry Smith comments, 'she's been to all those war zones round the world and there she is, comes to Wapping and gets beaten up. Their cameras were smashed, they were shining great searchlight torches at them so they couldn't get pictures.'

The *Guardian* reported the speeches came to 'a chaotic end' when 'Police on foot charged into the square, with the terrified crowd slipping and sliding as they fled across the uneven and muddy ground. A group of twenty who had run onto the stage to protect themselves were attacked while others who fell were hit repeatedly by police.'[67] A first aid worker on a trade union bus turned medical hub said, 'They are now smashing the windows of the bus. The children are screaming. The ambulance men are unable to reach the bus to take our injured because of the police presence all around.'[68] By 11 p.m. the area was cleared.

A printer, Paul King, was one of those arrested that night, and was initially taken to the police station before going to hospital. 'Whilst I was in Guy's Hospital I was diagnosed as having bruised kidneys from a kicking and trapped nerves in my wrist.' On leaving he was shown 'a ward that looked like a medical clearing station from the First World War. Men and women in there who had come from the demonstration ... bodies everywhere, there were stretchers on the floor, heads bandaged, arms in plaster, legs in plaster, it was horrendous … wives [got a] battering because they'd gone up to Wapping to support their husbands and they had no understanding of what went on and how brutal the police could be.'

The police left the site around 2:20 a.m. Three tonnes of rubble and other items were collected, including a 'spear' that looked like a trade union banner pole. These items were displayed on national television by DAC Jones the next day. He said his officers had 'acted magnificently' and that any accusations of ID numbers being covered up were 'simply not true'.[69] There was no mention that rubble had been used, not as weapons but to build a defensive barrier to stop the police horse charges. Nor was there any mention of the forty protesters known to the police as hurt, with over half having head injuries and twenty-nine going to hospital.[70] Instead, Murdoch's *Times* reported that the police said 'there were no known injuries to civilians' as a result of the horse manoeuvres.[71] Police injuries at Wapping on 24 January increased from initial figures to 194, with thirty-nine officers going to hospital, two of whom spent the night.[72] Some of the injuries were the result of mounted officers falling from their horses.[73] Brenda Dean, the SOGAT trade union leader, whom no one could describe as a radical, said she did not believe these figures.[74] The Police Complaints Authority (PCA) report published in 1990 stated that 'the true figure for civilian injuries will never be known,' but they confirmed that nearly 200 protesters were injured, a fivefold increase on the Met Police figures reported at the time.[75]

DAC Jones said the use of mounted police was 'to remove the demonstrators from the source of further ammunition'.[76] Jones maintained that the police 'would have suffered even worse injuries' if horses had not been sent in; 'The sky at one stage was

completely darkened ... because of the array of horrendous missiles thrown at us.'[77] This was nearly identical to the description
given by police chiefs during the miners' strike, after Hunterston
and Orgreave.

The majority of the sixty-five arrests were for threatening
behaviour and other summary offences. Thirteen were printers. Notably, the charges of unlawful assembly and riot which
had been used unsuccessfully in the miners' strike were missing from the Wapping charge sheets.[78] At least five of the cases
against printers fell away when the police offered no evidence or
doubt was cast by the PCA on the charges. Paul King was told
to bring an overnight bag 'because you're going to go down'.
Just before he appeared before the magistrate, King was offered
a bindover, including a ban on him being within one mile of
Wapping. He calls the experience 'exceptionally edifying'. Some
of the wronged eventually received financial recompense, including three printers who won £87,000 over their unjust arrest and
treatment. On top of the agreed settlement, new Met commissioner Paul Condon offered an apology and to pay their costs.[79]

On 28 January 1987, the BBC submitted a formal complaint to
the police regarding the assault on their reporter, Kate Adie.
Within a few hours, the Met commissioner, Kenneth Newman,
announced that Chief Superintendent Wyrko of Nottinghamshire
Constabulary would lead an inquiry into the complaint and that
it would be supervised by the newly formed PCA. The PCA
confirmed to the Home Office that it had 'every intention still
of examining the use of mounted police and "snatch squads"'.
A redacted Home Office memo considered to be from the home
secretary Douglas Hurd's private secretary states: 'he hopes
that the examination into the use of mounted police and "snatch
squads" will extend only to conduct and not to tactics.'[80] Hurd

backed the police in Parliament. After the weekend violence, on Monday, 26 January 1987, the *Independent* reported that the home secretary declared he had 'looked carefully into the use of mounted police. "Attempts were made to give warning of that operation in advance. A loud hailer was used but there was so much noise about that [the] warning did not have any effect."'[81]

There were over 400 complaints to the police for that night alone.[82] These included complaints from the BBC and ITN. The Soviet Embassy wrote to the Foreign and Commonwealth Office asserting that 'a cameraman for Soviet television was the subject of an unprovoked and rough attack by policemen.'[83] Their complaint of equipment being deliberately broken echoed complaints raised by the UK press. The NUJ believed that the police were preventing the press from recording protesters being 'beaten by police when exercising their lawful right to demonstrate' – 'The suppression of press freedom in Britain is no longer a threat but a reality.'[84] The NUJ added its voice to calls for a public inquiry.

Years later, a summary of the PCA report was issued after a leak to the BBC, who published sections of it. Before the summary was formally released, Commissioner Imbert met with the PCA to object to 'errors of facts' and express his concern on the morale of the police. No changes were made to the report, but its release was delayed by a day. A Home Office note confirmed the Met Police's press statement says the commissioner would 'accept and welcome' the report, question its evidence gathering and findings, and include some motivational statements around officers, but would 'not refer to the discussions of the last 48 hours'.[85]

The PCA findings included a lack of warning to the crowd, the impact on innocent bystanders and an escalation of violence that resulted from 'the behaviour of missile throwers or the actions of police officers'.[86] In private, a Home Office note confirmed that the lack of 'effective warnings' crops up 'after every large incident' and is something 'we have banged on about for years'.[87] The PCA also found evidence of officers' 'indiscriminate use of truncheons', and that police officers were 'uncontrolled and unsupervised.' A breakdown in the command structure included the on-site commander's vehicle not being used, which meant that he did not have 'an overall view' of events or officer actions, hindering the operation.[88] Allegations of obstruction and violence towards the media were also founded despite earlier denials by DAC Jones.[89] NGA leader Tony Dubbins said the report was 'a complete vindication of the demonstrators' peaceful conduct on that night'.[90]

These findings could not have been a surprise for the Home Office. In April 1987 the chair of the PCA, Sir Cecil Clothier, met with Douglas Hurd. Clothier was a 'man of integrity' who had during his tenure received four votes of 'no confidence' from the Police Federation.[91] He provided the insight that

> young officers found themselves running around, not being told what to do, not knowing the local geography ... they mounted charges on people who had nowhere to escape. Those directing operations were far away at headquarters ... officers were simply not sufficiently physically fit for public order work ... police officers set off to chase ringleaders, had to give up ... obesity brought on by huge meals and gallons of beer.[92]

In the same month the Home Office opened a new file, 'Dismissal of unsatisfactory police officers (recommendation of Police Complaints Authority)'. It included a handwritten note on House of Commons paper to Secretary of State David Waddington, in late 1989 or early 1990, suggesting that such an approach would lead the government into 'major conflict with the police'. This was because the police 'had stood by the Government during the miners' strike and other disputes' and that 'a deal is a deal.'[93] It confirmed a lack of independence between police and government despite decades of public protestations to the contrary.

Some other matters of concern were not investigated by the PCA as there was insufficient proof to support a complaint at the time. In the conclusion to the Haldane Society report, Lord Tony Gifford QC accused the home secretary of being a 'police mouthpiece' and that if 'agent provocateurs' were present they 'must be exposed'.[94] Years later, a spy cop, Bob Lambert, admitted he was a regular at Wapping demonstrations.[95]

Trade unionists have also long suspected the army were deployed at Wapping. We know the police had secret paramilitary tactics, but had they gone one stage further and secretly deployed the military? Gifford concluded in the Haldane Society report that from the planning stage, 'police commanders ... saw it as a *military operation against an enemy*, not as a public order exercise.'[96] Stories of policemen shorter than the then requirement or army sons of friends being spotted in the police lines are repeated often, even now, but remain unproven. The police can call on the army to support them in peacetime under a process known as MACP, Military Aid to the Civil Power. They had done so overtly in 'no less than 36 industrial disputes since 1945'.[97]

In 1981 (at the same time as Thatcher's Civil Contingencies Unit were making their detailed plan withstand a miners' strike), discussions were going on behind the scenes between civil servants and the army about potential military support in riot or continuing public order situations.[98] The suggestion was that if there was approval by the Home Office, the army could be 'integrated with the police operation' through joint training. The then home secretary, Whitelaw, agreed a 'cautious but mildly positive approach to this initiative'.[99] Discussions around joint working of the military and police included reference to 'public demonstration' attacks. Recommendations of theoretical and on-base training were replaced in the *Police and Military Joint Tactical Doctrine for Home Defence Operations in Periods of Tension and Conventional War* by training that included 'home defence exercises'; that is, training outside police or army training centres.

At a meeting between the home secretary and Commissioner Newman, two weeks after the 3 May 1986 demonstration, they discussed the 'continuing difficulties of the situation' at Wapping and the meetings between DAC Wyn Jones 'recently' held with ministers. Newman was 'grateful for the support of Ministers'. Whether the army were deployed under MACP or for joint training at Wapping or earlier protests remains an unknown. What is now known is that the Thatcher government and civil servants not only seriously considered it as an option for the police but also facilitated greater cooperation and joint training between police and armed forces. Was MACP therefore the reason for the meetings held between DAC Jones and ministers? Without access to these minutes these questions remain open.

Of around 1,000 police officers involved in the Wapping anniversary, over many months the PCA inquiry 'whittled down to about 230' those relevant to their complaints investigation. Despite many officers on the night not wearing their ID numbers, Wyrko's team identified the actions of nearly a fifth of those responsible for keeping the 'queen's peace' deserving of investigation. Some 114 were interviewed. After fifteen months of investigation, Chief Superintendent Wyrko and his eleven-strong investigations team sent sixty files to the CPS for consideration in relation to charging police for their actions on 24 January 1987.

Wapping was about so much more than the introduction of new technology or a new newspaper that its management claimed it to be. Murdoch planned to rid his companies of trade unions, a move that was supported by the compliance, connivance and silence of many. Nearly two weeks before strike action was called, Woodrow Wyatt wrote in his diary that Murdoch was undertaking 'a high-risk manoeuvre to stop the printing unions from printing the *Times, Sunday Times, News of the World* and the *Sun*'.[100] Despite Wyatt being a journalist, Murdoch's ruse and the fact that police had stored shields in a warehouse near his plant were kept secret in his diary until after his death, when his diaries were published in three volumes. Thatcher was reportedly 'delighted with Murdoch's plans'.[101] In the few days between his lunch with her at Chequers and the sacking of 5,500 workers, she wrote to thank Murdoch for the 'beautiful' red roses he had given her.[102] As a result of the move to Wapping the value of Murdoch's papers reportedly rose from $300 million to $1 billion. UK profits increased 85 per cent.

Twenty years after the dispute, Andrew Neil said of Wapping: 'It was just so important and I feel very proud ... We saved the British newspaper industry, no question.'[103] With the unions out of the way, media manipulation in the UK would not only solidify but go much further. When Claire Tomalin, the distinguished literary editor, refused to go to Wapping, she wrote to Andrew Neil, 'You have become the mouthpiece for a ruthless and bullying management which regards all employees as cattle.'[104]

Ann Field a retired national officer for Unite the Union (formerly of SOGAT), reflects, 'Rupert Murdoch did not "save"

the newspaper industry. He wrecked it and the jobs and jour-
nalism that went with it.'[105] Twenty-five years after the dispute,
the proofreader John Bailey concurs: 'if there were still strong
unions at Wapping, perhaps the recent catastrophe [phone hack-
ing] might have been avoided.'[106]

At the Leveson inquiry into the hacking scandal, Murdoch
tried to debunk under oath the view that he 'used the influence
of the *Sun* or the supposed political power to get favourable
treatment'. He said, 'I have never asked a Prime Minister for
anything.'[107] In his written evidence to Leveson, Andrew Neil
countered Murdoch, stating Murdoch had told Neil 'that he had
gone to Mrs Thatcher to get her assurance ... that enough police
would be made available to allow him to get his papers out past
the massed pickets at Wapping'. Neil wrote that Murdoch also
told him he could not achieve this from the New York mayor or
police.[108] Whatever Murdoch said about his influence, it is obvious that generations of prime ministers thought he had it. From
the time he arrived in Britain in 1969 and bought the *Sun* and the
News of the World, to the time of Leveson in 2011, he had seen
off eight prime ministers.

The Home Office and police chiefs knew of the police failures at
the first big demonstration at Wapping in May 1986 yet the police
were allowed to continue unchecked. After the last big march of
24 January 1987, instead of holding the police to account, Home
Secretary Douglas Hurd said they had his 'full support ... for
the police action'.[109] He provided considerable public resources
to 'protect' Murdoch's plant and commercial operations. The
Police magazine was self-congratulatory, saying the Met had
'dealt with the mob without firing a single baton round, squirt-
ing one water canon, discharging one CS canister, or ... firing
live ammunition'.[110]

Calls for a public inquiry to examine the mistakes and responsibility on both sides of the dispute were made by MPs and trade unions. Ron Leighton MP said,

> As 'Thatcher's Britain' becomes more unpleasant, more violent and more brutal, there are those in authority who see increased use of the police as the remedy to social problems and industrial disputes. They want to transform the nature of the police service and to escalate its use of force ... Instead of the neighbourhood bobby or the citizen in uniform, we are to have a paramilitary force to suppress the symptoms of social stress caused by Government policy.[111]

The cost of policing Wapping was £10 million, with 1.2 million hours of overtime. Considering this and the government's approach to the dispute, it is hardly surprising the Home Office wanted to hide what they knew. A public inquiry post-Wapping would likely have highlighted the fact that senior officers and the Home Office had failed to ensure that the police operated appropriately, and instead secret, questionable and brutal tactics were applied. Moreover, police 'dispersal tactics' were used not to facilitate protest, but to clear the area of all protesters and 'protect' Murdoch's business.

The future director of public prosecutions (DPP) and future leader of the Labour Party, Keir Starmer, wrote at the time, 'After Orgreave, no one should have been surprised when "paramilitary" policing methods emerged in Wellclose Square ... policing of any sort that is unaccountable stands directly in the path of any progress towards social emancipation.' Starmer asked what 'role the police should play, if any, in civil society. Who are they protecting and from what? Who controls them and for whose benefit?'[112]

℞

After the PCA sent their files to the CPS, twenty-six police officers were charged, constituting the largest group of police officers ever charged in relation to a single incident.[113] Finally the police were being put on trial.

The police commissioner, Sir Peter Imbert, was informed of the pending charges by the DPP's office in December 1988. The next day, on 13 December, he arranged a private meeting with the home secretary, Douglas Hurd, in an attempt to stop the prosecutions. Commissioner Imbert had previously been one of the senior officers involved in extracting 'confessions' from the Guildford Four. In 1975 Imbert also received information from IRA men who admitted the Guildford bombings, exonerating the Guildford Four. Imbert 'did nothing to bring it to light at the time' and they spent fifteen years in prison for a crime they did not commit.

In relation to Wapping, Imbert told the home secretary he believed that if the police were 'in jeopardy of proceedings' by deploying current tactics then new tactics such as water cannon would need to be considered. He said Mr Condon had been 'invited to re-examine' the manual, including the introduction of new tactics 'in light of the Wapping affair'.[114] The minutes obtained by Freedom of Information (FOI) request reveal that Douglas Hurd was more than sympathetic to Imbert's private lobbying and the Home Office contacted the DPP but got nowhere. Then suddenly, after a committal hearing in the magistrate's court, the cases came to a halt.

All serious London cases in those days started off at Bow Street Magistrates' Court. The first batch of the twenty-six police officers to be prosecuted was listed before resident magistrate Ronald Bartle, former Conservative candidate. Bartle accepted an audacious defence submission, that they could not have a fair trial because of delays in getting the case to court.

A couple of years later, Bartle also discharged (on the same basis of delay) three police officers involved in the Guildford Four case, also charged with perverting the course of justice. Chris Mullin MP, who campaigned for the Birmingham Six, another appalling miscarriage of justice against Irish people, criticised Bartle and sought assurances he would not be involved in their case. Years later, Bartle, clearly still smarting, responded directly to Mullin, in his book *Bow Street Beak*, asserting, 'I have never been biased in favour of police officers as such.'[115] However, the former judge was being economical with the truth. In a previous book, *The Law and the Lawless*, Bartle wrote, 'in combatting crime and maintaining public order the police are doing the work of God ... the ultimate line of defence between order and chaos and between civilisation and barbarism.'

Bartle also argued in *Bow Street Beak* that Mullin was wrong to criticise him because 'the judiciary is independent of the executive.' The foreword to his book was written by none other than Lord Hurd, who had known Bartle 'since Cambridge days', where they both were students in 1949. Lord Hurd was indeed the former home secretary who sympathised with the advances of Commissioner Imbert seeking to discontinue the Wapping police cases. The effect of Bartle's decision was that the cases against all twenty-six Wapping officers were thrown out and they walked away scot-free.

5

The Tinderbox

Anti–Poll Tax Protest, 1990

To avoid any possible misunderstanding, and at the risk of disappointing a few gallant colonels, let me make one thing absolutely clear: I haven't come to Cheltenham to retire.

Prime Minister Margaret Thatcher, Cheltenham
Town Hall, 31 March 1990

Ladies and Gentlemen, [voice breaking a little on 'Gentlemen'] we're leaving Downing Street for the last time after eleven and a half wonderful years, and we're very happy that we leave the United Kingdom in a very, very much better state than when we came here eleven and a half years ago.

Former prime minister Margaret Thatcher,
28 November 1990

Saturday, 31 March 1990 was not a good day for Deputy Assistant Commissioner David Meynell. The gold commander police officer was in charge of the poll tax demonstration that 'erupted into the worst riots seen in the city for a century'.[1] In the two months prior to the London demonstration there were 6,000 protests against the poll tax across the UK. Ten thousand people had demonstrated in Tunbridge Wells, and 8,000 in Plymouth, more than turned up to see the local football team, Plymouth Argyle. Over a million leaflets were printed and distributed before that day in London, resulting in 1,000 coaches travelling to the capital from over 600 towns and cities, as well as two chartered trains from Cornwall. In the build-up the chief stewards met with the Metropolitan Police, telling them to expect around 30,000 people; the police chief laughed as their intelligence suggested far fewer.[2] It turned out they had all badly underestimated the turnout.

For Prime Minister Margaret Thatcher, Saturday, 31 March was an even worse day. She was facing a backbench rebellion and leadership bids within her own party from Michael Heseltine and the right-wing loyalist Norman Tebbit. Still, she was determined to implement the poll tax, which in her view was necessary for making efficiencies in local taxation; instead it caused widespread civil unrest around the country.

In an attempt to steal the headlines away from the planned march in London and keep on track her beloved 'Community Charge' (as she and her government referred to the poll tax), she went to the safe Tory seat of Cheltenham to speak at a stage-managed event. Thatcher railed at the rostrum for forty minutes, interrupted by applause a mere twenty-four times by the 1,000 constituency activists. She declared, 'To avoid any possible misunderstanding, and at the risk of disappointing a few gallant colonels, let me make one thing absolutely clear: I haven't come to Cheltenham to retire.'[3]

Her bravado could not conceal the overwhelming opposition across the country to a flat-rate tax that was not based upon ability to pay. Most people knew the poll tax was regressive and unfair, in particular for the lower-paid. The unfairness was summed up by the benefit to the Duke of Westminster, whose usual rates on his estate of £10,255 were to be reduced under his new 'Community Charge' to £417 – it was said that 'his housekeeper and resident chauffeur face precisely the same bill'.[4]

While Thatcher thought she would be among friends in Cheltenham, opposition to the poll tax was so big that, even there, she was met by 3,000 protesters organised by the Gloucester Anti-Poll Tax Federation, and a fracas outside the town hall led to fifty-two protesters being charged. A hundred miles away in south London the sun shone brightly as the masses assembled in Kennington Park. There was a happy sense of unity with nationwide opposition brought together. London had not seen such a large demonstration since the mass CND demonstrations of the early 1980s.

The poll tax march crossed the Thames into Westminster, making its way into Trafalgar Square. There was a carnival atmosphere, with a mixture of people who represented the wide societal range affected by the dreadful tax: trade unionists and punks walked alongside the 'respectable' middle class. At around 3 p.m. there was a sit-down protest outside Downing Street, and within a short space of time the whole scene had degenerated into a riot.

Once the day was over DAC Meynell was left to assess the fallout. Some 408 protesters had been arrested, three buildings and six vehicles were damaged by fire, and dozens of shops in the West End had been looted. The event was formally declared a riot under the 1886 Riot (Damages) Act, allowing uninsured small businesses and householders to receive compensation from public funds. The government ended up paying out £9 million in compensation for the damage; seventy-five tonnes of debris was found on the streets.[5]

The following day, DAC Meynell had to compose a draft report on the riot for his boss, Commissioner Sir Peter Imbert; the home secretary; and the prime minister. Meynell was seriously hampered in being able to explain what happened at the London protest. While he had the police log of communications on police radios, there was a problem. Despite recommendations following the miners' strike that police radios should be much improved, the Met still only had a few radio channels and basic radios, so police communication was very limited.[6] The police communications log lacked detail or coherence. The deficiencies in communication contributed to the failure of the police operation on the day.

The failure of the gold–silver–bronze police command structure, introduced after the problems at the Broadwater Farm riot in 1985, was a further contributing factor. This system was supposedly designed for the policing of sudden events during public disorder. The 'gold' commander, normally an assistant chief constable or higher rank, had overall charge, setting strategy for policing the demonstration, located with a team in the control

Poll Tax demonstration, London, 31 March 1990.

room. The 'silver' commander reports to the gold commander and is typically a superintendent, who oversees the event, devising tactics to match the 'gold's' orders, which are then passed on to the 'bronze' commanders who are on the ground with the protesters.

The log confirms that there were no communications from the silver commander after 16:07, which was when the riot started.[7] It also reveals a complete lack of control and leadership, for which DAC Meynell as the gold commander had responsibility. For instance, the log entry at 16:29 said, 'Crowd being pushed towards Trafalgar Square where officers are under attack. This is the wrong strategy.' As the officer in charge, DAC Meynell was not ready to admit this in his report to his superiors. Instead Meynell concluded his report with an attack on 'a disruptive hard core of individuals who were at the vanguard of the violence and sought to incite others'. According to Meynell they were identifiable 'by a particular style of appearance ... and their possession of anarchist flags and symbols'. He said that these 3,000 people had undermined the cause of the majority of the 40,000 demonstrators, and instigated the riot. He stated the trouble started when a group of them sat down in protest outside Downing Street in Whitehall at around 3 p.m.

In the House of Commons the next day, Home Secretary David Waddington declared, 'All responsible members of society will wish to join me in paying tribute to the police for the courage and restraint which they showed in dealing with some of the most ferocious violence we have ever seen on the streets of London.'[8] He confirmed that he had requested a full report from the commissioner 'on the day's events'. The police were also setting up a team of 100 officers under Operation Carnaby to bring any rioters to justice. All sides of the House joined the home secretary in condemning the violence.

But some voices on the backbenches called for a public inquiry rather than an internal police review. They included Jeremy Corbyn, Dave Nellist and Tony Benn, who had all been present at the rally in Trafalgar Square. Benn was particularly well placed to make such a call as he had walked from the stage in Trafalgar Square along Whitehall, passing through a police line which was blocking the road from Trafalgar Square into Whitehall. Within the fighting on Whitehall he found a senior officer with a crown on his shoulder (superintendent rank), whom Benn asked, 'Why don't you let them go by?' The policeman replied, 'They won't move.' Benn's diary records,

> Well that wasn't true. He claimed there had been a lot of violence. I think that what they had done was to break the march up, squeeze the people in the middle and frighten them, and then no doubt some bottles and things were thrown. It reminded me a bit of Wapping.[9]

DAC Meynell was called to Downing Street on 3 April 1990 with Commissioner Sir Peter Imbert to meet the prime minister and the home secretary. Thatcher had cancelled two appointments in order to hold the meeting. Briefing the prime minister for this meeting was her private secretary, Andrew Turnbull. He confided in Thatcher, 'Although the police were under great pressure and showed great courage, it cannot be said that their handling of the event was faultless. Although some congratulations are in order, you will also want to probe how a repetition can be avoided.'[10]

The official record of this meeting makes no mention of any probing into mistakes made by the police. Meynell's initial line prevailed, that the riot was just created by some anarchists, without the involvement of a wider section of the protest. No one could explain why anarchists who had been present on all the previous demonstrations had been able to take over this one and cause mayhem on a scale not seen for over 100 years.[11]

The Downing Street meeting ignored the backbenchers' call for a public inquiry. Instead they confirmed that the police would carry out their own investigations, first into those they suspected of causing the riot and second into the lessons the police could learn from their operation on the day to improve policing of future protests.

That there would be a public inquiry was an assumption made by a senior barrister at 11 Kings Bench Walk Chambers, who had been the adviser to the Scarman report (believed to be Richard Auld QC). He wrote to the home secretary, David Waddington, offering his services for any future inquiry into the policing of the poll tax riots. The home secretary's response corrected him: 'it is not expected that there will be a role in this process for people outside the Metropolitan police. It will of course be very different from the Lord Scarman Inquiry after the riots in Brixton.'[12] The home secretary was certainly correct about that, given that he had sanctioned the police-led review into themselves, shielding the police from the criticism of the kind made by Scarman.

David Waddington's approach was also tested by an irate lord, who wrote immediately after the poll tax riot, expressing concern about police violence against peaceful protesters witnessed by his daughter (4'11" in height) who was on the demonstration.[13] He included in his correspondence a letter from the *Independent* magazine from another protester who also had a traumatic experience. Mrs R. A. Sare was on the way to the theatre when she witnessed 'a group of mounted police charged at full gallop into the rear of the group of protesters, scattering them, passers-by and us and creating panic.' Then 'another group of riot-squad police appeared, in a most intimidating manner.' More horrific was the fact that 'four of the riot-squad police grabbed a young girl of 18 or 19 for no reason and forced her in a brutal manner on to the crowd-control railings, with her throat across the railings.' The riot squad involved 'were *not* wearing any form of identification. Their epaulettes were unbuttoned and flapping loose.'[14]

The home secretary asked the lord to refer his comments to the police commissioner, and so the lord was forced to plead in a second letter to the home secretary,

> The point I feel justified in putting to you with all the force I can is that it is no longer right to leave the judgement of such complex matters in the hands of the police themselves, whose conduct has been criticised and will continue to be criticised. When it comes to the inquiry – ascertaining what happened – the conduct of the police ought to be examined by an authority outside the police.[15]

The prime minister received a similar letter about the nature of the policing from a man from Clifton, Bristol, who described himself as 'neither a radical nor an anarchist', and as 'sickened' by the violence of some protesters later that day.[16] He witnessed what happened in Whitehall, where at first the march was 'good humoured, festive mix of mothers with children, the disabled, a jazz band, people marching under banners proclaiming "ordinary people oppose the poll tax" ... I could see the gates of Downing Street ... at no time did I see missiles thrown, or any evidence of disturbance.' What he witnessed next is recorded in compelling detail.

> As we passed up Whitehall, without warning, without explanation, the police began a series of obviously pre-planned manoeuvres, which cut the march, and encircled a group of some hundreds of

us in the area between Richmond Terrace and Whitehall Place. As they did this I saw no provocation of any sort on the part of the crowd around us, no missiles thrown, no police officers assaulted...

At this point fully equipped, mounted riot police were brought to the edge of the uniformed cordon ... the uniformed officers parted, rode at speed into the crowd, batons raised, driving the crowd before them... It is difficult to describe exactly how frightening it is to be charged by a dozen helmeted, shielded, stick wielding mounted policemen, nor the sense of outrage it induces. You should try it sometime!

As he ran he saw people fall in their attempt to scramble to safety, and a woman who failed to get her three young children away. All escapes were blocked by the police. He goes on to describe,

One man in a wheelchair must have been overrun by police. I do not know what became of him... Three times riot police entered the crowd in this manner, until we were pressed so tightly together we could scarce breathe, and only now did I begin to see missiles thrown...

Within half an hour as the mounted police charged at a gallop into the crowds at the entrance to Trafalgar Square a peaceful demonstration became an uncontrollable riot ... I ask you to consider the consequences of a situation in which the sympathy between the public and the police is lost, and in which the police are seen to be out of touch with the moods and sentiments of the normal populous [*sic*] of the country, and the political impartiality of both the police authorities and those that guide them, called into question.[17]

Thatcher's response to the Bristolian mirrored that of her home secretary to the lord; she referred the harrowing letter to the police for any comment. From the outset both the prime minister and home secretary had convincing independent evidence of serious police violence on 31 March. They chose to ignore it by failing to place it before a public inquiry that would have considered external evidence independently from the police.

The line taken by the senior police was not easy to maintain. Shortly after the riots, a riot squad officer, WPC Fiona Roberts, was put up for a press conference on the ITN news, presumably to elicit sympathy for officers on the ground. At one point she let slip, 'I think we lost it.' The Metropolitan Police were embarrassed and refuted her claim.[18]

The nature of the police review ordered by the home secretary came under scrutiny from an unlikely source, the Conservative-run Westminster Council. They wrote formally to the home secretary in June 1990 seeking a ban on any future poll tax demonstrations in central London. In their letter they made a seemingly mild request to see the outcome of the review undertaken by the Metropolitan Police commissioner.[19] Imbert's deputy chief commissioner, John Metcalfe, was tasked with providing this report. His remit was to report on the lessons from the policing on the day. The report was ordered by the home secretary but controlled by the commissioner, who had already written to the Home Office about 'the inappropriateness of publishing the results'.[20]

The Westminster Council request thus caused some embarrassment and a flurry of activity at the Home Office. On 28 June 1990 the Home Office's 'F8 Division' affirmed the police's steadfast position: 'We will be informed of the outcome of the review but it is not intended that the conclusions should be made public.'[21] The home secretary replied to the commissioner that there was likely to be a general interest in their findings (including from backbenchers), which led to a compromise from the police, who then planned 'to produce a summary ... suitable for publication'.[22] The implication in what clearly looks like a cover-up was that a longer report to the home secretary might contain matters which the wider public should know about but would be intentionally withheld. A letter to Westminster Council stated that a summary report would be provided to them in due course when the review was complete. They would have a long wait before they would see even that, as the report was not drafted for another year.

Meanwhile, on 29 January 1991, Sgt Roy Ramm (tasked by DAC Meynell) published his report into the prosecution of suspects. Ramm had been busy, arresting new suspects in the months after the demonstration, which led to a further 100 people being charged. Despite it being outside his remit, Ramm could not resist providing his own analysis of the demonstration and made the dubious suggestion that violence was caused by people being offered money to join in.[23] Police conduct was not criticised, and contrary to the memories of the witness from Bristol, Ramm said the police dividing of the march in Whitehall was achieved 'peacefully'; but this statement was accompanied by a rather contradictory one that this tactic 'appeared to be the catalyst for the wider spread of disorder'.[24]

Ramm's report also did not mention how innocent demonstrators were swept up in the process, including the case of Roy Hanney, a television engineer who was taking photographs when arrested by the Territorial Support Group. The TSG was primarily used for public order situations, having been in force since 1987 after it replaced the disgraced Special Patrol Group.[25] Hanney was accused of throwing a brick and charged with affray. The evidence against him came from two police officers,

PC Ramsay and PC Egan, who were cross-examined at trial by defence counsel Dexter Dias. There was a striking similarity between their notebooks. PC Ramsay insisted the similarities were a 'coincidence', and that he could not possibly have copied his colleague's statement because he had described Hanney's hair as 'close-cropped', whereas PC Egan had said it was 'shaven'.

As journalist David Rose commented, 'it was an unfortunate example to choose as evidence of his originality.' Dias asked him to look at his handwritten version, from which a transcript had been prepared. It showed he had crossed out 'shaven' and substituted 'close-cropped'. 'At that moment, the credibility of PC Ramsay's allegation ... was somehow diminished.'[26] The next morning the jury had a discussion in the lift and sent a note to the judge, the effect of which was that the trial came to a swift halt. Hanney was free to go.

Hanney's case was not dissimilar to Alistair Mitchell's. He was a director of a wholefoods cooperative and was at the protest taking photographs for his girlfriend, who was making a film about the poll tax. At around 6:30 p.m. he saw a police officer grip a protester by the neck in a chokehold that he had previously read could prove fatal. He shouted to the officer involved, 'You could kill in eight seconds.' The policeman responded by grabbing him and shouting, 'In six seconds you'll be dead.' He was charged with and convicted of assaulting the two officers, including biting one of them. Three years later the conviction was quashed in the High Court at judicial review. *Private Eye* described him as 'the only man in British legal history to be convicted of biting a policeman – with someone else's teeth'.[27] Despite his ordeal Mitchell managed to forge a career as a barrister and become Queen's Counsel.

Metcalfe's report into what lessons were to be learnt about policing on the day was kicked into the long grass by taking a year to conclude. During this lengthy delay Metcalfe was awarded a Queen's Police Medal on 31 December 1990.[28] A twenty-page summary report was published on 4 March 1991 and put into the public domain, with a longer report sent to the Home Office for private consideration. The summary report made some interesting findings.

A year on from the riot, the police were finally prepared to admit what they had previously denied – that they had lost control. Maybe this admission was made because of some dissent among the police rank and file, including some junior officers who had threatened to take civil action against the Metropolitan Police. Their argument was that health and safety laws were violated, leading to officers receiving needless injuries during the riot.[29]

Metcalfe accepted that for those on the front line, 'officers working under different lines of command were often unaware of tactics used by other officers on different units. These difficulties were exacerbated by inadequate communications systems as attempts were made to coordinate police movements' from silver and gold command.[30] There had been no plans for the serious disorder that took place, and on the day the command structure suffered because 'some senior officers felt inhibited by the presence of more senior colleagues' from making the immediate decisions that were necessary to prevent the disorder escalating.

Metcalfe also accepted that the use of police vehicles 'raised the temperature of the crowd and coincided with an increase in the level of violence directed towards the police', and that 'police vehicles should avoid travelling through large crowds in congested areas to reduce the possibility of escalating violence.'[31] Finally there was official recognition of the size of the crowd that Metcalfe's fellow ACPO officer, DAC Meynell, had played down in his original report. Tens of thousands had come from across

London, and thousands more travelled from all over England and Wales.

Metcalfe's summary report was nevertheless woefully inadequate. It did not properly address why the police lost control and why there was a riot. His investigation, consisting of thirteen full-time officers who interviewed 1,445 people, was desperately one-sided. Three pages were given to police injuries with not a single mention made of any injury to a demonstrator. How could anyone begin to understand the violence on the day without even considering the position of the protesters? It was reported that seventy-five civilians needed hospital treatment, which was not surprising given the police use of batons, horses and vans.[32] This compared with fifty-eight police injured recorded at the last entry of the police log.[33] Metcalfe came to his own conclusions on how the violence materialised, and apparently did so by relying solely on police accounts. There is no doubt the police were at times in fear, including when scaffolding poles and masonry was thrown at them, but the fact that they policed with fear was airbrushed out.

A public inquiry could have exposed fundamental failings by the police, the first of which was that a riot could have been avoided if the authorities had listened to the organisers of the march. On the Monday prior to the Saturday demonstration the All Britain Anti-Poll Tax Federation asked for the march to be redirected from Trafalgar Square to Hyde Park.[34] At that stage they knew the support for the march had grown so much that it was going to be far bigger than their original estimate of 30,000 and would be upwards of 100,000.

The Secretary of State for the Environment, Chris Patten, said the redirection was impossible because seven days' notice had not been given. This bureaucratic foolishness placed protesters in a dangerously overcrowded situation, which should have been avoided. This may well explain why the police's official estimate for figures at the protest was so ridiculously low. DAC Meynell's report suggested there were 40,000 there. Any proper assessment would confirm it was around five times that based on the simple fact that Trafalgar Square itself takes 60,000 people when full. All the footage confirms that Trafalgar Square was packed and overflowing, with full streets and feeder marches from neighbouring streets. At the time the main march was filling Trafalgar Square, people at the back of the march were still leaving Kennington Park nearly two and half miles away. The protest of 200,000 people was thus funnelled into a space that only took 60,000. Such congestion was completely unnecessary and dangerous.[35]

Most importantly, a public inquiry would have focused on why a demonstration of all ages with a carnival atmosphere transformed quickly into a riot. The Trafalgar Square Defendants' Campaign that formed to provide legal support for those arrested by Operation Carnaby stated from the outset the cause of the riot was 'due to the incredible police stupidity and brutality in driving horses into an ordinary sit-down protest at Downing Street'.[36] The idea of using mounted horses against a relatively small sit-down protest was obviously going to start a reaction. It was the tinderbox.

The demonstrators reacted. Unconscionable policing did not stop there; the police in charge repeatedly grasped for excessive measures against an enormous crowd of protesters, which further inflamed the crowd, the most shocking of which was described by a constituent of Dawn Primarolo MP, who wrote, 'We saw a white police van, which seemed to come from nowhere, drive down the road so fast we only had time to turn our eyes … to see it hit several people … I screamed … as another van careered down the road hitting a man down before our very eyes.'[37]

Despite Metcalfe's criticism of this tactic, what was not mentioned in reviews of his report was that the ACPO 1987 tactical options manual recognised the 'tactical use of vehicles' for dispersal of a riotous crowd by driving into them. The idea that the police have a recognised tactic that they can drive a vehicle at a crowd to disperse it, and that this was sanctioned privately by a cabal at the Home Office, is extraordinary.

It is inconceivable that Parliament would have voted for such an obviously dangerous and extreme manoeuvre, which feels more like an army tactic imposed in Northern Ireland. A public inquiry would have exposed these secret guidelines to public scrutiny. Many witnesses said the vehicles were driving at around thirty miles per hour. The manual provided for driving at fast speed but only if they stop before reaching the crowd.[38] This did not happen in this case. The use of vans without warning, at such speed and without stopping, could only cause injury and understandable anger. It is ironic that the police had promoted an anti-speeding campaign with *Funeral Blues*, the first advert to use real footage from a funeral, showing drivers being encouraged to reduce their speed by children after the death of one of their friends.[39] The option to use vans required the authority of the senior officer at the scene. We still do not know today who gave the order.

In addition to vans, the police also sent horses into the enormous crowd in Trafalgar Square. Thirty years on, Tracey Bent, then a twenty-two-year-old speech and language student, cannot forget it. She was in the middle of the crowd in Trafalgar Square with her sister and boyfriend. They were chatting to tourists, a Canadian couple who came with their children: 'All of a sudden, police were charging us on horses, massive horses, from nowhere, with no reason as to why. There was no trouble anyone could see. There was no warning. They were suddenly swiping down with their batons. I saw a woman struck on the head. Nobody knew why they came or was prepared at all. It was absolutely terrifying. It was like some medieval jousting competition, they were leaning forward, charging through the crowd hitting people with their truncheons who were just standing there.'

The use of mounted police was covered under Section 21 of the 1987 manual, as was their use for crowd dispersal. The preamble states, 'Their deployment may trigger a worsening in crowd behaviour' and

> a risk of injury both to foot police working alongside and also to members of the public when the horses are in close contact. These injuries can be serious and even fatal … It would be inappropriate to use such manoeuvres against a densely packed crowd. The risk of injury to everyone concerned increases proportionally to the rate of advance.

The way mounted police were used in Whitehall and Trafalgar Square was in breach of this preamble. The seriousness of a 'fast rate of advance [that] may subsequently need justification as the risk of injury is considerable' was evaded because the police, the prime minister and the home secretary conspired to avoid a public inquiry despite many injuries to the public.[40] The horses at the poll tax protest were used for crowd dispersal at a canter, which can only be sanctioned by an ACPO-rank officer. If DAC Meynell sanctioned this tactic he never had to account for doing so as the rules he was supposed to apply remained secret.

If the police had studied their own intelligence reports in the few weeks before the 31 March 1990 protest they would have known that they were going to be facing a protest so vast and so angry that any excessive policing was going to set off a large section of the crowd.[41] In an attempt to undermine the strength of the protest, DAC Meynell in his initial report underestimated the size of the march as 'if it seemed smaller, then in could be written off as a demonstration of political activists, not a mass movement, and the aggressive tactics of the police would appear more legitimate'.[42] But the police were on notice as to what might provide a spark.

In the run-up to the Trafalgar Square protest there had been a series of protests at town halls as local councils, to the frustration of their constituents, complied with setting a rate for the poll tax. The police intelligence reports for these smaller protests reveal a similar attempt by police to pin any violence on the left organisations, but failing to do so. The widespread public anger was so visceral it was not possible to blame organised agitators; it was far bigger than their immediate political reach. The anti–poll tax movement was vibrant and campaigning groups formed in communities and in estates across the UK.

The poll tax had caused enormous anger because it was so obviously unfair. It came after many other attacks on welfare and working-class communities. There was a tremendous resentment against the government. An internal report on the town hall demonstrations from the Home Office F8 Division written just a few weeks before the national protest stated,

> From the reports we have received there is no indication of national co-ordination of the demonstrations. The leftwing demonstrators seem likely to be the most vociferous and active where they are present but it is evident from the reports we have received that they have been joined by other demonstrators wishing to show their disapproval at the setting of the community charge.[43]

There was also resentment within the general public over the stance taken by the official opposition, the Labour Party. While the biggest movement of civil disobedience in Britain in the twentieth century persuaded hundreds of thousands of people to resist the tax by not paying it, the Labour Party had taken a novel approach to resisting the poll tax, by paying it. The comedian Linda Smith derided the Labour Party campaign as being 'Pay the poll tax – but while you're doing so – oooo you give that clerk SUCH a look.'[44] Labour's approach was the antithesis of the determined mood of the anti–poll tax demonstrators across the country to get rid of the tax.

To start charging at a sit-down protest and then at an enormous, congested crowd with horses, batons and vans was only ever going to incite a reaction. In this case the police started and fuelled a response, a popular revolt that they could not control. It took them a year to admit they lost control but still, despite the evidence, the police failed to admit they had provided the tinderbox.

Despite numerous requests, the longer Metcalfe report that went to the Home Office has not been disclosed. We can only speculate about what the full Metcalfe report might include concerning the police's private view of the lessons to be learnt and whether or not there were concerns as to the legality of their tactics. We do know that private discussions continued between the police and the Home Office beyond the report's issue.

A letter from the Home Office to the Leader of the House on 21 June 1991, after Metcalfe's report, said that the ACPO tactical options manual 'has been "redrafted" over the last year and is now in final draft form awaiting formal approval from ACPO Council in mid-July'.[45] This confirms a pattern (as in 1983 and 1987) of the top brass in the police and the Home Office deciding the method by which the police use force at protests and how its citizens should be policed, without the involvement of Parliament. It appears that in 1991 yet again another set of secret rules was being established for use by the chief officers in ACPO, unbeknown to anyone else.

Publicly the police and government were not shy to float ideas that could seriously undermine protest and dissent. In the conclusion of his summary report Metcalfe argues for 'more use of existing preventative legislation'. He sought a further tightening of venues for assemblies and rallies, and routes of marches, recently made more stringent under the 1986 Public Order Act. As Statewatch commented, Metcalfe 'also ominously suggests that: Perhaps society should consider whether, where there are already many alternative means of influencing public opinion, it wishes to allow marches with a potential for violence and disorder to take place in the heart of the capital'.[46]

While the police and their erstwhile allies, the prime minister and home secretary, contrived to keep secret both the police rules and how they were misapplied at the poll tax demonstration, the police promoted restrictions on the right to protest. The home secretary also privately suggested that if the commissioner sought 'a ban of any community charge march ... it would receive his careful and sympathetic consideration'.[47]

The story of the poll tax protest challenges some theories held on the left about the police. The organisation Militant were at the forefront of the excellent All Britain Anti-Poll Tax Federation. They were, however, initially critical of the protesters who fought back against the police. Militant held the view that the police were 'workers in uniform'. On 31 March 1990 the police behaviour exemplified what they have done throughout history. The police on the ground followed their orders no matter how crass and dangerous they were. At the other end of the scale there has been a view that the police are all-powerful and that we live in a police state, doomed to defeat. Again the poll tax protest shows the opposite – that ordinary people can challenge the police and they can win. Over time, Militant changed their minds.

Opposition to the poll tax grew even stronger after the demonstration. The All Britain Anti-Poll Tax Federation inspired a non-payment campaign. In Strathclyde Regional Council alone 520,000 people refused to pay the poll tax. The campaign started to challenge poll tax summonses in the courts. This was a good tactic not least because such was the support for non-payment that 4.7 million summonses and 3.3 million liability orders were issued in England and Wales between 1990 and 1991.[48] Despite opposition leader Neil Kinnock distancing himself from the protest (and campaign), Labour's lead in the polls actually increased after the Trafalgar Square protest, with a Gallup poll in the *Daily Telegraph* putting Labour a staggering twenty-six points ahead of Thatcher's Conservative Party.[49]

During her reign Thatcher empowered the police by increasing police numbers by 9,500 and upping their wages, approving a 45 per cent pay rise straight after entering office.[50] She also ensured they were well equipped. In return, the police had turned out in force with their secret tactics to defeat the unions. However, Thatcher overreached herself with her flagship policy of the poll tax. It was such a brutal tax that cemented large numbers together, and even galvanised the middle class. Rather than taking on one section of the working class at a time, as outlined in the Ridley plan, she took everyone on at the same time. Despite the police using the most brutal tactics derived from their secret manual, by driving horses and vans at speed towards dense crowds, the sheer volume and anger of the protesters led to their defeat.

Nonetheless the police chiefs and the Home Office still contrived to maintain the secrecy of their secret tactics by resisting any independent public accountability. It was enough to save their hierarchical tactics for future battles but not enough to save the prime minister.

At the Conservative Party conference on 12 October 1990 Thatcher was still rattling the sabre: 'For years council after council has been hijacked by socialist extremists. The residents wanted litter-free zones, but what they got was nuclear-free zones. The Community Charge is making them more accountable and less electable. No wonder Labour councillors don't want it [applause].'[51] The following month Thatcher announced her resignation, and six days later, on 28 November 1990, she left Downing Street in tears.

The first act of her successor, John Major, was to call in Michael Heseltine and appoint him as the new minister for the environment, with a brief to get rid of the poll tax, which he did less than a year after the anniversary of the poll tax riot. As Martin Luther King once said, 'a riot is the language of the unheard.' There is little doubt that without the revolt at Trafalgar Square on 31 March 1990, Thatcher and her wretched poll tax would have carried on regardless.

Part II.
Major: Back to Basics

6

The Trap

Welling, Anti-racist Protest, 1993

The police acted with astonishing bravery, as is their custom, and according to the highest standards of their profession.

Minister of state, Home Office, Earl Ferrers,
House of Lords, 18 October 1993

The police were out of control. What did they expect? People were tremendously angry. The police should have handled it less aggressively. This is no way to negotiate, by hitting the chief steward round the head with a truncheon.

Julie Waterson, chief steward, Anti Nazi
League, *Independent*, 16 October 1993

It was a beautiful sunny day at Winns Common in Welling, south-east London, when Hossein Zahir took the stage. Everything had been set up for a small rally. However, 60,000 turned up. He recalls, 'I don't think anyone expected those sort of numbers. The Common was packed with people. The idea of a speech – just forget about it, the first fifty rows might have heard vaguely what was going on. I remember saying something that got quite an excited response and people cheered and you can see it, this rolling of placards. Standing there those people at the back had no chance of hearing but were waving their placards. I couldn't see where the crowd stopped.'[1]

The early 1990s was a particularly frightening time to be black in London. Derek Beackon, the first councillor ever elected to represent the British National Party (BNP), won a by-election in Tower Hamlets. The slogan for his campaign was 'rights for whites'. The BNP victory emboldened racists, leading to an increase in serious and fatal racist attacks. In south-east London, racist incidents rose by 300 per cent in 1993.[2] Vicious racist attacks also rose after the opening of the BNP 'bookshop' in 1989 in Welling, a traditional white working-class suburb.[3] The 'bookshop' was in a private house surrounded by residential roads and was understood to be the BNP headquarters where members' meetings were held.

Lois Austin, a local activist in the Labour Party Young Socialists, grew up around the corner. She says, 'It wasn't a bookshop at all it was like a house that had steel shutters at the front. It didn't have a shop front or anything in the window. Richard Edmunds lived upstairs.' Edmunds was known as a long-standing fascist, having stood for the National Front, and was a founding member of the BNP. In 1993 he told the *Guardian*'s Duncan Campbell, 'we [the BNP] are 100 per cent racist.'[4]

By 1993 Lois was national chair of the anti-racist campaign Youth Against Racism in Europe, organising locally against the 'bookshop' since it opened. Austin recalls that in the early 1990s, 'Marching in Eltham we were outnumbered by the fascists. I recognised some of them from my school; one of them when he was a teenager came with us on holiday to Ireland, when he was my brother's mate. Derek Beackon was also there. We lobbied the council many times to close it down and they refused. Some argued that if you leave them alone, what harm are they doing?' But there was an Indian family that moved in near the bookshop and we had to organise our own round-the-clock security to protect them.'

Appalling events continued to unfold in the area. In Thamesmead, in February 1991, fifteen-year-old Rolan Adams was on the way home with his brother Nathan from a youth club. They were waiting at the bus stop when they were chased by a gang of fifteen white teenagers, some of whom were shouting 'niggers'. Nathan managed to escape but returned to find his brother dying in a pool of blood with his table tennis bat by his side. He had been stabbed in the throat. In July 1992, Rohit Duggal was on his own standing outside the kebab shop in Well Hall Road, Eltham, when a group of white youths set upon him. He was stabbed in the heart and killed. Peter Thompson, a white youth, who was later jailed for his murder, was carrying leaflets produced by the BNP.

In the very same road in Eltham less than a year later another devastating racist murder took place. On 22 April 1993, three miles from the BNP 'bookshop', Stephen Lawrence and Duwayne Brooks were waiting at the bus stop to go home when a gang of white youths approached and one said, 'What, what nigger?' Stephen was engulfed by the gang and stabbed to death.

There was an immediate local reaction to Stephen's murder. A few weeks later, on 8 May, 6,000 people marched to the 'bookshop', demanding the place be closed down.[5] The police protected the building and there were reports of nineteen people injured. The home secretary, Kenneth Clarke, expressed sympathy with those who were opposed to the 'bookshop' but said he was powerless to do anything. Unstoppable momentum grew for a national march on the BNP 'bookshop', alongside a call for justice for Stephen Lawrence and the victims of the other racist murders. The Anti Nazi League, Youth Against Racism in Europe, the

Indian Workers Association, Searchlight and many other organisations called a unity demonstration for 16 October 1993.

The Anti Nazi League (ANL) had previously organised successful demonstrations and Rock Against Racism concerts in the 1970s to help defeat the National Front.[6] The ANL used their experience to galvanise support for this demonstration. The march was built across the UK with other anti-racist organisations and 550 coaches were booked for the day.

John Siblon was a national organiser for the ANL. He lived with his mother in Eltham but had to move out to protect her after he started receiving threatening calls from the far right targeting him because of his role and the colour of his skin. In the run-up to the demonstration, John remembers being invited to the U2 Zoo TV tour gig at Wembley Stadium to promote the ANL and the demonstration. They handed out leaflets and in the break a rap video promoting the demonstration was played to the 72,000 crowd.[7] Rage Against the Machine invited John onstage at a concert at Brixton Academy to encourage people to go to the Welling demonstration.

The 16 October 1993 demonstration was a sea of iconic ANL yellow lollypop placards demanding 'Close down the BNP', the link between the presence of the racist BNP and the growing number of racist attacks an obvious focus of those demonstrating. The demonstrators were led from Winns Common by a solid police cordon in yellow vests with a further line of police horses in front of them. As the march reached a crossroads at the top of the hill on Upper Wickham Lane the police escort dissipated. The march was so big that the back could not see what was happening at the front. The front of the march was met with large numbers of police lines at the crossroads. A police line blocked protesters from entering an 'exclusion zone' and going past the BNP 'bookshop'.

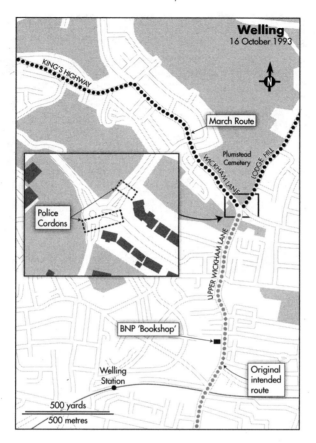

What happened next was witnessed by only a small contingent at the front. The ITN news reported,

The march had gone off largely peacefully until it reached a suburban road leading to the BNP bookshop three quarters of a mile away. A section of the demonstrators surged forward in an attempt to breach the police lines and gain access to Welling and the BNP ... It turned into a violent and ugly confrontation. But despite police charges the minority of rioters at the front held their ground. Mounted officers were deployed as the crossroads became virtually a battlefield.

Police confront protesters at the junction of Lodge Hill
and Upper Wickham Lane, Welling, 1993.

The fighting at the front lasted for hours in what was described
as a 'tactical hiatus', and at one stage someone let off on orange
smoke bomb that the police horses went through.[8]

The ITN footage confirmed the police's half-mile exclusion
zone around the BNP 'bookshop', and the redirected route. The
new route imposed by the police led protesters away from the
'bookshop' along Lodge Hill to the 'finish' at Clam Field Rec-
reation Ground. It was imposed as the police said they wanted
to protect the area, to stop violence. ITN interviewed two senior officers in charge. An angry commander, Hugh Blenkin, was
filmed at the scene picking up a brick, asserting that the police
actions were correct: 'If this march had been allowed to go past
the bookshop you can see what would happen in the far more
confined spaces.' Commissioner Paul Condon was later filmed
at a press conference looking sombre, complaining about the
protesters being 'a cowardly mob of extremists'.

BBC news led with a very similar report: 'Protesters trying

to break through police lines threw bricks and bottles, mounted officers charged the crowd … But police rerouted the march … the police blockaded the road [to the 'bookshop'] to force marchers in the opposite direction. Violent clashes were inevitable.' Blenkin was interviewed. 'We wanted to police a peaceful demonstration and this is what it turned into. But our tactics have held.' The BBC, like ITN, did not interview a single protester or organiser. They showed a similar graphic to ITN's, with added red arrows highlighting the police reroute, stating that the protesters had refused to take that route.

The next day the national Sunday press continued in the same vein. They carried photographs on their front pages of the mounted police amid smoke bombs. The *Sunday Telegraph* reported, 'Mounted riot police faced a barrage of sticks, bottles, bricks and smoke bombs as the march's progress was halted … Scotland Yard said 31 people were arrested, including four women; 41 others were taken to hospital … Wearing fireproof overalls and riot gear, police made several charges at the crowd.'[9]

By Monday the headline on the *Daily Mail*'s front page screamed, 'Black PC victim of anti-racist mob', which claimed a black officer, PC Turner, was singled out for attack by the crowd. The *Daily Telegraph* gave a detailed report of the Met commissioner's premonition that the march might end in violence. The commissioner explained that the organisers failed to accept his rerouting of the march imposed in the week before the protest, when

Mr Condon invoked his powers under the Public Order Act …
He prescribed a route not too dissimilar from the original one except that the marchers would be blocked some 400 yards before

the bookshop – as they came down the incline of Upper Wickham Lane – and directed back up Lodge Hill where there was more open land.[10]

In briefing the press about potential flashpoints, Mr Condon professed that they had 'nothing to hide in their preparations'. According to the *Telegraph*, 'between 3.00 and 3.15pm the main body of the marchers reached the junction of Lodge Hill and Upper Wickham Lane – manned by officers, 83 on horseback, carrying shields, batons and dressed in riot gear … A combination of events now led to the main outbreak of violence.' March organisers sought to persuade the police that they be allowed to follow the original route, 'but reluctantly agreed to take the alternative route.'[11]

Another group apparently started throwing missiles, while Julie Waterson, the joint chief steward, called on the protesters to sit down. At 3:20 p.m. came the first police baton charge. She was hit on the head during the second or third wave and needed stitches. The *Telegraph* interview with Condon concluded his 'loathing of racism is known, but even if he had more sympathy with the genuine protestors than those he was protecting, his role was to keep the peace'. Condon said, 'The hypocrisy of the organisers knows no bounds.' A couple of brief paragraphs were given to the organisers' complaints of a police riot but more space was given to Commander Blenkin to attack the Socialist Workers Party and Militant for being responsible for the violence.

The *Daily Telegraph* printed the same route of the march as was shown by ITN and the BBC. They praised the 'brave horses saddled with the task of quelling violent mob', detailing the, '83 horses, none of which was injured, passed through police lines to break up the front ranks of violent protestors and then brought calm to the area by charging up Lodge Hill and dispersing the remaining crowd.' Some of the same horses were veterans of the 1986–7 Wapping dispute and the 1990 poll tax riot in Trafalgar Square.

Six days later, on 22 October 1993, a very different account of the protest was published in the *New Statesman and Society*, written by its political editor, Stephen Platt. He had been at the front of the march, unlike the other journalists, who, if present at all, were behind the police line. He stood alongside Leon Greenman, a Holocaust survivor. Platt reported that the police had unilaterally decided late in the day to reroute the march so that it could not pass the BNP 'bookshop'. Greenman and other survivors were tasked with speaking with the police at the crossroads to allow the march to proceed on its original intended route, which was refused. Platt wrote this account:

> To the police, television and, almost without exception, the press, the story was simple: a mob of extremists, well-prepared and hell-bent on violence, tried to storm the police barricades ... The nearer it got to the planned re-routeing [*sic*], the heavier the police presence became ... not the usual political-demonstration presence ... it was ... stark, intimidatory ... communicating an intention not so much to keep the peace but to win the war that senior officers had convinced themselves was bound to erupt.[12]

Hossein Zahir remembers a tense atmosphere: 'The police were in riot gear from the get-go, and they were very aggressive. They thought we shouldn't be there.' Platt continued, 'As the march made its way up Wickham Lane ... Like something out of a cowboy film, massed ranks of police cavalry were silhouetted against the sun on the hillside to the right. On the left, behind iron-railing-topped walls, police dog handlers patrolled the slopes of Plumstead Cemetery ... At the crossroads itself, confusion reigned. All three exits were blocked by lines of police. The one to the right, which led to the BNP HQ, had the most fearsome presence of all, but the barricade straight ahead was almost as daunting. Most significant of all (a fact that, in the plethora of press reports, only the *Guardian* mention) a line of police had also closed off what was supposed to be the diverted route down Lodge Hill.'

Lois Austin led the march holding the Unity banner: 'we get to the crossroads and there is a police blockade but they blocked off every road. The route was always disputed with the police, but why did they block off every exit route? There was nowhere to go, we couldn't go back because we had 60,000 people behind us. It was a police trap. There was nowhere to go.'

Platt describes scuffles breaking out, and a few 'light plywood and cardboard' placards being thrown. He continues, 'Some marchers surged forward. Stewards tried to get people to sit down. Some of us did so – briefly. And then the horses moved in ... people were trampled underfoot. Police riot squads followed the horses into the crowd. Stewards attempting to calm the marchers were indiscriminately clubbed about the head ... By the cemetery, a wall collapsed under the sheer pressure of people trying to escape.' A small group threw some of these bricks at the police in response to the police actions; others tried to escape. Platt reported, 'Children were dragged sobbing out of the melee. A man in a wheelchair tried to steer a route away from the trouble. A wire fence cordoning off a small area of open space was torn down to try to relieve the pressure of the crowd ... a line of riot police moved forward to push the marchers back.'

Even though the crowd had nowhere to go, according to Platt they were repeatedly pushed around, clubbed and charged by police, milled about with little clue what was happening and even less about how to do anything about it. At no point did the police make any attempt to defuse the situation ... to make it possible for those wishing to leave to do so, or to enable the march to reform [*sic*] and set off along the diverted route. The police and loudspeakers remained silent throughout.[13]

The day after the *New Statesman* article, on 23 October, a forthright letter from Commander Blenkin was printed in the *Independent*. Writing as 'the Force Ground Commander at Saturday's march', he said the organisers were forewarned, 'On 11 October a letter from the commissioner was served on them prescribing the route. This took the march along Upper Wickham Lane and then left into Lodge Hill.' He claimed 'it was only when the first sticks and then stones came towards us that I replaced those officers with others in full riot gear, and brought in the Mounted Branch as support'. He then made this categorical statement: 'At no time was a barrier or cordon placed across Lodge Hill. The blockade referred to was caused by some of the more peaceful members of the march turning round and coming back down Lodge Hill into the junction.'[14]

David Osland, the deputy assistant commissioner, wrote to the *New Statesman* on 5 November 1993. As the 'officer commanding police operations on the day', he questioned whether Stephen Platt was at the same demonstration, given his report was not supported by the rest of the media. He also asserted, 'Lodge Hill was never blocked by the police.' Who was telling the truth? Platt's response was printed on 5 November:

As for the claim that Lodge Hill was never blocked by the police, I understand that an application has been made for TV film taken on the day. I am sure that this will confirm the evidence of myself and other first-hand observers, who testify that ... all exits – including the approved police route down Lodge Hill – were blocked by the police.

On 15 November 1993, a full month after the protest, a *World in Action* documentary, 'Violence with violence', was aired. The programme contained footage not previously shown by ITN or the BBC. *World in Action* showed that both Upper Wickham Lane and Okehampton Crescent were closed off by police. Then the camera swept across to show the third road, Lodge Hill. There in technicolour glory for all to see was a wide police cordon across the whole of Lodge Hill. Behind it was another line of mounted police. Stephen Platt's account has been corroborated and both police commanders' claims demonstrated to be false.

There had been no way through for anyone on that enormous march; it was a dead end created by the police. Yet the police repeatedly blamed the organisers, saying they were served with a Section 12 public order notice to divert the march.[15] Such notices are not standard, but are used to impose conditions on a march as set by the police. Usually they are served in advance on the organisers, and it is a criminal offence not to abide. In this case, the order was served just days before. The *Guardian* reported Commissioner Condon's reasoning that 'he feared mayhem if the demonstrators went past the British National Party bookshop', Osland also referred to being behind the decision to serve the notice.[16] Was this the first march in history that was diverted by police order, with threat of imprisonment, towards a police blockade with horses? No prosecutions of protesters followed for breach. It would, of course, have been impossible for the police to prosecute the organisers for a breach of an order that the police themselves had made it impossible to comply with.

Nowhere in the police accounts was any mention of the police blocking the march route entirely. To direct a march of up to 60,000 people along a small road into a dead end is extremely dangerous. To then repeatedly charge into the densely packed crowd with mounted police and then riot police with truncheons shows a complete disregard for protesters' safety.

Not for the first time, journalists chose to ignore what was before their own eyes and reported events to fit with the preset police agenda. They published maps showing the police approved route even though the reroute was not an option, because the police had blocked Lodge Hill. The police had given the opposite case and virtually all of the media reported that version of events. The organisers remain shocked at the police approach to the anti-racist protesters.

John Siblon remembers, 'I thought if we remained calm the police would think twice about charging, there was a strange calm before the storm. I remember saying, "Don't worry they are not going to charge". Then they charged with horses first, then later on the ground with truncheons. I remember a woman who was screaming having a panic attack having been knocked to the floor ... pulling people off the floor. It was very frightening.'

Lois Austin had tried to highlight the danger, 'I had been flattened twice, riot police hitting me. I said to them [the police] this is a death trap. Someone's going to get killed. In the end they opened up Lodge Hill. We were the last to leave ... police horses were still going into us ... Nobody in the media told the truth.'

The officers in charge that day had orchestrated the police operation in the weeks before. The senior officers were members of ACPO, including force commander, Hugh Blenkin. He was

supported by fellow ACPO officers DAC David Osland and Met
Police commissioner Paul Condon. However, the chief officers
had obviously not applied some of the lessons from Wapping,
including giving 'warning messages' to the crowd before
mounted police or baton charges were deployed. At the blocked
crossroads at Welling the police had rigged up a loudspeaker
system. There is no evidence it was ever used.

The singer Billy Bragg was there, and wrote to the *Guardian* on 23 October 1993, 'when the fighting broke out and the
mounted police began charging, up and down, it looked as if we
were being deliberately penned in, and thousands of peaceful
demonstrators were left with no choice but to try to resist the
baton wielding [*sic*] riot police that were attacking them.'[17]

An FOI request elicited the 1987 manual in redacted form
(from the College of Policing) and unredacted (from the Home
Office).[18] This manual was a revision of the 1983 one. In the
Home Office version the secrets of the manual are revealed, with
much detail on 'Mounted Police' tactics, objectives and considerations, with sixteen different tactical manoeuvres described
– only three were apparently released to the court during the
Orgreave trial.[19] As previously noted at Orgreave, Wapping and
the poll tax protests, the use of horses is an 'inappropriate' tactic when the crowd is densely packed. However, the tactic can
be used 'to confront a hostile crowd with a display of strength
to discourage riotous behaviour ... hold or ease back a solidly
packed crowd, preserving police lines, gaining ground or protecting buildings'. Warnings in the 1987 manual include the risk
of serious injury and to life. A lesson from the miners' strike and
Wapping leading to a revision in the manual was, 'A fast rate of
advance may subsequently need justification as the risk of injury
is considerable.' What the police did at Welling would not fall
within any version of a reasonable manual.

At Welling the avenues of escape had been closed off by a police cordon and mounted police. The manual's Mounted Police Option 11 requires the 'authority of ACPO rank' for 'mounted police advance on a crowd in a way indicating they do not intend to stop'. In capitals, it warns, 'THE CHIEF OFFICER MUST BE CERTAIN THERE IS AMPLE SPACE INTO WHICH THE CROWD MAY DISPERSE.'[20]

To use Option 11 at Welling was therefore in blatant contradiction of the wording in that section. It seems inconceivable that Blenkin and Osland, the commanders in charge, would not have known this.

There was nowhere for the demonstrators to disperse or retreat at Welling. Therefore, the decision to strike with batons, as with the mounted police, cannot be justified or proportionate to the circumstances. The command to send in baton charges was therefore another breach. As the manual requires, no one would describe the baton use that day as 'delivering light blows'. The London Ambulance Service said seventy-four people were taken to hospital.[21] Twelve of them were police officers, and it was reported that one was very seriously injured; however, two days later, the government statement in Parliament said all the police were out of hospital.[22] The nature of injuries to the protesters is also not explored much by the media, even though six times more protesters were injured.

The police were lucky that no one died that day, as had happened in previous anti-fascist demonstrations. In 1974, Kevin Gately, a second-year maths student at Warwick University, died from a blow to the head at a protest against the National Front in Red Lion Square. In 1979, Blair Peach, a teacher, died on an Anti Nazi League protest in Southall against a National Front meeting in the town hall. Witnesses saw Blair being struck by a police baton.

The police operation at Welling was stage-managed and had extensive funding, with all police leave cancelled and more than 3,000 officers present. There were almost as many in reserve (7,000 in total, according to the *New York Times*, a quarter of the entire Met).[23] Eighty-three police horses did not turn up by chance. The police likely intended to use them. Police dogs were also present.

The police say they had 'intelligence' that serious troublemakers were out to cause unrest and alleged that a sizeable minority were intent on violence. Years later, in 2014, Peter Francis, an undercover officer who was present at Welling, turned whistleblower about his activities. He believes that the Met were seeking to protect one of their own, another undercover officer who was embedded in the BNP in the 'bookshop', one of seven undercover officers present in Welling. Francis's theory is plausible and accounts, to a degree, for the senior officers' motive on the day. However, his theory does not take account of the police not only blocking the route past the 'bookshop', but also choosing to close off the very route that took protesters in the opposite direction from the 'bookshop'.

Stephen Platt gives a further clue: 'I tried with others, to argue with police that their tactics were sheer madness … they were making things far worse … The responses from the police came thick and fast, "Why did you come?" "It's your own fucking fault", "You knew there was going to be a fight, and that's what you got", "now fucking move" … I protested that I would rather be arrested – and safe – than allow myself to be pushed back into the front line. I refused to move, and held onto a fence to avoid being hauled away. A riot shield was brought down hard onto my hand, breaking a bone in my thumb. The officer exclaimed, "Now fucking do what I tell you!"'

The aggression shown to the protesters strongly indicates

that the frontline police were briefed by their senior officers that everyone who turned up was a 'violent extremist' and they were fired up to deal with them accordingly. Police clearly felt they could act with impunity with support from their senior officers. To understand how craven were the tactics at Welling we need to have a closer look at the senior officers in charge that day.

The 'top brass' responsible on the day were Paul Condon, David Osland and Hugh Blenkin. Seven months before the Welling demonstration, in February 1993, Paul Condon became the Met commissioner – the highest-ranking officer in the UK. He immediately announced a more 'caring and courteous' police force, and a drive to raise ethical standards.

Condon was already infamous among the black community. In 1988 he was deputy commissioner for west London. Officers answerable to him raided a community music club called the Mangrove, run by Frank Crichlow, a respected Trinidadian activist in Notting Hill Gate.[24] The illegal drugs the police found were said to be planted. Crichlow was awarded record damages of £50,000 after the case against him was thrown out. He never recovered, while Condon went on to run the Met for seven years from the start of 1993 to 2000.[25]

Condon's time in charge of the Met was most characterised by cases concerning race. Under his command there were black deaths in London at police hands, too numerous to list individually but include the following men: Shiji Lapite, Wayne Douglas, Brian Douglas, Ibrahima Sey and Roger Sylvester. Joy Gardner, a woman with mental health problems, died in August 1993; police gagged her with thirteen feet of tape, and used a belt to restrain her, all in front of her five-year-old son. No police officer has ever been convicted in any of these cases. Condon presided over a police force that showed no signs of improvement when it came to how it treated black people in police custody.

The second most senior officer in charge at Welling was Condon's deputy assistant commissioner, David Osland. On retirement, he became a Tory councillor for Coulsdon West, and held senior positions within Croydon Conservatives. Hugh Blenkin had started as a force commander in south-east London, just a few months earlier in June 1993. From Yorkshire, he played for his local cricket club and was later a captain of his golf club in Kent.[26] All three of these senior officers were also involved in the very case that brought such large numbers to Welling on 16 October 1993 – Stephen Lawrence.

After the murder of Stephen Lawrence on 22 April 1993 his family hoped the police would bring the killers to justice. But police failed to act against named local suspects at the outset. The family realised early on that something was very wrong with the police investigation and that they were going to have to campaign to make things happen. They enlisted the support of the fearless lawyer Imran Khan. In May 1993, nearly three weeks after Stephen's death, they met with Nelson Mandela, who publicly supported their case. The police instantly reacted and arrested five of the named suspects. Two were charged with murder. The Crown Prosecution Service subsequently dropped the charges saying the identification evidence was unreliable. The Lawrence family had no option but to resort to a private prosecution, against three of the men, but this too failed.

The Lawrence family did not give up. Over the next few years public support for their campaign grew massively. The home secretary, Jack Straw (famously depicted as a police officer by the cartoonist Steve Bell) responded to the public outcry and in 1997 instigated a judge-led public inquiry, under William Macpherson.

The Macpherson inquiry considered the police approach at the outset of their investigation, primarily the failure to arrest the suspects and search their properties. The inquiry did not answer all the unresolved questions but the police were interrogated in full public glare. It was a very uncomfortable time for the Met.

As a result, we now know a lot more about the three leading officers who were also in charge of the Welling demonstration. But for the Lawrence Family Campaign this information would have remained hidden. What Macpherson revealed was that the role of these senior officers was anything but the superlative that Commander Hugh Blenkin used for his rank-and-file officers – 'magnificent'. His inquiry revealed overwhelming evidence of these three officers' lack of respect towards the Lawrence family, who were overlooked and patronised. The police's treatment of the family came at exactly the same time as their hostility and dishonesty towards 60,000 anti-racists seeking justice.

The inquiry scrutinised a 1993 internal police review of the Stephen Lawrence murder investigation. Pressure had been building on the commissioner from those officially seeking answers on behalf of the Lawrence family, including from inside government. Reassurances were sought and so DAC David Osland commissioned a review of the Lawrence investigation. The Lawrence case was the first murder case in the history of the Met to be reviewed. Six officers declined to conduct the review. Finally a seventh agreed, Detective Chief Superintendent John Barker.

Barker told Macpherson that after agreeing to take on the review he discussed the matter with Commander Hugh Blenkin, who was in charge of operational matters in Eltham in 1993, and who read him the terms of reference. Barker said that Blenkin had told him upfront that the review should be carried out sensitively and should not criticise any officers, particularly Detective

Superintendent Brian Weedon, who was then one of the senior investigating officers of the Lawrence murder case.[27] In other words, just two months before the Welling demonstration, the officer tasked with a review into the Stephen Lawrence murder investigation says that Blenkin was trying to limit any criticism of the police. Blenkin's senior by rank was DAC Osland; he stipulated that Barker should complete his review in ten weeks.

The Barker review concluded that the Lawrence murder investigation had 'progressed satisfactorily and all lines of inquiry correctly pursued'. The review was provided to Osland, who wrote a note on 9 November that reiterated that Stephen Lawrence's murder was 'competently and sensitively investigated'. He circulated the report to the other senior officers.[28] Apparently, no general or formal discussion was convened. Osland said he discussed the review with Blenkin and the commissioner. On 17 November 1993 (a month after the Welling demonstration), the commissioner himself endorsed the Barker review: 'Seen. Thank you.'

The Lawrences were operating in a parallel universe, trying to get the police to prosecute the murder suspects. The private prosecution having failed, they moved to make a comprehensive police complaint that led to an investigation in 1997 by Kent Police, whose report contained some criticisms of the Barker review. Then followed the Macpherson inquiry, which sat through much of 1998. Michael Mansfield, the family's Queen's Counsel, submitted to Macpherson that the Barker review demonstrated 'the capacity and propensity of senior officers to collude with each other to manipulate and engineer a desired result'.[29]

Macpherson went much further than Kent Police and roundly criticised the review as little more than gloss over the serious errors made at the beginning of the case, a critical period in any murder investigation. He found the Barker review 'a flawed and an indefensible Review' that 'must be condemned', and noted 'not a single question was raised by any officer receiving the Review.'[30] The Macpherson report made damning criticism of the three officers who had ended up in charge at Welling:

> it is difficult to understand how senior officers involved in its reception could fail to raise at least some of the significant and obvious questions generated ... to satisfy themselves as to the adequacy of the investigation, and therefore of the adequacy and accuracy of the assurances that they might give to others based upon it ... they did fail to do so.[31]

The Macpherson inquiry was struck by how unusually the commissioner

> had become personally involved. As an example of his involvement his letter of 22 September 1993 [less than a month before the Welling protest] to Mr Khan indicates 'May I assure you that I have taken a close personal interest in this case from the outset, and that I am absolutely determined that everything possible should be done to bring those responsible to justice.'[32]

Richard Stone, chair of the Jewish Council for Racial Equality and a kindly, softly spoken GP, was a panel member of the Stephen Lawrence inquiry, as an adviser to Sir William Macpherson. In his book about the inquiry written sixteen years later, *Hidden Stories*, he highlighted the commissioner's role:

> I am most fascinated by one detail which was not included in the Report to the Inquiry, which shows the extent of his involvement. The copy of the [Barker] review that we were shown had on the top right-hand corner of its cover the initials 'PC' in red ink, with a neat tick alongside them. We were told that Sir Paul Condon

used red ink for notes and PC were of course his initials; this
was his standard mark on documents that he had seen and signed
off. So it does seem that the Commissioner saw and signed off a
review that had missed a glaringly obvious episode of abysmal
failure on the part of his own police force.[33]

During the Macpherson inquiry, when asked if Sir Paul
Condon should resign, Doreen Lawrence, Stephen's mother,
said, 'He was there from the word go supporting his officers and
therefore I think he should resign.' Neville Lawrence, Stephen's
father, said, 'The Met claim that things have improved since
1993, but plainly this is not true.'[34]

Following his retirement in July 1994, Osland could not resist
writing letters to the press to object to the Lawrence complaints.
In December 1997, in an interview with the *Croydon Advertiser*,
Osland said the police should consider legal action against the
Lawrences for accusing them of racism, as they 'seem happy to
accept the findings of the report where it suits them but not where
it does not'.[35] He asserted, 'There comes a time when enough is
enough ... how long do we have to suffer these allegations of
racism? ... maybe one way of sorting things out finally would
be to take action against Mr Lawrence.'[36]

When these comments were read out in the inquiry, Mr Lawrence left the chamber. The journalist Paul Foot wrote, 'The
irony in the notion that police officers who had not brought
Stephen's murderers to justice should secure damages from his
parents was plainly lost on Mr Osland.'[37] Macpherson found
Osland's attitude 'reprehensible'.

Osland's attack was particularly appalling given he was com-
plicit in the failures. There are 165 references to Osland in the
Macpherson report and a whole chapter devoted to him. Stephen
Kamlish, junior counsel for the Lawrence family, cross-examined

Osland, and asked why he took it upon himself to write a memo, on 8 September 1993, to Commissioner Paul Condon, while the review was in place. In it Osland complained, 'Our patience is wearing thin ... not only with the Lawrence family and their representatives, but also with self-appointed public and media commentators.'[38] This memo was written just five months after Stephen's murder and a month before the Welling demonstration.

Osland had also said at the time he would communicate the result of the Barker review to the Lawrences, but failed to do so, claiming at the Macpherson inquiry that the relationship had broken down. Given the review's contents, and his ongoing public complaints about the Lawrences, it is not difficult to see why Osland avoided making contact. The inquiry said it was 'almost six months later, that the family were given information relating to the Review', but only after pressure from their lawyer, Imran Khan. The impact of stonewalling the family was not lost on Macpherson, who named and shamed the senior officers responsible: 'Mr Osland ... also ... those above him including the Commissioner himself.'[39]

Macpherson held Osland responsible for the breakdown of relations with the family:

Because of his unquestioning acceptance and repetition, even in the public arena, of the myths about family liaison, Mr Osland should not be surprised that some who heard his evidence might regard this as another example of institutional racism at work. Collectively the officers involved failed to treat the family and their solicitor appropriately and sensitively. The evidence that this is so is plain.[40]

Macpherson also reported that Mr Blenkin used the word 'coloured' and that Blenkin was surprised that this expression was not acceptable to describe those from minority ethnic communities, leading to this damning recommendation: 'It is evident that a lack of racism awareness and training extends from the bottom to the top of the MPS [Metropolitan Police Services].'[41]

The revelations in the Macpherson inquiry surrounding the Barker review confirmed the family's long-held suspicions. The police had covered up the failings in their own investigation. They would have to fight on for another thirteen years until finally two of the original suspects, Gary Dobson and David Norris, were convicted for their son's murder.

The Macpherson inquiry, the first such comprehensive review of its kind into whether the police were failing in investigations concerning race, changed the landscape of criminal justice. It unusually found, against the wishes of the commissioner, what the black community had known for years, that the Met was 'institutionally racist'.

This shocking police behaviour involving senior officers Osland, Blenkin and Condon was taking place at the same time that 60,000 anti-racists attended Welling to close down the BNP and demand justice for the victims of racism. These three senior officers worked together on the Welling march where all routes were blocked. The result was a riot – a police riot, which they in turn used to undermine and tarnish the fight for justice by the Lawrence family and anti-racists.

At Orgreave the police lied about their role in starting and escalating the violence. At Welling they went to another level. They were prepared to lie to undermine those who claimed that the police were not doing their job properly in prosecuting local racist thugs. At Welling it appears that the police motive was to protect their reputation through engineering a situation in which they were dealing with a 'mob', to distract from their own failings around the recent murders. At exactly this time the police were also sitting on the Barker review. Their focus on 'violent protesters' helped remove the spotlight from failings in the Stephen Lawrence murder investigation.

On the Monday following Saturday's demonstration, before there was any chance to assess what had actually happened, a politician rose to his feet in the Lords to add his support for the police. He took the commissioner's account at face value. A former home secretary, with a secret – he had sanctioned the secret manual for chief officers with guidelines for policing protest. The manual was again misused at Welling. The loyal Thatcherite, now promoted to viscount, Willie Whitelaw, said,

> My Lords, I am sure that among all the people in this country there will be a wide acceptance of one simple fact concerning this disgraceful behaviour: that the Commissioner of the Metropolitan Police and his officers not only knew what was happening by means of good intelligence but also knew how to deal with the situation and save a great deal of trouble. The Metropolitan Police deserve the greatest congratulations. They are so often criticised. Sometimes they are rightly criticised, but on an occasion such as this they should receive all the credit they deserve.[42]

A week after the Welling demonstration, the Met Police chief Sir Paul Condon visited his secret Special Demonstration Squad (SDS) at a 'safe house' in London's Balcombe Street and gave each of the 'hairies' a bottle of whisky as a thank-you for the apparent accuracy of their intelligence.[43] One of the 'hairies' was Peter Francis. In 2013 he turned whistle-blower. Asked to spy on the Lawrence family, he knew that the police did not disclose this spying to the Macpherson inquiry. The Met denies his claims, saying they were spying on anti-racist groups around the Lawrence campaign.

Despite the police antics of looking out for themselves, the anti-racist movement grew in strength. After Welling, Derek Beackon lost his seat in Tower Hamlets. The Anti Nazi League organised a carnival in Brockwell Park, South London. Previously, in 1978, at Victoria Park, east London, the Clash headlined the Rock Against Racism concert, where, the '80,000-strong audience was the biggest crowd the group had yet played for'.[44] In 1994, 300,000 attended to hear the Manic Street Preachers and the Levellers. The Welling protest spurred a movement that helped marginalise the fascists. Finally in 1994, the BNP 'bookshop' was closed.

Lois Austin tells what it felt like locally: 'Welling was a victory. The BNP were pushed back for a decade really. My dad confronted ones we knew. One responded sheepishly, "I'm not with them any more, I'm not with them any more." After that big Welling demo they knew they couldn't carry on in the same way. It all evaporated away.'

In 2012 the other chief steward at Welling, Julie Waterson, died from cancer, aged just fifty-four years old. She never obtained an apology from the police for her injuries, but in the year 2000 did obtain £5,000 in damages, having taken a civil action. She retained the services of a vibrant solicitor, making a name for himself, at the civil rights firm Christian Fisher. Years later he was to become mayor of London. In settling the case Sadiq Khan said,

> The police on the day acted in an arbitrary, oppressive and unconstitutional manner. The payment of these damages and legal costs is a vindication to Ms Waterson and all the innocent demonstrators who were injured on this day due to the manner in which this demonstration was policed.[45]

7

A Succession of Repetitive Beats

Battle of Park Lane, Criminal Justice Act, 1994

We will never be deterred by the disgraceful riots like those we saw in London last weekend. And the sooner the Labour leadership disowns those Labour MPs involved in organising and speaking at this event, the sooner we may be prepared to take seriously some of their strictures on crime.

John Major, prime minister, Conservative
Party conference, 14 October 1994

Police tactics were monumentally ill-conceived.

Jeremy Corbyn, Labour MP for Islington
North, *Independent*, 11 October 1994

Castlemorton Common is the largest remaining tract of unenclosed public land in England. It does not belong to anyone. On 22 May 1992 there was a festival at the common. Music journalist Simon Reynolds described the event in his seminal book, *Energy Flash: A Journey through Rave Music and Dance Culture*:

Gradually, we realize we are no longer alone; our car has become part of a convoy, and the breathless anticipation, the sense of strength-in-numbers grows until almost unbearable, as does the fear that the police will thwart the rave. Our destination is Castlemorton Common ... set to be the high-water mark and absolute climax of this crusty–raver alliance. Previous Spiral-instigated parties have drawn crowds in the region of five or six thousand. But arriving at the darkened Common, it quickly becomes apparent that the event has escalated beyond all expectations ... Castlemorton is well on its way to becoming the biggest illegal rave in history. Estimates vary from twenty thousand to forty thousand.[1]

The response from some quarters outside the festival was less than enthusiastic. As Reynolds describes,

During the next five days of its existence, Castlemorton inspires questions in Parliament, makes the front page of every newspaper, and incites nationwide panic about the possibility that the next destination on the crusty itinerary is your very own neighbourhood ... Novelist Antony Burgess (mis)informs his *Evening Standard* readers that New Age travellers like to listen to New Age music, and decries the outdoor rave phenomenon as 'the megacrowd, reducing the individual intelligence to that of an amoeba.[2]

The reaction to the festival was to change the rave scene forever. The BBC reported 'police faced angry questions at a public meeting in Castlemorton village about how they had responded.'[3]

Five months later, John Major took to the stage of the 1992 Conservative Party conference in Bournemouth to a rapturous standing ovation. Background television footage of their hero entering Downing Street from April's general election had delegates ecstatic. His shock victory had confounded all the polls. Just two years previously, Margaret Thatcher had resigned in tears when her senior colleagues had cast her adrift as a liability, along with her flagship policy, the poll tax. Now, post-election, the Tories were cock-a-hoop, and in a mood to legislate. Major removed his jacket – the grey monotone meant business. Top of his agenda was crime, and specifically a threat to the landed gentry, 'There's another problem we are dealing with – the illegal occupation of land by so-called "new-age travellers".'

As it was not illegal to have a festival on common land, a Criminal Justice and Public Order Bill was hastily drafted that aimed to abolish 'raves'. Extraordinary legal drafting was required in order to single out this genre of music. Within the new law the power to remove persons attending a rave applied to gatherings at which 'amplified music is played during the night' and 'by reason of its loudness and duration and the time it is played, is likely to cause serious distress to the inhabitants locally'. 'Music' was defined thus – 'includes sounds wholly or predominantly characterised by the emission of a succession of repetitive beats'.[4]

The editor of *politics.co.uk*, Ian Dunt, included the Criminal Justice and Public Order Act in his ten worst British laws of all time, 'For many young people growing up in the late '90s, this Act was totemic of a government which did not understand their culture and was in fact actively conspiring to dismantle it.'[5] Dunt's outlook is confirmed by the debate in the House of Lords:

EARL FERRERS: 'To draft a clause which would catch a rave party but would not also catch a Pavarotti concert, a barbecue or people having a dance in the early hours of the evening. It is very difficult. I entirely agree with my noble friend that some loud music is deeply offensive, but when we start to tell people that they must not play such music under any circumstances and even during the day, that is quite an intrusion into their life. The real danger comes at night-time and that is the reason why we have limited the provision to night-time.'

LORD MCINTOSH OF HARINGEY: 'I hope that the noble Earl is
not accusing Pavarotti of emitting "sounds wholly or predominantly characterised by the emission of a succession of
repetitive beats".'

LORD HARRIS OF GREENWICH: 'I hope that we shall also do our
best to avoid sending Pavarotti to prison for three months.'[6]

The music community responded to this boorish elitism with
creativity. Autechre, part of the new Intelligent Dance Music
scene, produced a sleeve insert for their CD stating, '"Flutter"
has been programmed in such a way that no bars contain identical beats and can therefore be played under the proposed new
law.' The prominent dance music duo Orbital released a track
'Criminal Justice Bill' which consisted of four minutes of silence.
A Taking Liberties compilation CD included the support of top
bands the Shamen and the Prodigy, who were less subtle with the
chorus of 'Their law': 'Fuck 'em and their law.'[7]

The Criminal Justice and Public Order Act went much further
than outlawing ravers and New Age travellers. Home Secretary
Michael Howard drew up a wish list of a '27-point plan to crack
down on crime', to include in the bill. The most controversial of
these points was the removal of the right to silence for suspects.

The Runciman report, recently published in 1991, followed
the Royal Commission on the Criminal Justice System. The
commission had been set up after a spate of appalling miscarriages of justice cases quashed at the Court of Appeal, including
the Birmingham Six, the Guildford Four, the Tottenham Three,
the Maguire Seven, the Cardiff Three and the Taylor Sisters.
Common to many of the cases were police malpractice and false
confessions.

Despite this, the commission failed adequately to protect 'the right of silence', leaving it vulnerable to criticism, which Howard capitalised on.[8] He worked alongside ACPO, who on the eve of the first reading supported his bill by publishing their own *Right to Silence* briefing paper: 'Five pages of tables with little explanatory material which were faxed to newspapers and news organisations and attracted considerable publicity. Although this document had the appearance of a press release, no fuller report of the research has ever appeared, making it impossible to assess the methodology adopted.'[9] ACPO had no qualms in ending the right of silence despite police complicity in the miscarriage cases.

Other sections of the bill dramatically increased police powers, several impacting directly on protesters. These included giving conditions of bail prior to any court hearing; sweeping police search powers; and a brand-new offence of aggravated trespass, directed at hunt saboteurs and road protesters. It also reduced the age of consent for gay and bisexual men to eighteen, denying parity with heterosexuals, and introduced sanctions directed against travellers, Gypsies and squatters.[10]

No wonder Andrew Puddephatt, general secretary of Liberty, described the bill as 'a collection of prejudices bundled together with no internal logic'.[11] Even a Police Federation spokesperson spoke against some of the bill.[12] The *Daily Telegraph* journalist Auberon Waugh commented on the 'ludicrous mismatch of a Bill, which has caused the Government almost as much unpopularity as Mrs Thatcher's poll tax'.[13]

The shadow home secretary was a rising star in the Labour Party, a young barrister and something of an enigma. He had seen himself as on the 'soft left' and in 1982 wrote to the left-wing leader Michael Foot describing himself as having 'come to socialism through Marxism', before winning the Sedgefield seat in 1983. Tony Blair talked in enthusiastic but crafted phrases.

When it came to crime he was 'tough on crime and tough on the causes of crime'. No one quite knew what that meant.[14]

In January 1994, at the second reading of what would become the Criminal Justice and Public Order Act (CJA), Michael Howard, boasted it was 'the most comprehensive package of measures to tackle crime ever announced by a Home Secretary.' He taunted the opposition for their 'truly feeble reasoned amendment ... If the amendment fails, the Opposition will presumably vote against the Bill'. Blair, with exuberant confidence, retorted,

Of course not. If the Home Secretary accepts our reasoned amendment, we will support the Bill. The Right Honourable and learned Gentleman may want to support the amendment which he thinks is so feeble. If he does not accept it, the Opposition will abstain on Second Reading and table our amendments in due course.[15]

Another young barrister, Keir Starmer, criticised Labour in measured terms. He contributed to a lengthy academic paper that complained of Labour's abstention on the bill for 'strategic considerations', as 'much depends in an adversarial political system on robust opposition'.[16] The paper identified that there was inadequate time given in Parliament to debate despite the bill nearly doubling in size from its inception, with some 480 government amendments, which were 'often introduced late'. Starmer's academic paper complained that 'Labour as a party did nothing substantial to seek to gain extra time for effective scrutiny.'[17]

In Parliament Blair boasted, 'I wish that Conservative Backbenchers could have seen the Rt. Hon. and learned Gentleman's face drop about six inches when we told him that we did not intend to oppose the Second Reading.'[18] The human rights lawyer Michael Mansfield (who represented many of those victims of miscarriages of justice) could not hold back his fury, declaring

Blair had 'allowed a fascistic piece of legislation almost certainly to become law'.[19]

It was therefore left to extra-parliamentary activity to oppose the bill. One protest group, the Freedom Network, a loose coalition of travellers and squatters, developed from nowhere. It quickly flourished across the country with over ninety branches from Shetland to Plymouth.[20] They swiftly organised a big protest in London on May Day 1994 that finished at Trafalgar Square.

A Coalition Against the Criminal Justice Bill was also set up combining the many different interests and groups under one banner, with support from some trade unions and MPs. The organising meetings took place in a large empty disused hall on Electric Avenue in Brixton, which was being squatted. Mirroring the various issues in the bill, it was an eclectic mix of road protesters, miscarriage-of-justice campaigners, squatters, LGBT groups, ravers, the Socialist Workers Party and the Advance Party (a collective defending the right to party). The chair of the campaign, Weyman Bennett, recalls, 'We would debate … starting at five o'clock and finishing at one o'clock in the morning. One felt like you needed special superpowers in order to get through the debate; it was all done by consensus.' A sharp contrast to the minimal debate in Parliament.

On 24 July 1994, a second demonstration against the bill took the same route to Trafalgar Square as the previous one. It was twice the size, at around 40,000 people. The protesters were a mixture of young, lively people who came to rave against the bill. There was trouble at the gates of Downing Street (perhaps unsurprising given the absence of a parliamentary opposition to the bill), which caused some damage, but it did not last long before the police restored order.

☙

As the bill was nearing its final reading, a third demonstration was called for 9 October at Hyde Park. Just like at Welling the year before, it was a balmy sunny October day. The demonstration travelled the traditional route from the Embankment to Hyde Park. Mary-Ann Stephenson, who worked for Liberty, attended in a fluorescent vest marked 'Legal Observer'.[21] By chance she was given some warning of what was to come, 'Earlier on I was outside the McDonald's near Marble Arch tube. McDonald's was a target because of the McLibel case. I had seen the police; you could see all the riot police in all the vans parked round the corner and I saw police officers pulling their numbers off their shoulders so they were hanging down so they couldn't be identified.'[22]

The march was nearing Hyde Park with a festival atmosphere. The late 1980s–early 1990s rave vibe was rooted in peace and love, which the police did not appreciate. The Advance Party organised three hi-tech sound systems, each needing their own articulated lorry. Their presence on the march had been 'agreed in advance with Scotland Yard', but there was no agreement for them to enter Hyde Park. At around 4 p.m. the police managed to escort the first sound system away. Ravers gathered by dancing around the second because they wanted the party to continue in the park. The police resisted, charging at the people around the lorry to stop it entering the park, brandishing their truncheons. The crowd responded, throwing beer cans and bottles, but the police didn't stop. Eventually the police relented and let the sound system into Hyde Park.

Inside the park there was a rally with speakers from the campaign against the bill. The chief steward, Weyman Bennett, had just finished speaking: 'I left the stage and I was walking through the crowd with all these people sitting down. It was a hot day. I looked across to the gates at Marble Arch, and saw a commotion.

Horses came into the park; there was no need for them to be brought in. They then started galloping around. People were saying "sit down", "don't get involved". These were people from the traveller community who believed in non-violence and were saying just sit where you are. I immediately ran away towards a gate further down the park. The police were doing a wide sweep to clear the park moving down from Marble Arch. There was mass panic; it was terrifying.

'I looked back and saw the horses charging into the crowd aimlessly, and then officers on foot behind, riot police using truncheons, beating people, saying, "leave the park" – but there was absolutely no way to exit. They caused mass panic.'

In Hyde Park Danny Penman was working as a journalist for the *Independent*. He stepped away from the crowd and went further into the park so he could get a broader view of the scene. He saw lots of young people dancing in a carnival atmosphere: 'The Criminal Justice Bill brought together groups of different

Mounted police charge at demonstrators protesting against
the Criminal Justice Bill, Hyde Park, 1994.

people who wouldn't normally associate with each other. I remember there were a lot of young people who were just wanting to, you know, enjoy life and not be hassled. Then there was a coterie of more politically orientated people.' The huge crowd included two coachloads bringing eighty people from Somerset aged between fifteen and nineteen from six council youth clubs, organised by the council.[23]

Suddenly riot police sprang from behind Penman; they were everywhere and swept through the park: 'I assumed they were going for the main crowd. One of them swung a baton at my head, luckily I dodged out of the way, I turned away and lowered myself so he missed. As I did so another one came in, and aimed a blow at my waist which struck me.' In those days not many people had a mobile phone, but Penman brought one for his work: 'It was a chunky thing in my pocket. The baton hit the mobile phone with such force that it broke in half. That phone saved my kidneys. And then I was hit about three times on my right side. It took me some time before I could start moving again.'

Penman could not see anybody doing anything illegal, but they 'just battered everybody. There was no justification to start what the police did there.' The previous ACPO public order manual from 1987 sanctioned such truncheon charges 'to disperse a crowd', but specifically stated 'truncheons must not be aimed at the head' and that 'no more force should be used than is necessary', in line with the general doctrine of self-defence.[24]

Asad Rehman, a civil liberties campaigner who worked at Amnesty, said, 'There was a huge noise, and this helicopter with lights on was suddenly above us and it came so low, it felt like it was going to land. They were using it to try and physically disperse people. I have never seen anything like it. It felt like *Apocalypse Now*.' The manual only envisaged helicopters being used to illuminate a scene. Here they were apparently being used to intimidate a crowd by flying low in a tree-lined park. This went beyond the manual's warning of 'restrictions on low flying [*sic*] helicopters' in 'urban areas', increasing crowd tension.[25]

Mary-Ann Stephenson remembers there was violence from anarchists on the day (who had put out a leaflet before the demonstration saying 'keep it spikey'); however, this was not in her view the main cause of the police violence that day. She was over by Park Lane and saw one woman 'being attacked by the police; she was sat on the floor, refusing to move but was not in any way violent or aggressive and was just beaten by officers with batons and the whole atmosphere was very, very, scary.' This may have been Liz, aged sixteen, who later recounted,

> As we got near Hyde Park there was a row of military police ... a group of us – girls – went to the front to try and diffuse [*sic*] the situation. We sat down cross-legged in front of them but they ran at us and beat the shit out of us. I was dragged into the park by two police, and the girl next to me had her dog killed in her arms.[26]

As it got dark, Stephenson was observing by the railings of Hyde Park next to Park Lane. She remembers there were a group of people inside the park being pushed back by the police, who were marching in formation. They were pushing people back with riot shields and truncheons until the protesters were right up against the railings that formed the park's perimeter fence. People were trying to climb over the railings but there were officers on the other side beating them back. People were trapped, and they were being squashed. Nobody could get out because the park gate was locked. Stephenson climbed up onto the railings, and shouted down to the officers on the other side, 'Remember what happened at Hillsborough? This could happen again; we are being forced against these railings.' She finally managed to get the attention of an officer, who replied, 'No, you need to get back, you need to go back into the park.' She replied, 'We can't go back.' Because it was dark the police couldn't see everything that was going on. Another officer then said, 'Actually I think she's right.' When the police realised the situation they created an outlet for the protesters. It remains a haunting memory to this day for Stephenson, 'being trapped against the railings and being very scared'.

According to the BBC *Nine O'Clock News* the police claimed that following a stand-off on Park Lane they let people leave. Joe Rollin, a sixteen-year-old apprentice printer, had travelled down from Barnsley, South Yorkshire, along with three coachloads. He tells it differently, with the police charging from Park Lane at the protesters behind the park railings – 'It was scary.' The stand-off led to a battle all the way down Park Lane. All the coaches waiting to take thousands of people back across the country were also parked all down Park Lane and were due to leave around 6 p.m. But police were not allowing the protesters out of the park to get on them. When Joe finally got onto Park Lane the Barnsley coaches had already left but he was lucky as he managed to find a Sheffield bus, and rang for a lift from his parents when he finally got back to Sheffield.

Mary-Ann Stephenson's overriding memory of the protest was that it was 'really, really quite terrifying'. The policing was a 'shambles … Different groups of police officers didn't really seem to know what other groups of police officers were doing.'

After the demonstration there was complete disagreement about who was responsible for the violence. Weyman Bennett said the police had broken their agreement, 'That buses taking people away from the demonstration could assemble at Park Lane but they then blocked that off.'[27] Jeremy Corbyn MP said, 'police tactics were monumentally ill-conceived', that police deliberately charged demonstrators when everyone was leaving, and a number of people, including children, were seriously hurt.[28] He also called for the officer in charge to be disciplined.

The senior officer in charge of the protest, Chief Superintendent Cullen, was on the evening news that night in front of the railings at Hyde Park. He denied any police provocation and said that those who triggered it were 'the same people who provoke it on every occasion in London'. He later accused Mr Corbyn of 'relying on the political rhetoric of the moment' and getting his facts wrong. He said, 'My officers acted with admirable restraint. I dare say some officers retaliated. You can't expect police officers to come under such violent attacks and not retaliate.' Weapons used against officers included sharpened staves, scaffolding, bricks, bottles, cans, gravel and 'almost anything you can think of', he said. On the BBC news, Michael Burke described a riot with twenty-five injured, including eight police officers. Twenty-four protesters were charged with various offences.

Speaking at a press conference the next day, Jeremy Corbyn MP countered the police narrative: 'A lower-key approach, not forcing people to leave the park, not forcing people to rush up to that corner of the park, would have helped to defuse the situation. A lot of people would have gone home at that point, there would have been far fewer people around and I submit less trouble.'

The following day the *Independent* published a letter from MPs Jeremy Corbyn and Tony Benn that complained,

We disagree strongly with the police statement that anarchists turned our rally into a riot. People attempting to leave the park peacefully were attacked by riot police on horses. The only group intent on organising a riot was the Metropolitan Police, whose incompetent and aggressive policing led to a trail of violence and

destruction … We are demanding an inquiry into the policing of
our demonstration.[29]

Cullen's superior, Assistant Chief Commissioner (ACC)
Tony Speed, the second-highest police rank, said the police were
responding to the 'despicable behaviour of the minority'. Speed
added, 'I am proud of the way my officers reacted in the face of
extreme violence.'[30]

So proud was ACC Speed that just two days later he privately
commissioned Commander David Kendrick to carry out an
internal police review of the policing of the demonstration.
Despite the public pronouncements by Speed, his remit sought

1. To examine the strengths and weaknesses of the policing
operation.
2. To enable any lessons available from planning, strategy and
tactics to be debated and developed amongst Commanders (Operations) for the benefit of future events, and for any appropriate
matters that arise to be incorporated into public order, management, planning and training.

Speed was careful to make clear, 'This will be for internal MPS
[Metropolitan Police Service] use only and your internal report
will not be published or your conclusions made public.' Kendrick provided his report to Speed in December 1994. It remained
secret for twenty years until it was unearthed following an FOI
request. The seventy-page report makes for interesting reading.[31]
Its contents led to one incontrovertible conclusion: the policing
of the protest was indeed 'a shambles'.[32]

The report confirmed that the background to the protests
raised no particular risk of violence. On that basis fewer officers

were deployed than for the previous smaller protest on 24 July. On that protest, trouble at Downing Street involved 'no more than 100 at any one time'.[33] 'The Special Branch threat assessment seemed to endorse' the reduction of police numbers, by over 400 officers.[34] Six days before the demonstration, on 3 October, a tactical meeting was held by the police, 'intended to be for Gold and Silver to discuss and agree tactics with the Bronze Commanders'. 'However, it appears that only Superintendents or above were invited to the meeting as principals ... two Bronzes, who were Chief Inspectors[,] were not invited.'[35] This included 'the marching Bronze (a Chief Inspector) as a principal' and meant 'attention may not have been given to the rally and subsequent dispersal.'[36]

Kendrick identified the cause of the trouble as the decision to allow the large sound systems to travel up Park Lane, adjacent to the rally in Hyde Park. This 'was a mistake'. This was sanctioned following the Special Branch Threat Assessment, suggesting that the sound systems might 'reduce the likelihood of any antagonism of police by the demonstrators'. Kendrick's rather telling recommendation was that if the police did not want the sound systems to go into the park they should not have let it get near the park entrance.[37]

Kendrick made an apposite description of the crowd very different to the one previously given publicly by his senior officers Cullen and Speed: 'It is a remarkable feature of this event that on many occasions officers in ordinary uniform were able to pass through a hostile crowd relatively safely. Whilst the same crowd were seen to throw missiles at "fully kitted" officers.'[38] This corroborates that the cause of the trouble was that people wanted to continue their party in the park but the riot police resisted.

The most significant comment within Kendrick's report is the concession about the dispute that led to the violence: 'It is a matter of fact that a large prolonged confrontation between police in full kit and revellers occurred, with the end result being one sound system was diverted and one was allowed in the park. The gain from the whole confrontation for police was negligible.' The *Daily Mail*, in a two-page splash, focused on the sound systems being the cause of violence, 'There is no doubt the music they were playing acted as a rallying cry for thousands of young protesters, many of them bent on violence.'[39] In contrast, Commander Kendrick wrote, 'It is also a matter of fact that the large sound system that did enter the park, once inside, caused no additional policing problem of note.'[40]

Kendrick confirmed there was 'antagonism and even open conflict' amid police ranks, and chronicles events outside any police training, where some serials were having difficulty withdrawing through the park gate due to the number of officers entering the park at the same time. He records that there was no overview, and the big picture 'had clearly been lost ... The situation became more confusing and chaotic with mounted, vehicles, Level I and Level II officers now inside the park confronting various hostile crowds.[41] This situation lasted for some time with no-one apparently in control and officers acting independently of others.'[42]

The situation degenerated as the police abandoned vehicles in the Park Lane carriageway that was the pick-up point for people to get their coaches home, causing an obstruction. There were also continuous problems of 'discipline and supervision amongst' the police. Despite regular discussions between senior officers, they 'failed to ensure that everyone would act together with a common purpose'.[43]

Prior to the day, a plan had been agreed that if police were going to attempt to clear the park they would do so via the south side away from Oxford Street. On the day this changed to a new plan of a 'simultaneous north and south push to send demonstrators east to Park Lane'. Kendrick confirms the 'hostile demonstrators would have been either pushed into the serials they had been attacking for some hours, or they would have been squeezed against the chest high [*sic*] railings.' At Park Lane, 'Commanders present ... had no knowledge of this plan and subsequently believed that had it [the new plan] been executed correctly there could have been serious implications for public safety and disorder.'[44]

The new plan implemented on the day didn't work. These two simultaneous sweeps from the north and the south were hopelessly executed and badly communicated. An officer assumed the role of higher command than authorised, and many officers were not in fact where senior officers thought they were. No one had knowledge of the big picture.[45] The sweep from north to south was not ready and therefore the sweep from the south charged, striking the crowd with their truncheons. This led to a push from south to north-east, onto Marble Arch. Thankfully for all involved, the north was not ready because this avoided a pincer movement which would have pushed all the crowd towards the railings at the same time. If they had been successful it is unthinkable what would have happened to the young crowd.

Another incompetent feature of the policing operation was the use of a helicopter: 'The aerial pictures from the helicopter ... were still unusable and continued to be so until 1735 hours due to transmitter difficulties.'[46] It was not clear what was the purpose of a helicopter. Whether it was for surveillance or crowd control, it failed on both fronts. The communication between the aircrew and the key commanders on the ground was 'at best to be mainly one-way' by a crew who had no 'specific briefing'.[47]

One can only imagine what the aircrew were saying on the day given the Kendrick recommendation that the audio facility within the aircraft should be switched off. 'The recording of any commentary given by the aircrew may well be vital evidence. Anything less than the highest professional standards is not acceptable.'[48] Given its ineffectiveness, Kendrick advised the police to get a new helicopter costing a mere quarter of a million pounds.

As with the aftermath of the poll tax protest, the police masked their failures through an internal review that would not be made public. And what became of the hapless Commander Cullen? He was never held to account publicly for the failures recorded in Kendrick's report. Instead he became head of the police training school.

The police used maximum force at Hyde Park against many protesting, or in this case dancing, for an alternative lifestyle. Their behaviour was reminiscent of the attack on the travellers in the Beanfield in 1985. On this occasion the larger operation by inner city police was also characterised by incompetence. David Kendrick, though, made a prescient observation that the police suffered from an 'apparent cultural abhorrence' for tactical withdrawal, where 'many of the "fully kitted" officers seemed reluctant to withdraw ... some ... responded in an uncoordinated manner advancing towards the demonstrators whilst others were withdrawing.'[49] The psychology of the Met Police seemed to be geared up to all-out offence. They had been let off the leash. That the CJA provided extensive new powers to the police was surely relevant to the orders dished out that day. The senior officers had a self-interest in ensuring the safe passage of the CJA.

The Criminal Justice and Public Order Act passed into law on 3 November 1994. Rather than stop activism, the demonstration galvanised a movement that became known as the DiY Culture, around issues such as the environment.[50] However, as Jeremy Corbyn and the organisers of the protest asked at the time, 'If this is what happens before the Criminal Justice Bill becomes law, what are we to expect when the police are given even more powers?'

The CJA included a new offence of aggravated trespass that was first used in earnest in July 1995 when protest camps were established against the proposed A34 Newbury bypass in Berkshire. This occurred 'when protesters breached a cordon of security guards and climbed trees or chained themselves to machinery'.[51] This reflected a new spatial strategy by the police where they used private security firms to help police the area. People were arrested under the Act for being in the wrong place, and then under pre-court bail conditions, denied access to the area.[52]

The road cost £74 million pounds to build. Some £25 million was spent on private security, and £5 million was spent on the policing. They achieved the removal of 10,000 trees from the countryside to create nine miles of road. Thousands of protesters were involved, including locals, in the building of twenty-seven camps to try and protect the land.

During the 'third battle for Newbury' (chosen in reference to the English Civil War battles that took place close to the town in 1643 and 1644) between January and April 1996, 988 arrests were made, 356 of which were for aggravated trespass. This was the greatest use of the CJA provisions thus far. Fifty-nine were cautioned and 258 prosecuted, just over half of whom were convicted.[53] The wide use of this offence against anti-road protesters was sanctioned by Assistant Chief Constable Ian Blair of Thames Valley Police, while he claimed to be strictly 'bipartisan'.[54]

The police started using the Act in earnest; for instance, Devon Police even sent a helicopter to prevent an 'illegal rave' – a birthday barbecue of fifteen family members.[55]

Section 60 of the new Act allowed the police to stop and search any person or vehicle without giving reasons. Bizarrely, the police used it the following year to stop a coachload of Cardiff City football fans just short of Plymouth to avoid them seeing their team play Plymouth Argyle. They were spared a goalless draw, but their case was taken up by Football Fans Against the Criminal Justice Act.[56]

The Conservatives often pontificate about the vagaries of the state playing an interfering role against the free market in issues such as health and safety legislation. However, at the same time, they have placed an increasing number of police powers on the statute which have infringed civilians' right to freely protest. These measures were introduced on the back of a moral hysteria about raves. Were they really necessary?

On the weekend after the Hyde Park demonstration, 16 October 1994, there was another protest of thousands in Manchester against the Criminal Justice Bill. The sun shone, they had a party, burned a twelve-foot-high reproduction of the Scales of Justice, and left, picking up the rubbish on the way. The officer in charge, Malcolm George, assistant chief constable of Greater Manchester, was delighted at the peaceful result and said, 'sometimes we pray for rain at events such as this, but not this time.' He put it down to his close contact with the organisers on the day and the police keeping a low profile. He smugly asserted, 'We have an excellent reputation for handling public order situations in Manchester. On Saturday, we said we would not interfere with the march provided it stayed within the law. And that's how it went.'[57]

Surely policing by consent would have been a more sensible stance at Hyde Park, as at the rave at Castlemorton Common in 1992, when David Blakey, the chief constable of West Mercia, took a 'softly, softly' approach because, 'Faced with ... the number of people that there were, there was no way I'm going in with riot shields, with public order gear, to move them off.'[58]

Part III.
New Labour: Tough on Crime

8

The Commissioner's Kettle
May Day Protest, 2001

The limits of tolerance are past when protesters, in the name of some spurious cause, seek to inflict fear, terror, violence and criminal damage on our people and property.

Prime Minister Tony Blair, morning press announcement, 1 May 2001

For many journalists the discrepancies last Tuesday [May Day] between the endless clichés about violent anarchists and dogs on strings and the reality – of several thousand people from all walks of life held against their will for seven hours by riot police – must have been painfully apparent.

Jessica Hodgson, *Guardian*, 7 May 2001

When Tony Blair's New Labour abstained on the 1994 Criminal Justice Bill, many saw it as a betrayal of civil liberties. Others thought it was a short-term electoral ploy. Alan Travis, the home affairs correspondent for the *Guardian*, raised a pertinent question in response to civil liberties lawyers at the time: 'The real test of whether Michael Mansfield is right or not will be, how much of the legislation Labour dismantles if it gets into power? For that we will have to wait until after the election.'[1]

On May Day 1997, Blair's New Labour won a landslide victory with a 179-seat majority. The youngest prime minister since 1812 had inflicted the most humiliating electoral defeat on the Tories since 1906.[2] There was a real sense of optimism.

During Labour's time in government, how many of the new offences and police powers in Michael Howard's Criminal Justice Act were removed? None. Rather, Blair created a relationship with the chief police officers of which Thatcher would have been proud. ACPO seemingly got what it asked for. Blair's government's 'frenzied law making' enacted 3,000 new criminal offences, one for every day they were in office.[3] He went way beyond Michael Howard. With Blair at the helm, seventeen additional criminal justice bills were introduced, more than in the entire post-war period.

Whole communities were criminalised under sweeping terrorism powers. Between 2000 and 2008 more than 100,000 people were stopped and searched under the 2000 Terrorism Act; not a single one led to a terrorism conviction. One in three of them was a member of an ethnic minority.[4] Any protest near Parliament was also restricted under Section 132 of the Serious Organised Crime and Police Act 2005, leading to the conviction of a young woman for reading aloud the names of the ninety-seven British soldiers who died in Iraq.[5]

Exactly four years after Blair's victory, on May Day 2001, there were protests in the streets of central London, campaigning 'against capitalism'. Blair's New Labour were now the 'party of business' set on establishing 'the most business friendly [sic] environment in the world'.[6] Even prior to his election, Blair in 1995 had travelled across the world to meet Rupert Murdoch and News Corporation executives to successfully solicit support for Labour.[7] The similarity between the two main parties was reflected in the defection of Shaun Woodward MP from the Conservatives to Labour. Woodward had played a key role in the Conservatives' 1992 election campaign. Labour's hierarchy found him a safe seat in St Helens South for the general election in June 2001.[8]

So it was no surprise that Blair denounced the campaign against capitalism: 'It is not idealism. It is idiocy. It is not protest, it is crime pure and simple.' For Blair, the protests represented a 'spurious cause' and he gave 'absolute and total backing' for the police.[9]

The 2001 May Day protest was based on the game Monopoly, where famous locations on the board game would be targeted for protest. The Monopoly protest allowed for different groups, organisations and individuals to decide which element of the system they wanted to criticise and what statement they wanted to make. The nature of each protest was not declared to the police in advance.

Paul Condon's troubled time as Metropolitan Police commissioner came to an end in February 2000 when he was replaced by John Stevens. Stevens's tenure was marked by a close relationship with the Murdoch press. Since 1986 Neil Wallis had been working at Murdoch's News International (during the News International Wapping dispute), where he took on various editorship roles. Wallis offered Stevens free public relations advice and credited himself with facilitating Stevens's appointment as commissioner.

Wallis had to account for his close relationship with top police officers during the Leveson inquiry, where he boasted, 'I advised Lord John Stevens throughout the application and interview process in which he was ultimately successful. I recall having a number of discussions with him on the subject of his candidature.'[10] He told Stevens to stress he was a 'copper's copper' or 'thief-taker'. After Stevens retired as commissioner in 2005 his close relationship with Wallis continued and he was given a weekly column on his paper, the *News of the World*, at a cool £7,000 per column, with Wallis as his ghostwriter.

Stevens likewise had to account to Leveson for his close relationship with the Murdoch press. Stevens was also said to have formed a strong relationship with Rebekah Brooks, who, having started her career with Eddy Shah's newspapers, rose to become editor of the *News of the World* and then the *Sun*.[11] At the subsequent Leveson inquiry, he was specifically asked how many times he had met with named newspaper editors. Top of that list was Rebekah Brooks. He accepted that he had met with various editors through this period but no specifics were provided as his social diaries went missing.[12]

Stevens also formed a close relationship with top politicians:

> During my time as Commissioner we invited all the Home Secretaries and their wives, along with the Prime Minister, to the NSY [New Scotland Yard] mess to thank them for what they did and explain to them what we were doing. I also had weekly meetings with the Chairman of the MPA [Metropolitan Police Authority]. I tried to appear in front of the media with him, and with the Mayor, as much as possible.[13]

Two months before 1 May 2001, Commissioner Stevens 'dined with a succession of newspaper executives' and briefed them against the upcoming protests[14] – presumably with a view to influencing the press headlines, given that the Met were criticised after May Day 2000, when an unpoliced McDonald's had every window smashed by a group of protesters. There had also been press hysteria about a clump of grass placed on the statue of Sir Winston Churchill's head in the shape of a Mohican. Jack Straw, the home secretary, demanded an explanation from the Royal Parks agency and English Heritage on why they had ignored police advice to cover up the Cenotaph and the statue of Churchill.[15]

The meetings Stevens had in 2001 with newspaper executives certainly had the desired effect.[16] The *Sunday Telegraph* ran the headline 'Police mobilise for May Day mayhem' and the *London Evening Standard*, 'Anarchists to loot Oxford Street'.[17] The *Sunday Telegraph* focused on the 'Wombles' (White Overall Movement Building 'Liberation' through Effective Struggle), stating that 'Special Branch officers believe that the Wombles is a highly trained and dedicated organisation' involved in 'the drilling of about 500 rioters in preparations for attacks on the police during the protests'.[18] Even the *Observer* 'reported some of the more fanciful police briefings concerning samurai-sword wielding [*sic*] protesters, and the police's willingness to use specialist firearms teams to counter this'.[19]

The police reinforced their strategy with press conferences, where Sir John Stevens (supported by the mayor of London, Ken Livingstone) adopted a 'zero tolerance' approach to protesters.[20] The chairman of the Metropolitan Police Authority (MPA), Lord Harris, mentioned that rubber bullets might be used if the situation got out of hand, although on the eve of the protests Stevens played this down, stating that the police had no intention to use baton rounds.[21]

A climate of fear had been created around the May Day event and communicated effectively to the public through various media channels. The numbers that turned out to demonstrate on 1 May were less than half the expected 10,000.

Chez Cotton, a newly qualified civil rights solicitor, worked just off New Oxford Street, a short walk from Oxford Circus (one of the Monopoly locations). From her office window she could see 'row after row after row of police in riot gear marching along followed by rows of mounted police, like some parade in Russia, or North Korea, giving a show of military strength. It was endless and chilling to see on a spring day in the middle of London.'

The commissioner had joined his troops at 5 a.m.; 6,000 officers were deployed, with 3,000 in reserve. At times there were twenty officers for every protester.[22]

The protests started at 8 a.m. with over 500 taking part in two Critical Mass bike rides from Liverpool Street and Marylebone stations, protesting against traffic pollution and congestion. More than thirty separate protests were planned across London 'against everything from capitalism to the banning of pigeon feeding in Trafalgar Square'.[23] There followed 'a veggie-burger giveaway outside McDonald's; the building of a temporary "cardboard city" in one of London's most affluent areas to highlight the problem of homelessness'; and an anti-privatisation picnic at Elephant and Castle.[24]

Just after 2 p.m. around 1,000 protesters demonstrating against the World Bank moved along Regent Street to Oxford Circus, dishing out Monopoly money as they went. The *Guardian*, who were running a 'minute-by-minute' online guide, confirmed 'the demonstration has remained peaceful.'[25]

Then suddenly, at 2:45 p.m., the police blocked off all exits from Oxford Circus. The side exits along Regent Street and Oxford Street were also blocked by police vans. The police then moved to pen in the crowd. Nothing on this scale had been tried before; nobody understood what was going on. The 3,000

© REUTERS / Alamy Stock Photo

May Day anti-capitalism protesters penned in by police, Oxford Circus.

protesters could not move outside the police circle; they were surrounded very tightly on all sides. They were *kettled*. A protester, Mick Gordon, from Cambridge, said, 'They seem to be turning this peaceful process into a potentially dangerous situation by penning people in.'[26]

The media appeared confused. One report said the protest 'developed into a stand-off that was to last for hours', and the early ITN evening report concluded 'the demonstrators showed little inclination to leave' – ignoring the fact that the protesters were not allowed to leave. The protesters were contained in what became known as a 'kettle', a metaphor, comparing the containment of protesters to the steam within a domestic kettle. Its modern English usage is understood to come from *kessel*, a cauldron or kettle in German, that describes an encircled army about to be annihilated by a superior force. The kettling tactic was not improvised on the day; it had been meticulously planned, with the officers on the ground fully briefed on its implementation. Many cameras were set up around Oxford Circus in order to capture the scene. Compared with May Day 2000 the police increased their observation capabilities with some 2,000 video feeds, including teams of roving police 'spotters' armed with cameras.[27] The commissioner had said, 'We are praying that nothing untoward will happen. If there is any trouble ... we have to have the resources ready to meet it.' But it turned out that they were instead ready to deal with any protester even if nothing untoward had happened.[28]

The idea of kettling had come from a former police officer turned Met Police researcher, who ironically shared the same name as the manufacturer of the board game Monopoly. Peter Waddington was known as 'Tank' due to his tall and solid build. The concept of a kettle had not even been contemplated when the 1983 and 1987 ACPO tactical manuals were drafted. Even the authors of the manual had not foreseen such an intrusion into the right to protest. 'Containment' tactics within the manual were all prefaced on a reaction to public disorder, not a pre-emptive tool when no disorder was taking place. In claiming credit for the theory of kettling, Peter Waddington argued that 'whereas with other kinds of methods of dispersal the police have to act aggressively, the great advantage of kettling is that it is a relatively non-aggressive form of containment and control.'[29] How did Waddington's theory play out on 1 May 2001?

A large section of kettled protesters understandably had had enough of being corralled, and attempted to push through police ranks. The news stated, 'under pressure the blue line buckled but did not break. There were some ugly clashes and the first casualties of the day.'[30] This commentary did not come close to describing what the coverage showed – a number of officers striking unarmed protesters around the head with long truncheons – people who were just trying to push their way past them to get out.

The *Independent* reported, when 'hundreds tried to break through police lines ... Police on horseback and in protective gear were involved in repeated baton charges against the demonstrators, leaving at least 50 protesters and three police officers injured.'[31] The overwhelming disparity contradicts Waddington's theory that kettling is a 'relatively non-aggressive form of containment and control'.

There was a further pernicious element to Waddington's kettling, as he submitted that you could restore public order 'by using boredom as its principal weapon, rather than fear as people flee from onrushing police wielding batons'.[32] Certainly the police successfully applied his tactic. The 3,000 protesters were all penned in for at least seven hours in a tight circle. They were denied food, water and toilets. No one was allowed to leave, including passers-by Geoffrey Saxby and George Black, who later took out a civil action.[33] The very public display of enforced boredom on 3,000 protesters would help to deter future demonstrators. The idea that outnumbering protesters with vast police numbers who could resort to violence to keep protesters penned in for hours is anathema to freedom of expression.

Following the protest, the police, media and politicians hailed the police operation as a great success. Home Secretary Jack Straw (a former radical student) boasted that 'a huge amount of effort has gone into the preparations by the police and due warning has been given to potential demonstrators who are going to be intent on violence.' He praised the "'very, very professional" operation and denied there had been an over-reaction'.[34]

Lord Harris of Haringey, the chairman of the Metropolitan Police Authority, said, 'I believe [the police] struck the right balance between facilitating peaceful demonstrations and deterring violent disorder ... The police tactic of containment in and around the flashpoint of Oxford Street proved to be the right one.'[35]

Jenny Jones, a Green Party member of the London Assembly Police and Crime Committee, criticised the use of kettling: 'I would argue it is never appropriate because it is very destructive, and can stoke up tensions ... I would argue it is very counter-productive.'[36]

Solicitor Chez Cotton was contacted by numerous protesters in the kettle, and took over forty statements in the following days. A picture quickly emerged that was in stark contrast to what was being reported. There were teenagers on their first protest, young parents wanting to collect their kids from nursery, office workers getting their lunch, individuals on the way to the bank, OAPs taking part in organised May Day events. It was completely indiscriminate. She remembers 'the shock that the police in Britain would hold you for seven hours, without a loo, or water, or food, when you were doing nothing wrong. It was unbelievable – this was meant to be democracy with policing by consent.' Who had sanctioned the use of kettling?

For 171 years the Met Police at Scotland Yard had been the responsibility of the Home Office. But in June 2000, Home Secretary Jack Straw told the inaugural meeting of the MPA that it was 'at long last bridging the democratic gap by making the Met locally accountable', and answerable to the MPA.[37] The MPA website boasted that its establishment 'marked a fundamental change in the policing of London and ensures policing is democratically accountable'. Chez Cotton asked a special MPA meeting, chaired by Lord Toby Harris, whether the MPA had been informed in advance of the use of a new policy of kettling. There was an audible gasp in the room when the answer came back, 'No'. This confirmed that the police continued to act as they had before the democratic gap was 'bridged' – it was the commissioner's kettle.

In the same meeting the police representatives strongly objected to Cotton's and others' use of the term 'kettling', refusing to recognise the term, and insisting it was 'a containment'. Containment did not begin to describe the experience of those detained for more than seven hours, which also included, as Cotton says, the 'dehumanising' effect where 'police officers would not answer questions or speak at all' to protesters seeking basic information.

A partner at Cotton's firm, Sadiq Khan, the future mayor of London, took over the civil cases, and later told the press, 'The actions of the police were neither necessary nor proportionate.'[38] The exceptional new method of policing protest led to a test case bringing a legal challenge against the use of kettling. Keir Starmer QC was instructed to lead the challenge. His submission was that the police tactic was a deprivation of the protesters' liberty and therefore a breach of Article 5 of the Human Rights Convention. This issue was to make its way through four different courts over many years. We shall see in Chapter 10 below how it progressed near the end of the Labour government at the 2009 G20 protest in London. Before that, the Met were deployed to police protest slightly further afield – Scotland.

9

Barriers to Protest
G8 Summit, Gleneagles, 2005

*Whatever I have done that some may find disagreeable, it is nothing
compared to the police.*

Dr Dónal O'Driscoll, protester at Geneagles, opening
statement, undercover policing inquiry, 5 November 2020

*People believe that police can only do what they are authorised by law
to do. And in fact that's not true. Police can do whatever they think is
necessary at the time, irrespective of the rule of law, it's just if they
act outside the rule of law, they are accountable for it, presumably in
either criminal court, or in civil court.*

Lothian Borders Police officer identified as LBP1

During the 1990s, meetings of the world's most economically
developed countries became synonymous with violent battles
between police and the growing anti-globalisation movement.
The World Trade Organisation (WTO) conference of 1999
was held in the centre of Seattle to agree global rules of trade.
Over 40,000 protesters arrived to meet them, with ten times
that number taking part in a virtual sit-in online.[1] The protests

related to the WTO's prioritisation of economic benefit over social issues, sustainable economies, workers' rights and the environment. They were initially unexpected, non-violent and successful, even preventing the opening of the conference and the cancellation of other events. Mounted police, dogs and armoured cars with pepper spray, rubber bullets and tear gas were used to break up peaceful protesters and some responded by throwing water bottles and sticks. A small group vandalised shops with graffiti and broke their windows.[2] Protests were banned in downtown Seattle in contravention of the US Constitution. Many protesters defied the ban and 500 were arrested and held in jail until the end of the summit. A protest demanding their release was held outside the prison for days.[3] Before the WTO talks eventually failed to agree a new global trade deal, thousands of protesters highlighted police brutality by holding sit-ins outside the Seattle Police Department. The heavy-handed police tactics were widely criticised, with the police officer in charge, Chief Stamper, later admitting, 'We saw what looked and felt very much like a war zone ... and in effect we started it.'[4]

The Seattle protests not only galvanised protesters but helped expand the anti-globalisation movement both at future summits and online. After a protester was shot dead by police in Genoa, Italy, outside the 2001 G8 summit, subsequent summits moved from town centres to more remote locations.[5] In 2005, under the presidency of UK prime minister Tony Blair, the G8 met at the historic and remote Gleneagles five-star luxury hotel, set beneath the picturesque Ochil Hills, thirty-five miles from Edinburgh.

Confronted by the prospect of significant public disorder, police forces in Scotland developed a multi-layered approach. According to Chief Constable Vine of Tayside Police, who was in charge of policing the summit, 'the Scottish approach to policing' would be applied, meaning protests would be 'facilitated' and a softer approach taken by police in Scotland than the police of other host countries abroad.

In the months before the summit, the Scottish police complained about how the media were creating hype about 'violent anarchists' descending on Scotland. Newspaper articles were reinforced with images that repeatedly showed the worst violence at previous global leaders' summits. Even so, in the run-up the police also presented similar footage to Members of the Scottish Parliament (MSPs) and made plans for the global leaders to retreat to a castle if the 'mob' overran.[6]

To implement the plans during the summit, considerable resources were made available to the police. All police leave in Scotland was cancelled and the largest ever police operation in Britain was mobilised with 12,000 police from forces across the UK, including 1,500 from the Met.[7] Unlike during the miners' strike of 1984, a change in the law meant English, Welsh and Northern Irish police could now legally cross the border to provide mutual aid.[8] A no-fly zone was put in place except for police helicopters that relayed video images of protesters to police on the ground.[9] The use of water cannons was considered but rejected. A five-mile ring of steel was built to cut across the Scottish countryside to protect the Gleneagles Hotel. Inside this fence, and nearer the hotel, a mile-long inner cordon built of concrete, steel barriers and supports was also set in place. According to the chief constable's report after the summit, 'This was the biggest ever deployment of this specialist, counter terrorism [*sic*] product.'[10] Edinburgh lawyers were reportedly advised not to 'wear capitalist suits' on the days of the summit and shops along the main street, Princes Street, were boarded up.

At a meeting three months before the summit, Chief Constable Vine reassured a committee of MSPs of the police approach. He confirmed that he thought the operation had enough powers and resources to keep roads open if they were blocked, as protesters had threatened; and unless circumstances dictated otherwise, he would use uniformed officers and provide a business-as-usual service. It was, he told the meeting, an intelligence-led operation. The 'threat to the summit from terrorists or from violent protest' was not 'high', although he acknowledged that this could change.[11] In answering MSPs' questions about military use, Vine thought that the only military support he would need would be specialist, such as electronics and surveillance. The military could be used, Vine explained, not routinely but as a contingency or when military expertise was needed. At that time he had 'no plans to call in any regular military assets'.[12]

What the committee of MSPs was not told was that Tayside Police had given consent for eighteen top-secret long-term undercover police officers mainly from England to work in Scotland around the G8. Tayside Police agreed to six undercover German officers.[13] Scottish police were therefore not only running the largest ever police operation in Britain, but also the largest-known gathering of spy cops.

As the 2005 G8 summit dawned, thousands of protesters had based themselves at a council-approved site near the town of Stirling, where they established an eco-camp. The river Forth ran around the site, and as such there was only one entrance in and out of the camp. From there it was a thirty-minute drive to Gleneagles and just over an hour to Edinburgh. The location allowed protesters to travel across Scotland to events arranged in the days before the G8 summit started.

The Scottish police called for 'responsible' organisations to engage with them and encouraged protesters to protest in a specific area built into the fence that surrounded Gleneagles. Two academics who observed the wider protests at the G8 stated that policing had changed from taking 'oppressive or coercive approaches to an emphasis on consensus based [*sic*] negotiation'.[14] Others agreed, but argued that there was an exception to this softer policing approach – international summits.[15] Such statements highlighted the possibility that police had moved away from aggressive tactics. This unwittingly confirmed that the police had been decidedly oppressive in public order situations previously, when both the police and government had spent many decades denying just that.

In the run-up to the G8 in Scotland, organisations such as Make Poverty History and G8 Alternatives did coordinate with the police and local authorities in advance. The G8 Alternatives (a collective that included CND, the Muslim Association of Britain, the Scottish Socialist Party, Stop the War Coalition and various trade unions) wanted to hold a march and rally as near as possible to the Gleneagles Hotel. The authorities preferred a static rally in a local park in the village of Auchterarder around two and half miles away. It took the G8 Alternatives many months of discussion before the council and police agreed, only a week before the summit, to a loop march that would pass in 'earshot of world leaders'.[16] The march would go past the fence protecting Gleneagles but the authorities limited numbers to no more than 5,000 protesters. Other groups agreed with the police to a 'protester expression area' that had been built specially into the cordon fence.[17]

In Edinburgh the pre-summit marches started on 2 July 2005 with the Make Poverty History (MPH) march, part of the Global Call to Action Against Poverty campaign which had grown around the world. On the same day, across the globe, concerts took place to further highlight the importance of and support for alleviating global poverty.

The police were expecting 100,000 people on the MPH march.

On the day, the march attracted 225,000 people, many wearing white, the symbol of the campaign. They marched to and from a park called the Meadows and formed a white ring of people around the city. The police were friendly, giving directions to toilets, smiling in flat caps and yellow jackets.[18] It was an eclectic gathering of over 400 aid agencies, charities, church groups, celebrities, trade unions and civic groups, who had come together over one year to place pressure on the leaders of the Gleneagles G8 summit, culminating in the Edinburgh march.

Earlier in the year, Nelson Mandela, though recently retired from public life, thought the issues important enough to give a speech in London calling on people to come together: 'The Global Campaign for Action Against Poverty can take its place as a public movement alongside the movement to abolish slavery and the international solidarity against apartheid.' He concluded, 'Sometimes it falls upon a generation to be great. You can be that great generation. Let your greatness blossom.'[19]

MPH brought a strong collective voice to Edinburgh which its spokesperson, Bruce Whitehead, described as a 'welcome [to] the G8 leaders'.[20] Not everyone was happy with this, or with celebrities cosying up to world leaders.

Chanie Rosenberg, an eighty-three-year-old 'veteran demonstrator', expressed her anger to *The Times* on the 10:26 a.m. G8 Express train which had been chartered from London by Globalise Resistance: 'I'm very disappointed to see Bob Geldof smiling in a picture with Tony Blair. It's appalling. What's Bob Geldof doing with a man who's responsible for so many of the world's problems.'[21] During the summit, Geldof was also photographed with world leaders at the Gleneagles Hotel. John Pilger, a veteran journalist, epitomised why many expressed their dissent at this and the G8 leaders: 'In the orgy of summit coverage something has been overlooked: the two men [Prime Minister

Blair and President Bush] at the heart of it, telling us how the world should be run, are the men responsible for Fallujah and Abu Ghraib.'[22]

In the days before the summit there were a number of protests – at Faslane nuclear plant on the west coast; at an asylum seeker detention centre near Glasgow; Stop the War; and other events in Edinburgh, including the Carnival of Full Enjoyment. The carnival protest was to highlight poverty levels of many workers and aimed to disrupt businesses by peacefully occupying the streets.

During these protests, the police in Edinburgh used cordons to corral protesters through the creation of a 'sterile area' using a mobile metal fence. Some protesters were delighted by the police blocking Princes Street, the main thoroughfare that separates the north and the south of the city – they helped the protesters achieve their aim. With cordons, police appear to have followed the tactics set out in the latest version of the manual, including both 'selectively allowing passage through' and 'prohibiting passage' of protesters.[23] However, according to observers, when such powers as 'stop and search' were ambiguous or unknown they were open to police abuse.[24]

Protesters complained that a number of police were not wearing their ID numbers, but this was not their only concern. During the Carnival of Full Enjoyment in particular, police were criticised for their indiscriminate use of Section 60 of the Criminal Justice and Public Order Act 1994 (an order imposed on central Edinburgh) used in conjunction with Section 13 of the Criminal Procedure (Scotland) Act 1995, and Section 44 of the Terrorism Act. According to the G8 Legal Support Group, 'They used these laws to arrest people, search them, and request their names and addresses.' It is only after the first few protests that they appreciated 'that this kind of information could only be requested if one has witnessed or committed an offence'.[25]

At the MPH march of 2 July 2005, few noticed that a group of sixty protesters dressed in black, commonly known as the Black Bloc, were corralled by police into a side street and held for over an hour. The press were denied easy access. As the media were excluded only a few photographs were found of riot police with the marking 'SP' on their helmets blocking roads surrounding the anarchists.[26] The Black Bloc were said by the police to be 'apprehensive, because being cordoned off abroad is usually a precursor to the police wading in, laying about with batons and making arrests. Whereas it was never our intention to even arrest them at that point.'[27]

As MPH marchers tried to return to Edinburgh station they found their path blocked. Without warning, the police 'raised their shields and charged, scattering protesters, including families with children'.[28] Frances Curran, an MSP for the Scottish Socialist Party (who at the time had six MSPs), said, 'The policeman I spoke to had his face covered, I could only see his eyes. These weren't ordinary police, they were specialised riot police.'[29]

Not content with controlling the space protesters could inhabit, there were some other curious operations that meant that some protesters didn't make it to the eco-camp or protest events at all. Scottish Parliament documents released in 2021 show that a month before the summit, the first minister of Scotland, Labour's Jack McConnell, and his ministers were briefed 'about the prospect of widespread disorder'. They were worried about 'small, hardcore elements intent on disrupting events'. It was noted in the Scottish parliamentary Cabinet minutes that 'the security services were working to deal with this threat as best they could.'[30]

This reinforces Chief Constable Vine's assertion to the committee of MSPs in March 2005 that the policing of the G8 summit was 'intelligence-led'. However, intelligence was being gathered in a way the Holyrood MSPs and MPs at Westminster may not have approved of, if they had known.

On the day of the Carnival of Full Enjoyment, a medically trained protester support team was stopped by the police. They were arrested from their vehicles and charged with breach of the peace. Lynn Watson, who often helped out by driving the group, was not arrested.[31] It transpired, years later, that she was one of the eighteen spy cops whom Tayside Police agreed to have operating in Scotland around the G8 summit.

Appearing in court, the medic support team, like many others arrested, received strict bail conditions that echoed those of the 1984 miners' strike. These required many to leave Scotland, or not return to named towns and cities, even though charges were never pursued.[32] If they went straight from court to collect their possessions or tried to leave Scotland by train, they would breach their bail conditions, and some were arrested for doing so.[33]

As the eco-camp was an hour from Edinburgh train station, volunteer drivers were required. Jason Bishop and Dave Evans, flatmates from London, were asked to collect people arriving at Edinburgh train station. Ten minutes after they collected protesters there was a 'significant police operation using helicopters, dogs and riot shields ... [they] seized the minibus and arrested all on board' for breach of the peace. Charges against Bishop and Evans were dropped minutes before they entered court.[34] A number of years later they were both identified as spy cops. While the police continued to claim facilitation of protest at the G8, they were also secretly stopping and arresting people on the basis of what might happen.

The authorities thus acted to delay or remove the right to protest through subterfuge that would be condemned if other countries undertook the same approach. The inquiry into undercover policing excluded investigation of these spurious police operations because they took place outside England and the terms of reference are limited to England and Wales.

Mark Kennedy, alias Mark 'Flash' Stone, was another spy cop at the G8, who had relationships with a number of women he was spying on. He later revealed the interest in his intelligence: 'My superior officer told me on more than one occasion, particularly during the G8 protests in Scotland ... that information ... was going directly to Tony Blair's desk.'[35]

Despite the remote venue for the summit, hidden away in 850 acres of Gleneagles estate surrounded by rolling Scottish hills, many protesters were still determined to get there. The G8 summit was also determined to thwart the anti-globalisation movement that had galvanised since Seattle.

The night before the summit officially started, and worried that the police would block the only exit from the eco-camp, many protesters left before midnight. On 5 July 2005, some of the protesters were dropped at sleeping points, others walked up to seventeen miles over the Ochil Hills through heavy rain. All settled in the undergrowth for what remained of the long summer night, plans in place for the following morning. 'Beacons of Dissent' were lit on two hills south of the Gleneagles Hotel at midnight; their flames not only buoyed the soaking wet travellers but were intended to send a message to the G8 that they were not welcome. As they hid, preparing themselves for the next morning, a helicopter occasionally flew overhead.

Less subtly, hundreds of other protesters, primarily dressed in black, including some of the international Black Bloc, walked out of the eco-camp en masse just before 3 a.m. They were headed west to a nearby motorway, the M9, which connected Edinburgh to Gleneagles. On leaving the campsite a cordon of around fifty riot police was there to meet them. Those at the front of the Bloc had padding in their clothes and large sticks, which they beat against the shields of the police, who retreated.

The protesters marched on, meeting the police at various points. Some of the international Black Bloc had collected a shopping trolley and filled it full of bricks which they then threw at the police. While trying to find a route to the M9, the Bloc found themselves in a shopping area full of national and international brands and restaurants, everything the anti-capitalist protesters were against. Windows were smashed, buildings were covered in graffiti and at least one police vehicle was attacked. Some of the media reported that the Bloc damaged personal property, but they deny this, and said local residents had helped them on their way by pointing out how best to get to the M9. These directions took the Bloc over a golf course, where they walked in single file after a Scottish voice shouted, 'Don't walk on the green.'[36]

At 7 a.m. the other groups of protesters who had slept in the woods dragged themselves from the undergrowth and set up blockades on roads. Some used branches, others drove cars on a 'go-slow' or, wearing bright yellow jackets, set out 'Road blocked' signs and locked themselves on to pre-prepared cars. They would create an effective blockade and then, when police appeared, move away, disappearing across fields and forests only to reappear with a new set of branches elsewhere.

BBC Scotland travel news confirmed that all roads to Gleneagles were blocked, except for a few minor roads. Railways were also blocked in two places. In some cases it took over five hours for the cutting crews to arrive and remove those fixed onto their cars. A kids' picnic took place on a bridge with clown protesters and a red bus; the police did not appear to know what to do with them. More than thirty people were arrested after blockading the few roads that connected Gleneagles with the rest of Scotland.

The Dissent! protest group estimated that over 4,000 people took part in the blockades over many hours. They nearly shut down the summit after severe delays for delegates, apart from the leaders who were flown directly into the venue. Adapting to a decentralised protest model reflected the remote locations that the G8 protesters faced. Multiple autonomous groups agreed to block the roads using their own initiative and methods. The police could not predict what would happen next or keep up with the protesters' action. As BBC travel news confirmed, the roads were paralysed.

At around 11 a.m. police announced they had cancelled the G8 Alternatives protest march for 'safety reasons'. This prompted Colin Fox of the Scottish Socialist Party to argue that 'the police nakedly tried to stop it from day one, even on the day.'[37] After the organisers said they would march on Edinburgh instead the police reversed their decision and agreed to let the march go ahead. It was then a struggle for the protesters to get to Auchterarder. In Edinburgh, the police stopped a G8 Alternative convoy of coaches from leaving. A number of other vehicles were 'stopped and searched crossing the Forth Road Bridge' and some roads were reportedly closed by the police.[38] After a few hours' delay, around 5,000 people gathered in Auchterarder Park to walk the agreed route. Those who had blockaded roads and managed to evade the police joined them.[39]

Tanya Bolton, at the time an NHS case manager working in mental health, was on one of the buses from Edinburgh to the G8 Alternatives protest. She was delayed a number of hours and so joined the march near the back as it passed through the village of Auchterarder towards the fence at Gleneagles. Tanya remembers a noisy but good-natured crowd who moved along a narrow road with perfectly trimmed hedges. They were watched by locals, who stood on their doorsteps outside stone cottages set back with

little paths down to the road and shouted good wishes to protesters as they passed. It was a cheerful, colourful demonstration,
with music from a number of groups.

Tanya recalls, 'At that time, I was coming from much more of
a "police are there to protect us" view ... We wanted to see what
was happening at the front of the march so moved up. As we got
closer to Gleneagles, there was a massive wire mesh fence ...
then you could see this big, long green area, like a lawn rolling
gently up a hill and there was a heavy police presence. Massive
police horses and riot police force [on foot]. It was quite intimidating. When I saw them ... when we got close ... I was just
like, oh God, the horses were massive. Riot police all uniformed
up looking authoritarian. A shield protecting them, a helmet,
and you're stood there in your normal clothes – it really kind
of wakes you up. It's terrifying. I was thinking, "I don't want to
be here."'

Suddenly, the double rotor of a Chinook helicopter was heard
overhead. Barry Wright, a seasoned protester, now a teacher,
who travelled to Auchterarder on the same delayed bus as Tanya,
said he was shocked to see 'a very different kind of police ...
what was particularly intimidating was they were lined up as a
wall each with their own radio communication device on their
lapels and whenever they got a message ... you got this line [of
police] with a little blue square all lit up at the same time. They
were ready for confrontation, an intimidation tactic ... high-tech
security – organised.'

The enormous helicopters landed time and again, bringing
riot police who piled out into the field. Barry took their message
as, 'You will not pass. We are going to carry on with this ... a
show of strength and intimidation.' Tanya recalls her response
to seeing the first Chinook helicopter: 'It was thunderous, low
... coming into the field. That was me, "I'm out of here".' As

Police reinforcements arrive by helicopter at
Gleneagles at the G8 summit, 6 July 2005.

Tanya turned to leave she met some aggressive calls of 'Don't
turn around, that's what they want you to do.'

Contrary to her direction, others continued on the prescribed
route and then veered off into a field where some had breached
a weak point in the fence. As protesters tried to cross the fields
heading towards the inner fence they were cut off by cordons
of police, many of whom were from the Metropolitan Police.
One person did manage to climb over the inner wall and was
promptly arrested. The sound of the double-rotor Chinooks,
which were commonly used in the war in Afghanistan, brought
more riot police reinforcements. Never before had military helicopters been used against civilians on mainland Britain.[40]

Some protesters pulled down parts of the fence. A force with
'SP' embossed on their helmets pushed back from the other side.
A thin wire fence that bent under the pressure was all that divided
them from each other. 'SP' officers were involved in the front line
at previous demonstrations in Edinburgh where police in riot

gear charged the crowds at both the MPH march and the Carnival of Full Enjoyment. Academics Gorringe and Rosie stated, 'Aggressive police in riot gear' were trying to clear the streets, 'charging the crowd, shoving interested onlookers with shields, shouting and swearing at people'.[41] A police officer later admitted that on two occasions at the Carnival of Full Enjoyment, despite having 700 police officers deployed, he 'almost lost control'.[42]

The 2004 manual has three pages dedicated to the identification markings of public order helmets that ACPO state are particularly important for 'ease of identification of officers engaged on Mutual Aid'.[43] The two-letter riot helmet markings identify the different police forces deployed across Scotland's G8 protests, including Central Scotland Police (AH), Lothian and Borders Police (ZH) and Fife Constabulary (ZT), all now part of Police Scotland; and a number from England, including the Metropolitan Police (MP). The 'SP' force, however, remains an enigma.

A Freedom of Information (FOI) response from Police Scotland states, 'SP – This is Police Scotland's identifier, however[,] we are unaware of whether it was in use in 2005.'[44] Police Scotland was not formed until 2013. Police Scotland wrote again 'having made further enquiry'. They were '*advised* that Strathclyde Police wore the "SP" identifier on their helmets at that time, before changing to "AS" post G8'.[45] A radio history expert who was last on the Strathclyde system in the late 1990s advised that he has 'only known Strathclyde as M2AS'. He explained that M2SP is 'listed as the Prison service college at Tulliallan' around twenty miles from Gleneagles. The change to airwave was in the mid 2000's … [when] many dropped the national M2'.

It has thus not been possible to properly identify who the 'SP' force deployed in Edinburgh and at Gleneagles in 2005 were. At this stage, all we know is that they were deployed on the front line, particularly when protests turned violent, or were expected to.

At Gleneagles on the first day of the summit, on the G8 Alternatives protest, the police cordoned the last 200 protesters in the field and moved them back to the road and the village. Observers were prevented from accessing the area during this stand-off, where subsequently it was reported that twenty-eight police were injured. It is unclear if this number includes the police officer who ended up in hospital after US president Bush knocked him over when the president was out riding on his bike. A year later, in his annual report, Chief Constable Vine confirmed there was no damage to private property, except to crops.[46] Over the week, 700 protesters were estimated to have been arrested and detained, with 366 arrested and charged; a number of these cases were subsequently dropped or abandoned.[47]

In the early hours of 7 July 2005, around 200 police officers mainly in riot gear surrounded the eco-camp where 2,500 people were sleeping. Television crews stood behind the police lines. Plans for the environmental marches on that day were therefore in doubt. However, tragic news of a terrorist attack on London's public transport led the protesters to hold a candlelit vigil instead. The G8 summit continued with their agenda regardless while Tony Blair returned to London. Subdued and often silent protesters packed up, but were only allowed to leave after the police used their stop and search powers. The campsite was also searched, to no avail. After the search, the police withdrew.[48]

The police, while repeatedly stating they would facilitate protest around the G8 summit, instead covertly and overtly tried to frustrate it. Most importantly, the summit was positioned in luxurious remote surroundings, which made it as difficult as possible for protesters to protest at the seat of power. Police were happy to facilitate protest that did not rock the boat, but that which sought to show dissent faced constant barriers. Tactics deployed were often led by the police's delineation of the right to protest, where and how.

The ambition of the majority who sought to get to the summit was non-violent direct action against a variety of issues, including global poverty and climate change. In 2005, while climate change was on the G8 agenda, it was not yet the mainstream issue it would become. George Monbiot, the *Guardian* columnist, describes such non-violent direct actions: 'Not a direct attempt to change the world through physical action, but a graphic and symbolic means of drawing attention to neglected issues, capturing hearts and minds through political theatre.' He warns such action 'will succeed ... only when it is part of a wider democratic assault on the policies which gave rise to them'.[49]

Around the Gleneagles G8 summit, this included the blockades of roads by protesters for up to five hours and colourful clowns protesting with non-compliant antics in Edinburgh. Some disruption is expected, almost inevitable, at a protest, even if the police don't self-determine whether or not the protest is legitimate or where it can be held.

The police approach was determined by the level of engagement protesters were willing to have with the police, and the intelligence received. The undercover officers who operated in Scotland were then supervised by ACPO (by then restructured as a company limited by guarantee).[50] Their spy cop operations had oversight from ACPO Scotland. Their deployment had been agreed to by Scotland's Tayside Constabulary, who were running the G8 policing operation. Additionally, a 'Tayside police officer was seconded to the NPOIU ... coordinated undercover operations at the G8 summit ... including that of six German undercover officers overseen by the National Public Order Intelligence Unit'.[51] Ironically the police determined what was legal protest, while the very presence of spy cops in Scotland was questionable.

While spy cops were operating north of the border in 2005, ACPO's scope of operations and objectives in legally binding documents lodged at Companies House was only expanded in 2006. The amendments included the coordination of the 'strategic police response in times of national need on behalf of all chief officers'. In 2013 (two years after the spy cops were absorbed by the Met Police) ACPO's objects were expanded again, to cover Scotland and an ambit of other powers that Blair's government had gifted them. The accumulation of these changes appears to have been done on advice, to make ACPO retrospectively compliant with their overt and covert activities.

Whether or not that change applies retrospectively to actions undertaken at the G8, eight years previously, should be a question for the undercover policing inquiry. However, despite numerous efforts by campaigners, the inquiry's terms of reference exclude Scotland. The UK government said in 2016 that it was 'not possible' to expand the terms of reference and include Scotland. Harry Halpin, one of the people Mark Kennedy spied upon, responded to this decision, 'It is a real shame that [Home Secretary] Theresa May did not extend the inquiry to Scotland and personally I think it is because she is covering things up.'[52]

The latent results of the overt and subversive police action at the G8 (combined with Blair ignoring a million people in London who marched worldwide against the Iraq War in 2003) would lead to a further breakdown in trust between police, government and the population. The effect, no doubt intended, could be a propensity for people to stop protesting because they feel they are not heard as the events become so anodyne that those in power can repeatedly ignore them.

Prior to and during the G8 summit at Gleneagles it is now apparent that the police used a number of violent tactics that frustrated protest in a series of different ways. Spy cop intelligence, excessive force, intimidation with vast deployments, the use of high-tech communications and the first use of the UK military against its own population on the British mainland were all implemented in the name of 'the Scottish approach to policing' and 'facilitating' protest.

People trying to express their objections to G8 governance through protest were quietly picked off, removed en route, arrested and then banned from being in Scotland during the summit. Others, intimidated by the use of military or police psychological and physical force, walked away. By building the largest ever police operation in Britain and using the military to implement their plan, a Labour government and the devolved Scottish Labour Party Executive upheld global economic governance by a small group of transient mainly white male middle-aged leaders.

The result showed that the police are willing to facilitate some public dissent, but only if they approve where, when and how. After tactics deployed by protesters around the remote location of Gleneagles caused disruption and were a headache for the police, the global leaders' summit of 2009 abandoned remote locations and moved to the City of London.

10

The MP's Kettle

G20 Protest, 2009

Part of the headlines should be ... 'Astonishing operation pulled off by the Met who did a first-class job'.

Commissioner Sir Paul Stephenson, 22 April 2009

They are using this more and more. Instead of sending snatch squads in to remove those in the crowd who are committing criminal offences, they contain everyone for hours. It is a retrograde step ... it is an infringement of civil liberties.

John O'Connor, former Met officer on
kettling, *Guardian*, 3 April 2009

On 1 April 2009, five MPs went to observe the G20 protest at the Bank of England in the heart of the City of London. They were leading members of the Liberal Democrats – four shadow secretaries and Baroness Shirley Williams. They must have looked slightly odd alongside anti-capitalist protesters. The protest had been called in opposition to the 2009 G20 London summit of the heads of state and government from the twenty largest economies, hosted by the new prime minister, Gordon Brown.

Representing 85 per cent of the world's GDP, and two-thirds of its population, these world leaders were meeting to discuss financial markets and the world economy.

This was the second meeting of the G20 following the world-wide financial crisis of 2007–8. There were protests across London to coincide with the summit, including a climate camp. At the Bank of England, 4,000 protesters were corralled by police. The Members of Parliament were denied access, unable even to view the demonstration. The MPs' trip would have been wasted but for the Liberal Democrat shadow secretary for home affairs, Tom Brake MP, who managed to get through the police line, accompanied by two members of his team. Once inside the demonstration the unfortunate Brake found he too was refused permission to leave. He was detained for five hours, despite identifying himself as an MP and a legal observer. As a result of being detained he missed a vote in Parliament. Alongside thousands of protesters the Member of Parliament was kettled.

Three weeks later, the Met commissioner, Sir Paul Stephenson, praised his force's policing on that day, saying it had been an example of an 'astonishing' police operation.[1] He claimed that 'the overwhelming majority of officers carried out their duties in a professional manner … [and] did a first-class job.' A spokesperson for one of the groups on the protest, the Campaign for Climate Change, responded, 'If that was a good policing operation it makes you wonder what a bad one would be like.' The following day the mayor of London, Boris Johnson, said in an interview on SunTalk radio, 'I worry that there are large sections of the media that are currently engaged in a very unbalanced orgy of cop bashing.'[2]

Despite the statements of the commissioner and the mayor, several official inquiries were launched into policing at the G20 protest, including a parliamentary investigation led by the Home

Affairs Committee (HAC). The HAC televised inquiry involved robust interrogation of witnesses summonsed before them, with a similar feel to court proceedings, demanding in this case senior police officers account for their actions.

As a member of the HAC, Tom Brake MP found himself in the bizarre position of being a witness to his own committee. He testified to what it was like to be kettled:

> [At] 3:45pm … we learnt that the police had decided to use the kettle tactic by detaining everybody. It was impossible to leave the area. All the roads were shut by a police cordon. Policemen were wearing helmets and protection. They did not explain why and when asked, could give no indication as to how long they expected the cordon to be in place.

Brake described how a series of people unsuccessfully sought assistance from him as an MP to ask the police to let them leave, including an apparent bystander who needed to go home to look after his elderly eighty-three-year-old mother, a young man who was a diabetic and needed to return home for medication, and an elderly couple who made the mistake of walking through the area and then feared for their safety. Brake filmed his experience and placed it on YouTube.[3]

Another man explained he had not had any water for more than nine hours. It was a sunny day, and a member of Brake's team formally asked the sergeant in charge of a police cordon to provide water. 'He refused to provide it, claiming that they did not have any. My team member pointed to a police van, with its door open, which contained many bottles of water.'[4]

The issue of kettling was raised by the HAC with senior police officers. This led to a petty and comical exchange reminiscent of that in 2001 between the Met and solicitor Chez Cotton after the May Day protest where the police refused to even recognise the use of the term 'kettling'. The MPs at the HAC got the same treatment. Sue Sim, ACPO lead on public order, told them, 'I do not understand the term "kettling". Kettling is not a British policing public order tactic, it is something that has been created apparently in the media.'[5] Asked what she would call grouping people together in this way, she stated, 'containment'. Sim maintained this position under robust cross-examination by the MP for Westminster North, Karen Buck:

> MS BUCK: 'Going back to the issue of kettling as a term, as a concept, it is something that has entered discourse in terms of crowd control probably since the May Day demonstrations at the beginning of the decade. In an earlier answer you kind of rejected it as a term. Are you saying, really, that this is a media invention and that actually there has been no change in the tactics of crowd control?'
>
> MS SIM: 'Kettling is not a term that is contained within any policing manuals or with any policing concept. The issue of containment is a public order tactic.'
>
> MS BUCK: 'Do you not think then that there has been any change in the techniques of crowd control in recent years: because that is certainly an assumption that is widely held, that there have been these changes, which is why the term kettling has come into more popular discourse?'
>
> MS SIM: 'Containment has been a tactic for a long time. On the issue of kettling, I do not actually understand how that has come into the terminology because it is not something that we would accept; containment is.'[6]

This issue of when kettling began was taken up by a Conservative MP. Once again Sim denied that the police kettled and asserted that 'the containment tactic has been around since the manuals began.'[7] Sim was supported by other senior police giving evidence to the HAC, who also stated that kettling was not a recognised tactic. The HAC asked to see the manuals but it is not clear whether they were disclosed. They are not referenced within the HAC report.

Sim's evidence was a distortion. She was suggesting that what happened on May Day in 2001 was not unusual. This is untrue. The enforcement of a tight encirclement by police, restricting all movement, thus denying exit for many hours, was, as Karen Buck MP pointed out, a new tactic. The police were trying to suggest otherwise. One recognisable flaw in Sim's argument is that it overlooked the unfortunate fact that Peter 'Tank' Waddington, the former police officer turned Met Police researcher, had invented kettling to expand the stratagems available to the police.[8] He boasted of having done so as a response to police failures at the poll tax demonstration in 1990.[9] In 1995 the police decided to test the tactic for the first time on disabled people protesting against discrimination in Parliament Square. It was then used in 1999 at a protest against the World Trade Organisation in Euston, before it was deployed on a large scale at the May Day protest in 2001.

Did the police manuals, as Sim claimed, contain anything akin to kettling? As the tactic was invented in 1990 it was obviously not present in the manuals of 1983 and 1987. In Waddington's obituary in 2018, *The Times* described that kettling meant

non-compliant protesters be corralled until such time as they became bored, tired and hungry. By forming large cordons of police officers who would move as one to contain a crowd in a limited area, he said it should be possible to leave protesters with only one exit, which could be controlled. Either that or the protesters would be prevented from leaving the area completely, with the effect of denying them access to food, water and lavatory facilities for an arbitrary period determined by the police.[10]

In the manuals created after 1990 that we have had sight of, there is nothing that correlates to this method of containment, denying dispersal of large numbers for hours and wearing protesters down.[11]

The proud inventor of kettling, Peter Waddington, reviewed how his tactic fared at the 2009 G20 protest. He argued that kettling had succeeded 'in restoring order by using boredom as its principal weapon, rather than fear as people flee from on-rushing police wielding batons'.[12] How did Waddington's analysis compare with Tom Brake's experience stuck in the kettle at the Bank of England?

Brake told the HAC that while they were being kettled:

[At] 4:30pm – The riot police charged without any warning. Most of the people in front of the police cordon at the corner of Threadneedle Street were peaceful protesters. They were dancing, listening to music and there was no apparent threat. The atmosphere changed, with people panicking. Some people were injured by the Police. People were running and trying to escape but with the cordon completely sealed, there was no escape route.[13]

Brake and his team decided to talk to officers in charge to find out why the kettling strategy had been implemented and why the police were charging into a kettled crowd without warning. They spoke to several officers on the ground who either did not respond or said they did not know who was in command.[14]

The police charge happened over three hours after an attack on a branch of the Royal Bank of Scotland, where some protesters smashed windows and set fire to blinds.[15] At 5:45 p.m. the police started to squeeze the cordon area. It was only at this point, according to Brake, that 'the tension rose significantly' and 'a small minority of around 50 to 100 people, [began] fighting with the Police'.[16]

Greg Foxsmith, civil rights lawyer and then fellow Liberal Democrat councillor, described the policing as a 'disgrace'. He was close to the kettle and witnessed an elderly gentleman being struck on the arm by a police officer in a balaclava. When he sought the officer's shoulder number he too was struck, on the chest, causing him to fall to the floor.[17] He went past rows and rows of police waiting to be deployed; 'it felt like being in a police state.'

Even *The Times* was critical. One of their journalists who endured 'seven hours of detention without food or water' within the kettle wrote,

> The police tactics were simple. At the first hint of trouble, they enacted a long-planned strategy – trapping and detaining all the protesters, violent or not. Once established, the cordon slowly squeezed – each police charge rolling past any protesters who refused to move, battering them. No one was released. If I were to design a system to provoke and alienate, I could not do better.[18]

Waddington's assertion that kettling was an alternative to 'fear' in what was an 'otherwise remarkably successful policing operation' was particularly ridiculous, given that it meant setting aside what he called 'two momentary episodes' which he failed to identify, one of which was the death of a man and a catalyst for the high-level official inquiries into the policing on the day.[19]

Ian Tomlinson was a forty-seven-year-old homeless man who helped out newspaper vendors around Monument Underground station. The vendors described him as 'a gentleman' who 'never hurt anyone'.[20] He was walking home to his hostel near Smith-field Market and not part of the G20 protest, when after 7 p.m. he collapsed and died. That evening the Independent Police Com-plaints Commission's (IPCC) London regional director agreed a Metropolitan Police press release that 'misleadingly failed to mention that there had been police contact with Ian Tomlinson before his death "but focused instead" on the apparently exag-gerated throwing of bottles by protesters at police administering first aid'.[21] The media initially and largely uncritically repro-duced this version of events. The *Evening Standard*, the very newspaper Tomlinson 'had been selling for two decades, ran the headline: "Police pelted with bricks as they help dying man".' It went on to claim, 'Based on the information at this stage the IPCC are satisfied that there is no evidence that the actions of those officers present in Cornhill contributed in any way to the sudden and untimely death of an innocent bystander.'[22] The go-to Home Office pathologist, Freddy Patel, concluded in his initial examination that Tomlinson had died of a heart attack.

G20 protests, London, April 2009.

© Kristian Buus / Alamy Stock Photo

By chance, an asset manager from New York, Christopher La Jaunie, who was in London for a conference, filmed the protest on his digital camera. The businessman soon realised that his video footage contradicted the official version of events outlined in the media which claimed that Tomlinson died of natural causes.[23] La Jaunie made contact with the *Guardian*, who, on 7 April 2009, six days after the protest, published the previously unseen video footage of what happened to Ian Tomlinson.[24] The news had an immediate impact, confirming that the Met Police statement was inaccurate and that, in fact, a Territorial Support Group (TSG) officer had struck Tomlinson with a baton to the back of his leg, and then aggressively pushed him from behind immediately prior to his collapse.

The video went viral and suddenly the tabloid media did a volte-face. Just after 7 p.m. the police had decided to end the kettle outside the Bank of England and disperse the crowd.[25] Tomlinson was struck soon after that policing decision. He had been trying to get home but met different cordons of police blocking his route, part of the wider kettling operation at the Bank of England.[26]

The TSG had replaced the controversial Special Patrol Group (SPG) in 1987, as the specialist police unit dealing with social disorder. The SPG had been disbanded because of ongoing criticism following an attack on a teacher, Blair Peach, at an anti-racist protest in Southall in 1979. Peach died of his injuries. An undisclosed police report found that Peach was almost certainly killed by an officer from the SPG.[27] No officer has yet been held to account. The TSG remains as controversial as its predecessor; between 2005 and 2009 it received more than 5,000 complaints, including 376 allegations of discrimination and 2,280 of 'oppressive behaviour'.[28]

Tomlinson's death was evidence of the police attitude towards the protesters. By 10 June 2009 the IPCC had received

276 complaints about the policing of the G20 protests, relating
to both police tactics and the use of force.[29] Further incidents
came to light via phone footage, including what was probably
the second 'momentary episode' Waddington had referred to –
the sturdy Sergeant Smellie was caught on film striking a much
smaller woman with the back of his hand.

One group that was singled out for special attention at the G20
protest was the press. The National Union of Journalists made a
comprehensive submission to the HAC on the police's treatment
of their members. Drawing parallels with the Beanfield events
twenty-four years earlier, the police prevented the press from
recording events. The Met later apologised, suggesting the press
were 'caught up' when the police used Section 14 of the Public
Order Act 1986 to move people away. This order was designed
to prevent 'serious public disorder, serious criminal damage or
serious disruption to the life of the community', which was arguably not justified in any event, certainly not against journalists.[30]

David Hoffman was one of the photographers moved away
under the Section 14 order as the kettle was formed.[31] He believed
that this decision was in part to avoid witnesses to police dogs
being deployed, but he nonetheless managed to get a photograph. This deployment of dogs was made despite concerns
raised three decades earlier and the warning in the 2001 manual
that 'dogs are unable to discriminate as to who is or who is not
breaking the law.'[32]

Having been shepherded away, sixty-four-year-old Hoffman
was confronted by another police cordon with officers in full riot
gear squaring up to several hundred protesters. He sought to
move into a space to the side and as he did so was hit with a police
shield in the back with considerable force. Even more concerned
for his safety, he moved further away to be on his own and separate from the demonstration. He collected himself and started to

get his camera ready to take photographs when an officer in riot gear suddenly left a group of officers he was with and headed towards Hoffman some metres away. He hit Hoffman in the face with his shield, causing injury to his jaw and his camera to fly around so that it was knocked and damaged. Hoffman had to have emergency dentistry on five fractured teeth.[33]

Luckily the assault was caught on a protester's footage, otherwise it would have been very unlikely that he would be able to make a claim for damages against the Met. Hoffman won £30,000 from the police, plus the cost of extensive dental repairs. He also received an apology (alongside a separate apology for having been wrongly moved in the first place under the Section 14 order) which said, 'The MPS [Met Police] confirms its recognition that freedom of the press is a cornerstone of democracy and that journalists have a right to report freely. The MPS apologise to Mr Hoffman for the treatment he received and have paid compensation.'[34] This was a surprising statement given that the Met Police in February 2008 had launched an 'anti-terrorist' poster campaign targeting photographers, leading to a vibrant opposition campaign, I am a Photographer not a Terrorist.[35]

David Hoffman mentioned in his civil action that he noticed the police officers did not have numbers on their uniforms. The commissioner, Sir Paul Stephenson, said this practice of some officers was 'absolutely unacceptable'.[36] The issue was raised in the House of Lords on 29 April 2009, and the Home Office parliamentary under-secretary of state, Lord West of Spithead, said, 'The displaying of identification numbers is not required by legislation. This is a matter for individual chief constable and force level guidance. Contravening force guidance on this ... is a disciplinary offence and cases are handled in line with the Police (Conduct) Regulations 2008.'[37] The mayor, Boris Johnson gave the same response a few months later to the London Assembly.[38]

A subsequent report by Her Majesty's Inspectorate recommended, 'Consideration should be given to making the display of police identification numbers a legal requirement.'[39] Yet nothing was done to implement this. No one, it appears, was even disciplined outside words of advice, and the practice of not showing shoulder numbers on protests, which was clearly no accident, given it had occurred across three decades at Orgreave, Wapping, the poll tax protest, the G8 and the G20, was allowed to continue without any change in the law.

Police not displaying their numbers was not the only issue as to the identity of officers at the protest. The first witness before the HAC, the gold commander for the protest, Bob Broadhurst, alongside the commissioner, was interrogated by Tom Brake:

TOM BRAKE: 'Presumably there were plain-clothes officers in the crowd. I would expect there to be to spot the worst trouble-makers.'

SIR PAUL STEPHENSON: 'I just have to say the idea that we would put agent provocateurs in the crowd is wholly antithetic to everything I have known about policing for the best part of 34 years.'

TOM BRAKE: 'Can I ask Commander Broadhurst, please?'

COMMANDER BROADHURST: 'I was obviously the Gold Commander. We had no plain-clothes officers deployed within the crowd. It would have been dangerous for them to put plain-clothes officers in a crowd like that. The only officers we deploy for intelligence purposes at public order are forward intelligence team officers who are wearing full police uniforms with a yellow jacket with blue shoulders. There were no plain-clothes officers deployed at all.'

TOM BRAKE: 'In which case, Commander Broadhurst, can I ask you what explanation there is for two men who I personally saw walking through the police lines where I had attempted to secure the release, if I can put it that way, of a number of people who needed medical attention for instance and not succeeded? What explanation can you give for the fact that those two men walked through the police lines without any form of challenge? Who were they and why were they allowed to walk through the police cordon?'

COMMANDER BROADHURST: 'I do not know who they are. They were not plain-clothes officers deployed by me or anybody on the operation. All I would say initially, and you can come back to me later on when I give evidence to you, is that there is an issue around the discretion used by individual officers, the message communicated to those individuals, how they interpret that. It may well be that the people you saw have gone through some officers who have used more discretion than others who are not letting anybody out. That is an issue I need to grapple with in our training and our work on such tactics.'[40]

Six months later the assistant commissioner of the City of London Police, Frank Armstrong, gave a very different account, that about twenty-five undercover officers were deployed during the protests. The HAC confronted Broadhurst about his previous evidence. He maintained that despite being the gold commander for the whole protest, he had no knowledge that City of London Police employed undercover officers.[41]

Things got worse for Broadhurst. In 2011, Scotland Yard admitted that he misled MPs at the HAC by denying that undercover officers had infiltrated protesters during the violent G20 demonstrations.[42] Acting Commissioner Tim Godwin apologised to the chairman of the Home Affairs Select Committee for giving false evidence. This apology did not come about because the police had a sudden bout of candour but in response to the unmasking of undercover officer, Mark Kennedy, who had been employed by the National Public Order Intelligence Unit to infiltrate a group of environmental protesters and had been asked to provide intelligence on the G20 protests.

Mark Kennedy was an undercover officer of a different sort. He was not there by chance on 1 April 2009 but had spent nearly seven years embedded in environmental protest groups. At the G8 protest his van was used to ship equipment to an eco-camp near Stirling. Years later, in 2018, the police finally admitted that Mark Kennedy's managers knew that he had deceived a woman protester into a long-term sexual relationship and allowed it to continue. It was not the only one.[43] None of this was divulged to Parliament in 2009 by the officers in charge of the Met when they had the opportunity. When women protesters unmasked a number of undercover officers who had formed sexual relationships with them (as outlined in the excellent book *Undercover* by Rob Evans and Paul Lewis), Theresa May, then home secretary, instigated a judge-led policing inquiry. It has proceeded at glacial pace. One day it may reveal how many undercover officers were present at the G20 protest which senior Met Police failed to disclose to Parliament in May 2009.

Given the controversy around the policing at G20, the ongoing use of kettling was in jeopardy. The Home Affairs Committee found that it 'involves a shift in power and control from the protesters to the police and should be used sparingly and in clearly defined circumstances'. They deferred as to its ongoing use as 'a matter for the courts' and to the police 'as a tactical measure [which] is to be addressed in the forthcoming HMIC [Her Majesty's Inspectorate of Constabulary] Report'.[44] The HMIC produced a lengthy colourful brochure of a report, *Adapting to Protest*. They commissioned opinion polls to suggest majority support for the use of kettling. However, relying on 'public support' is no way to decide on police policy, given that those polled were not subjected to the kettle. Relying on opinion polls for criminal justice policy would probably illicit capital punishment, which has often had majority support.

The HMIC also decided the silver commander's tactical plan for G20 was legitimate in that it relied on judicial support for kettling. Kettling as deployed at May Day 2001 had been subject to challenge through the courts up to the Court of Appeal, led by the human rights barrister Keir Starmer QC. In July 2008 Starmer made a surprise move to become the director of public prosecutions, and so was no longer able to represent the kettling challenge which had made its way to the highest UK appeal court, the House of Lords.

The House of Lords decided, in January 2009, that this form of containment, kettling, was lawful, if certain criteria applied: if the tactic is resorted to in good faith, if it is proportionate to the situation which has made the measure necessary, and if it is enforced for no longer than is reasonably necessary.[45] Lord Hope's judgment found that 'the restriction on the appellant's liberty that resulted from her being confined within the cordon by the police ... was not the kind of arbitrary deprivation of liberty that is proscribed by the Convention, so Article 5(1) was not applicable in this case'.[46] In other words, their Lordships found that despite those being held in a kettle for up to seven hours, nearly the length of a working day, their liberty was not at stake, and they were not unlawfully detained.

This decision was affirmed by the European Court of Human Rights in 2012. Clive Coleman, the BBC's legal affairs correspondent, explained: 'The essence of the judgement really is that kettling is lawful if it's done in the right way, if it's proportionate and is enforced for no longer than reasonably necessary and if it's being undertaken to avoid personal injury and damage to property.'[47]

A legal challenge to some of the kettling tactics applied at the G20 protest succeeded at first instance but was appealed by the Met.[48] The unelected Court of Appeal Judges found again for the police, deciding that the salient factor was the view of the officer in charge of the protest as to whether a breach of the peace was imminent. Therefore the courts left the police with a very wide discretion as to when and where they could use kettling as a legitimate tactic during protests.

History confirms that the police have not erred on the side of discretion when presented with new discretionary powers. The following year, in 2010, in the second of a series of demonstrations against tuition fees, thousands of school students left their schools to demonstrate in Whitehall. The response of the Met was to kettle them with 'no water or toilets or space to sit down' in sub-zero temperatures for seven hours.[49]

In the same spot ten years later, kettling was used again against Black Lives Matter protesters, on three occasions, following a mass outpouring of protest against racism after the killing of George Floyd by police in Minneapolis in May 2020. Protesters were held until after midnight, then photographed, and their names and addresses were taken before they were allowed to leave.[50]

Twelve years into a Labour government, the policing of the G20 protest in 2009 showed the police at the peak of their powers. So confident were the police that they did not need to rely on any manual; instead they could implement Waddington's creation, resorting to kettling, then deny it is a tactic. The police kettled large numbers of protesters for several hours, in 2001 and again in 2009, despite only a few protesters causing damage during the mass anti-austerity protests.

Waddington's theory that kettling was a more peaceful and safer way to police protest is undermined by the evidence of recorded police violence from inside and outside the kettle. The excessive and aggressive policing was supported by the controversial TSG, undercover officers, dogs and the intrusive surveillance gatherers in the forward intelligence teams (FITs). The police also applied improper use of the law, such as using Section 14 orders to move members of the press away.

For many years Tony Blair and his erstwhile home secretary, Jack Straw, had given virtually all the powers and resources that ACPO had asked for. After nine years under Blair, ACPO's budget had increased from £1.5 million to £19.8 million, an increase of 1,220 per cent.[51] ACPO were firmly established as a far-reaching 'Big Brother' bureaucracy, and were free to run their operations. In 2006 the near trebling of ACPO grants and funding correlated with their absorbing three units that infiltrated and spied on protest groups: the National Public Order Intelligence Unit (est. 1999), the National Domestic Extremist Team (est. 2005) and the National Extremism Tactical Co-ordination Unit (NETCU, est. 2004). NETCU was established after corporations, whose regulations had been relaxed by the Labour government, lobbied the Home Office.[52]

Vast amounts of taxpayers' money was being used to support business interests through ACPO in their endeavours against those who protested against business practices that impacted on the environment or animal rights.[53] ACPO had such a close relationship with the government that in 2006 they changed their company rules, with the rather contradictory description that they were 'an independent, professionally led strategic body ... in equal and active partnership with Government'.[54]

At the G20 protests of April 2009, the ACPO officers knew they had the complete backing of the higher echelons of government when they sent rank and file police officers onto the streets at the Bank of England to kettle the protest. In addition, Keir Starmer QC, the DPP, was faced with the decision whether the officer who struck Ian Tomlinson should be prosecuted. Starmer decided in July 2010 that no charges would be brought for his death, relying on the fact that Dr Freddy Patel's initial pathology report led to an 'irreconcilable conflict' with the other medical experts as to cause of death.[55] Just two months later, Patel was suspended by the General Medical Council, who found him guilty of misconduct in two other post-mortems and of deficient professional performance in a third.[56] Despite this, the DPP stubbornly maintained that he was 'not altering' his decision not to prosecute.[57]

Starmer was publicly criticised by his peers. A letter published in *The Times*, complained that his 'refusal to authorise the prosecution of PC Simon Harwood ... in the light of the suspect evidence of the police surgeon Dr Freddy Patel always struck me as incomprehensible, and the finding by the inquest jury of unlawful killing makes essential a reconsideration of the decision'.[58] Starmer relented on his decision, but the about-turn still did not bring a conviction.

For a brief period in 2009 the future of kettling was in jeopardy. The Home Affairs Committee put the police on trial for the policing of the G20 protest. The vigorous chair, Keith Vaz, repeatedly demanded that Sue Sim, ACPO lead on public order, answer his question as to whether she had concerns about the evidence she had just heard from protesters on the policing of the G20.[59] However, that vigour was absent from the subsequent HAC report, where the parliamentarians deferred to the unelected police inspectorate and the courts as to whether kettling should be permitted. When the Court of Appeal decided in 2012 that kettling was lawful, Vaz did an immediate U-turn and welcomed the decision. His capitulation confirmed that during the Blair years the police could now control the exact space in which you can protest – it may be legal, but not moral.

Most people did not expect the Blair years to be characterised by the promotion of neo-liberal policies and support for the 'filthy rich'.[60] As previously noted, Blair had courted the support of Murdoch before he was elected.[61] He later became godfather to one of Murdoch's daughters.[62] Privatisation flourished, with swathes of private finance initiatives across schools, hospitals and prisons, costing the public purse £300 billion for infrastructure projects said to be 'four times the size of the budget deficit used to justify austerity'.[63]

Years later, when Margaret Thatcher died in 2013, Blair admitted that he saw his job as being to 'build on some of Thatcher's policies'.[64] Certainly that was the case for the police and ACPO, whose reach and power increased under Labour. The Liberal Democrat home affairs spokesman, Nick Clegg, obtained figures of the New Labour government's 'frenzied approach to law-making, thousands of new offences ... an obsession with controlling the minutiae of everyday life'.[65] Just as Tony Blair's support for Rupert Murdoch would allow for the worst of press practices, hacking, to flourish (leading to the Leveson inquiry), so his unqualified support for the police gave them confidence to apply new draconian tactics against protesters, knowing they were safe from any criticism from the prime minister.

In response to the economic crash, the Blair and Brown governments pursued a wider neo-liberal agenda and outsourced public services. Companies who benefited from privatisation included G4S and Serco, who grew into vast multinational companies. They absorbed services across healthcare, probation and prisons, resulting in the shrinking of the welfare state. With privatisation and deregulation, employees' conditions and public services deteriorated. It was called free enterprise.

Conversely, the same Labour governments imposed a massive expansion of state power over the individual. Thousands of new laws were introduced, including the Anti-Social Behaviour Order (ASBO), criminalising anything that was 'likely to cause alarm', resulting in more than 1,000 children being imprisoned.[66]

In this era, with the government's blessing, the police moved to stop the population freely protesting against government policies. They built upon the power exercised since 1983 and collaborated with a new government to extend their control over protest. Under Blair this was encapsulated by chief officers feeling confident enough to mobilise vast numbers of riot police to trap protesters from the outset, restricting any movement or dissent. By this exceptional tactic, the police even went beyond their own secret manual. How far they had come from 'normal policing'.

Part IV.
Austerity Justice

11

Charged

Student Fees Protest, 2010

We did everything we could to facilitate peaceful protest and, in reality, while I'm sure the vast majority came here to want to protest peacefully, a significant number of people behaved very badly today.
Commissioner Sir Paul Stephenson, 9 December 2010

There were large numbers of protester casualties – and a smaller but still significant number of less severe police injuries. The casualties seemed to be a direct result of the change in police tactics. If these now become even more extreme, there will no doubt be more violence and more people hurt.
Susan Matthews, mother of Alfie Meadows, student protester who had brain surgery after being struck on the head with a police baton, *Guardian*, 28 January 2011

Every Liberal Democrat MP in the May 2010 general election signed a pledge to oppose any increase in tuition fees. Students were facing a change in policy that could see those fees rise to as much as £9,000 a year. As a result, the Liberal Democrats won 45 per cent of the university student vote, nearly double that of

Labour.[1] The election result left no party with an overall majority and the Liberal Democrats made the surprise move to form a coalition government with the Conservatives. The electorate had 'voted centre left, but the government they got was monetarist and right-wing'.[2] As part of their pact with the Tories the Liberal Democrats promptly reneged on their election pledge and backed an increase in tuition fees. Their leader, Nick Clegg, declared that it was 'not unreasonable' to do so.[3]

The prospect of exorbitant fees arising from this blatant act of treachery led on 10 November 2010 to a protest of more than 50,000 students in London. There was a feeling the government could be stopped in its tracks, leading to a new election.[4] The march went to Parliament Square, and several thousand continued to Millbank, where they occupied and ransacked the Conservative Party headquarters, all of which was caught on television cameras. The occupation extended to the whole building, including the roof, from where one college student on his first protest dropped a fire extinguisher.

The police had clearly underestimated the turnout and the mood of anger. They were working on an earlier National Union of Students (NUS) estimate of a 5,000 attendance and only deployed 225 officers for the entire demonstration.[5] Commissioner Sir Paul Stephenson admitted his force 'should have anticipated the level of violence "better", adding: "It is not acceptable. It's an embarrassment for London and for us."'[6] For the police to allow the governing party's headquarters to be taken over was unprecedented. It was not to be the only embarrassment suffered by the commissioner in the large student protests that dominated the next month.

A fortnight later, on 24 November, 130,000 protested across the whole country. In London thousands of children walked out of their schools and assembled at Whitehall. The police responded by kettling them for more than six hours into a dark freezing evening. The following day, at a Metropolitan Police Authority (MPA) meeting, the commissioner was challenged as to why police horses charged such a young crowd. His reply to the question, 'Had horses charged at the protest?' was as follows: 'I was at the debrief last night, there was no reference to that whatsoever and I have no reference to it.'[7]

Stephenson's response was, rather like the police statement made after Ian Tomlinson's death at the G20 protest, completely inaccurate. The official account was amended by a Met spokesperson later that day: 'Police horses were involved in the operation, but that didn't involve charging the crowd', and they may have been used 'to help control the crowd for everyone's benefit'. They added, 'police officers charging the crowd – we would say: no, they did not charge the crowd.' Unfortunately for the commissioner and his force, video evidence was then published in the *Guardian* that clearly showed police horses cantering into the crowd.[8]

Brian Paddick, a former deputy assistant commissioner, argued that serious questions had arisen from the policing of the protest, 'if there were school children, their parents and a pregnant woman there'. John Biggs, a Labour member of the MPA, complained, 'I think the explanation we've had so far just isn't good enough.' The commissioner maintained they got the policing 'right'.[9]

The police had form for charging at students with horses. On exactly the same date, 24 November, twenty-two years earlier, in 1988, just around the corner, another student protest was charged at by police horses. The tabloid press called it 'the Battle of Westminster Bridge'. Some 6,000 students had deviated from a march south of the river, to lobby Parliament against student loans replacing the non-repayable grants system. The student protest filled the bridge. Benny McLaughlin, president of NUS Scotland, said, 'The vast majority of marchers on the bridge merely wanted to be let through to try and peacefully lobby their Members of Parliament.'[10]

Scotland Yard said Commander Tony Speed (who instigated the internal police inquiry into the 1994 CJA protest) ordered a 'controlled dispersal of the large group of students', even though many coaches were due to leave half an hour later.[11] The suggestion that the police had given a warning before they charged was disputed by witnesses, including Ann Clwyd, Labour MP for Cynon Valley, who offered this prophecy: 'Some of us believe that the police are being conditioned to use extreme instances on occasions like this, and during the miners' strike. If this is true then future demonstrations can only be more violent.'[12]

One of the mounted police officers later wrote, 'apart from one injury to the public where a hefty lady was trodden on when one horse came down on the metalled road surface, the dispersal worked beautifully and was a tribute to our horse, our training

Mounted police at the Battle of Westminster Bridge, 24 November 1988.

and the horsemanship of the officers.'[13] In fact, twenty protesters needed hospital treatment, including Maria Franklin, who
had simply gone to meet her father, who was there as a mature
student. A quarter of an hour after she met him the police horses
charged: 'there was no warning, none at all ... I was standing at
the back of the crowd, on the south side of the bridge, I ran as
fast as I could but I wasn't fast enough; I fell to the floor and I
was trampled by a police horse. When I got up I was dripping
with blood, my trousers were ripped, my leg was ripped open, I
was carried away to an ambulance.'

She was taken to hospital and diagnosed with an extensive and
severe laceration fourteen inches long in the shape of a horse's
hoof which went to the bone. She lost three pints of blood and had
emergency surgery, which lasted two hours because the wound
was so dirty from the glass and gravel from the horse's hoof.
Franklin suffered PTSD and had a very long road to recovery.

Rhona Friedman, a student from Sussex University (now a
criminal defence solicitor), saw people being sick having witnessed the police violence. She saw a mounted officer 'charging
like something out of *Game of Thrones*, his baton raised and
swinging down from above his head, narrowly missing mine, it
made a swishing sound which I shall never forget'.

The subsequent 'independent' Police Complaints Authority
(PCA) inquiry carried out by the chief constable of Cambridgeshire 'commended' the police use of horses and described as
'naïve' the idea that the police could have waited half an hour
for when the coaches were due to leave.[14] The PCA news release
stated, 'the use of police horses in this manner is an approved
method of dispersal'. It did not record a source for the 'approved
method' for obvious reasons. The 1983 police tactics manual
was revised in 1987. Neither the revised nor the original manual
involved the elected representatives of Parliament. It is debatable

whether the police horse charge on Westminster Bridge complied with the 1987 manual. Any horse charge was supposed to give protesters an 'avenue of escape'. How did charging a packed crowd on a bridge where the 'avenue of escape' was a dangerous drop into the river Thames meet the minimum standards of professionalism required by the rules?[15] What is not arguable, though, is that these methods were never 'approved' by Parliament.

Ironically, despite acting under powers that had bypassed Parliament, the police partly justified their actions in 1988 by arguing that they were protecting Parliament. The approach of keeping protesters away from Parliament has since developed into something of a paranoia. In 2001 peace campaigner Brian Haw began a permanent peace protest in Parliament Square against military action in Afghanistan and Iraq. He lived there for nearly a decade. The Blair government introduced a law specifically to get rid of him. They created a new offence of demonstrating without authorisation within one kilometre of Parliament Square.[16] Unfortunately for the government the only person in the country to whom their new law did not apply was Brian Haw, as his protest had started before the Act came into force.[17] Even so, a Labour government had limited the rights of protesters to gather outside Parliament. The authorities continued to pursue Haw and five years later the mayor, Boris Johnson, won an injunction to remove him and other campaigners, because 'it is nauseating what they are doing to the lawn'. The campaigners were removed and some very ugly fencing was erected in their place.

In the run-up to the demonstration on 9 December 2010, students expressed their dissent through occupations of university buildings across the country. The leader of the National Union of Students, Aaron Porter (who years later moved into a 'higher education consultancy job' advising universities) promised to call a demonstration in London.[18] The 9 December 'official demonstration' (called on the day the MPs were due to vote on tuition fees) was changed to a glow-stick vigil on the Strand, away from Westminster. On the day, it only attracted a few hundred people.[19]

The London Student Assembly, a coalition of education groups across the capital, called a march to Parliament for the same day, which was supported by the new vibrant campaigns, the National Campaign Against Fees and Cuts and the Education Activist Network. Clare Solomon, the president of the University of London Union, recounted that 'fraught negotiations with the police produced a route that led us into Parliament Square, and out again to the "official" demonstration. The mood was determined. Police formed solid lines along the length of the demonstration, riot helmets at the ready.'

The march entered Parliament Square from Great George Street in the north-east corner. It was meant to continue up Whitehall towards the Embankment and the 'official' glow-stick vigil. Solomon explains,

> Thirty thousand students surged through central London, police running to keep up. The raucous, unrestrained crowd arrived in Parliament Square well ahead of the police schedule – and, much against police wishes, they stayed. Parliament was the target ... The fences were torn down and the whole Square occupied.[20]

Again there was music and dancing and chanting, reminiscent of the 'repetitive beats' that were played at the Hyde Park protest against the Criminal Justice Act in 1994.

Polly Curtis, reporting for the *Guardian*'s rolling live blog of the protest, showed how quickly the unrealistic police plan to keep people out of Parliament Square collapsed. She took photos, one with a near-empty green in the square's centre the other only three minutes later showing Parliament Square completely full.[21] Students protested at Parliament, and some missiles were thrown. The *Guardian* blog of reporters provided a recap of what happened in the next hour and a half:

> The vast bulk of the protest has been peaceful and good-natured, those on the ground say ... there have been some isolated skirmishes, mainly protesters using barriers to try and force back police lines. Some placards and flares have been thrown ... Scotland Yard says that so far there has been just one arrest (for drunk and disorderly) and no reported injuries, though both could change.[22]

Despite the fact that there were only 'isolated skirmishes' up to that point the police suddenly resorted to two tactical decisions that raised the ante. They kettled the crowd and soon after sent in the horses. What caused the change was not entirely clear. Battles then ensued between the police and protesters, which carried on into the night.

With the support of the Liberal Democrats the tuition fees bill passed into law at 5:25 p.m. with a majority of twenty-one – this obviously raised tensions further. The Treasury was attacked. Some students moved into the shopping area of the city around Regent Street, where the police decided, in what was another first, to escort the royal entourage directly into their protest. Paint and objects were thrown at the royal car taking Prince Charles and Camilla to the London Palladium theatre. If there is any official explanation for how they got this so wrong, it remains unclear.

In the aftermath of the protest the media and most politicians were quick to condemn the protesters. Four days later, Parliament called a debate on public order policing. It was led by the home secretary, Theresa May, who prejudged the issue, 'I want to be absolutely clear that the blame for the violence lies squarely and solely with those who carried it out … that police tactics were to blame, when people came armed with sticks, flares, fireworks, stones and snooker balls, is as ridiculous as it is unfair.' She reminded the House that UK policing was 'based on popular consent and trust between the police and the public. That must continue.' Shadow home secretary Ed Balls chimed in, 'It is important, too, that we recognise the bravery and commitment that our police officers showed … in the face of extreme provocation and physical danger. Without their professionalism and restraint, there would have been many more casualties.' [23]

A few dissenting voices raised questions, including the Labour MP for Bristol East, Kerry McCarthy, who, after acknowledging the 'very difficult job' of the police at the 9 December protest, gave voice to students at the University of the West of England: 'I was disturbed to hear their accounts of how they felt the police had overstepped the mark, to see video footage of horses charging

Mounted police charge student protesters,
Parliament Square, 9 December 2010.

into protesters, and told of injuries from truncheons and so on.'
McCarthy sought an assurance that if she provided the home secretary their personal accounts they would be taken seriously. May
said, 'Of course the hon. Lady is free to write to me about those
matters,' but appeared to palm off the information 'about the way
the police have treated them' to the 'formal process'.

However, the home secretary, without even seeing the students' accounts, maintained, 'we should not focus on how the
police responded. They should be accountable and complaints
should be investigated, but we must ensure that we focus on
those whose responsibility it was for violence to occur in the
first place. That was not the police; it was the protesters.'[24]

How did May know at that early stage what had happened?
She was briefed by the commissioner, and so presumably was
the prime minister, David Cameron, when he asserted the day
after the protest that the students had acted in an 'absolutely
feral way' and 'there were quite a lot of people who were hell-
bent on violence and destroying property.' He fulminated about
'police officers being dragged off police horses and beaten'.[25]
When events are fast-moving it is all too easy for history to be
rewritten. No media journalist corrected Cameron even though
a cursory view of events showed that only one officer became
separated from his horse.

If we follow the story of two young brothers implicated for
this attack on the mounted police a different record of the day
emerges. Chris and Andrew Hilliard travelled to the 9 December protest together from Manchester. Andrew had a homemade
placard promoting 'Strength Through Unity', and both wore
Guy Fawkes masks, which were in fashion at that time as a symbol of opposition. This mask became a bestselling item on the
Amazon website and had its origins in the film *V for Vendetta*.[26]
Chris had attended Parliament the year before from Teesside

University as part of an NUS delegation to lobby MPs against tuition fees, which coincided with Remembrance Day. He wrote up his 'personal perspective' for his student paper, 'I pray that these men and women, from forces all over the world, from the Police and other essential personnel that risked and gave their lives to save others at home to the men and women that serve in our armed forces, will never be forgotten.'[27] The Hilliards, who had friends in the police, both voted Liberal Democrat in the May 2010 general election because of their opposition to tuition fees.

The brothers entered Parliament Square from the north with the large crowd and made their way across the square towards Parliament on the south side where Chris had lobbied the year before. There was no way into Parliament this time, with four-sided metal barriers erected and police lines behind them. Some missiles were thrown from the crowd. Chris and Andrew moved back from the front of Parliament into the square.

After a while the crowd started moving towards Broadway Sanctuary, a street at the north-west corner of Parliament Square that merged into Victoria Street at the rear of the square. Chris and Andrew followed. The police formed a cordon across Broad Sanctuary to block the crowd. The official police account said that by chance at the very same time (15:00),

A unit of mounted officers were making their way to take a refreshment break when they passed through this area and observed the perilous state of the cordon. They took the decision to self-deploy to Victoria Street to support their colleagues on foot and formed up behind the police line to provide a 'show of strength'.[28]

Chris, who suffers with autism, had a sensory overload; he said, 'It was very surreal.' He and Andrew found themselves separated from the crowd and behind the police line.

The police record at this time stated officers and horses were attacked and 'one of the most serious injuries to officers occurred when one of the mounted officers was pulled from his horse'.[29] An inspector at the scene pointed out Chris and Andrew saying, 'These are the two that pulled him off the horse.'[30] The brothers were seized by the police and arrested. In the process both were assaulted.

At the station, they were interviewed and released with bail conditions not to return to the City of Westminster. The following month, when they returned to the police station, they were interviewed by the Counter Terrorism Unit and Homicide Squad officers. Video footage was shown to them placing them at the scene. They were both charged with violent disorder.

In the years before the student protests, it had become common practice to charge protesters with violent disorder under Section 2 of the Public Order Act 1986, the second most serious offence after riot, which carries a five-year maximum sentence. Despite the range of options and charges open to the police and the CPS, they had more recently resorted to using Section 2, treating protesters as if they were football hooligans. Keir Starmer QC was the director of public prosecutions during that period.

A year before, a number of protesters were charged with violent disorder following a large protest supporting Palestinians against the shocking bombing of Gaza. Dozens of them, who were predominantly young Asians, went to prison despite pleading guilty and being of good character. A number of students were also charged with violent disorder after the 2010 protests. For them and their families it was a very scary time given the experience of the Palestine protesters.

Due to the court being available, Chris and Andrew's trial was held at the Old Bailey, a court normally reserved for the most serious of cases of murder and terrorism. It was another surreal experience for the brothers. They said the surroundings felt like a 'comfortable museum', and they recall their trial passing quickly in a blur. After a fortnight the jury deliberated over three days but could not come to a decision. The CPS pursued a retrial.

The Hilliard family, who believed in Chris and Andrew's innocence, had a meeting to prepare for the retrial. Chris describes his family: 'Grandpa is a chemical engineer, Gran was into chemistry so that they're fairly, you know, sensible people. My uncles are both programmers. You know, so you're talking to a well-rounded family from a knowledge perspective.' They were marshalled by Jennifer Hilliard, the boys' mum, who worked in IT and was a former auditor – perfect skills for the job. Chris said, 'Mum was amazing.'

In the run-up, Andrew remembers his barrister insisting that the prosecution disclose copies of the police footage to the Hilliards so they could analyse it at home. This proved essential to preparing their defence. Together the family worked through the points made in the prosecutor's closing speech from their first trial. Their investigation led Jennifer to make their own video to counter the prosecution's arguments. Chris explains, 'We rapidly realised that what we needed was a grandmother test. If our Gran couldn't understand it, then no member of the jury was going to understand it. If we were trying to explain an area to them, then why are we trying to explain it verbally when we can hand them a map with it drawn on.'

The allegations against the Hilliards mirrored the claims made by the prime minister and home secretary against the protest as a whole: they were part of a violent crowd intent on violence who ignored the official route by invading Parliament Square; they tried to leave from the rear of the square rather than the original route; they assaulted and then pulled a police officer from his horse, causing him serious injury.

The retrial, in 2012, had been moved to the market town of Kingston upon Thames in Surrey. Just before the trial the defence received a letter from the CPS. The silver commander, Johnson, described to the parliamentary committee as 'one of the most experienced commanders in the MPS', having commanded over 350 operations, withdrew from giving evidence at the retrial. Johnson had also been unavailable to give evidence to the parliamentary Joint Committee on Human Rights that considered the policing of the student protest as he was on an 'extended period of annual leave abroad'.[31]

The jury were shown Jennifer's compilation video on behalf of the defence. It included previously undisclosed commentary from the police helicopter discovered by Jennifer. In the helicopter recording, silver commander Johnson could be heard saying, 'As discussed yesterday we want to give them the north side of the square, so allow the people coming down Great George Street to turn right ... as we agreed yesterday.' This confirmed that the police had a back-up plan that they were implementing. It suggested that the police thought they would need to be flexible because of the size of the protest on the day of the crucial vote in Parliament. They realised they would need to allow protesters to gather outside Parliament – something they should have facilitated from the outset.

This reveal in court completely undermined the prosecution's suggestion that there was an unexpected violent incursion into Parliament Square; instead the police planned and facilitated a reroute of the march in line with a back-up plan. The defence video then showed that the large crowd were led around the strange fencing in Parliament Square, into a dead end in front of Parliament, which was blocked by four-sided metal barriers and police.

Another aspect of the prosecution case was that the crowd had suddenly decided en masse to storm the rear of Parliament Square to cause disorder. This assertion was undermined by the work of a tenacious paralegal in the Hilliard legal team. After viewing extensive Sky TV footage he discovered images of a police officer on a loudhailer in front of Parliament making a forthright announcement to the crowd, 'If you wish to leave, leave from the rear. This is not a containment. If you wish to leave, leave from the rear.' This announcement was made at 3:16 p.m. The footage showed that students immediately followed the officer's announcement and started moving slowly in the opposite direction away from Parliament to the rear of Parliament Square, to Broad Sanctuary and Victoria Street.

When this evidence was shown to a police witness in court, Jennifer recalls that 'he was visibly shaken.' This evidence completely contradicted the Crown's (and government's) case that protesters, including Chris and Andrew, moved to the rear of Parliament Square to cause trouble. In fact they were merely following police advice. That the police advised the crowd they could leave from the rear of the square raised questions of the validity of the police kettle imposed on the whole protest in Parliament Square at 3:23 p.m, just six minutes after the crowd had followed that advice.[32] In the time it took for the crowd to make it to the rear of the square they were already kettled.

The final and most important part of the prosecution case that the Hilliards had to resolve was PC Cowling's statement. He said that the brothers had attacked and pulled him off his horse, Annabelle, which led to his serious injuries. This alleged incident took place just six minutes after the crowd were kettled. The original footage shown at the first trial confirmed that the brothers were behind police lines in the vicinity of the horse but Cowling's specific allegation was not caught on this film. It was PC Cowling's word, an officer of twenty-six years' experience, against that of two young students who were part of an angry protest where some had thrown objects at the police.

Jennifer made contact with the Legal Defence and Monitoring Group, who located records of a journalist who had been in the area, and he had some footage of the incident. This footage proved decisive. It contradicted the claims made by PC Cowling and confirmed the Hilliards' version of events, that Cowling himself was the aggressor. From his elevated position Cowling had (unlawfully) grabbed Andrew's hat, and then the masks from both brother's faces, which led to Chris losing his glasses. Cowling then grabbed Chris by his ponytail, wrapping it in a tight grip and pulled his hair. No assault against PC Cowling was shown on the footage. The video was played to PC Cowling for the first time while he was in the witness box in the second trial. His responses to questions from the Hilliards' barristers were less than impressive. Cowling struggled to explain the sharp contrast between his statement and previous testimony, on the one hand, and what was actually shown on the journalist's footage, on the other. He stuck to his original claims despite the new footage.

Hidden in the BBC archive is live footage from the day that further corroborates that the Hilliards should never have been arrested. In close proximity to the incident was a BBC reporter, Phillip Herd. On the rolling twenty-four-hour news channel he was repeatedly asked by the studio presenter about reports of an officer being knocked off his horse and injured. Herd confirmed he saw the incident and was adamant: 'I wouldn't say they were knocked off; what appears to have happened is the horse was scared by a firecracker and it bolted and the saddle came undone, so the officer was thrown off, was what I saw.'[33]

In May 2012, the Kingston jury quickly found Chris and Andrew not guilty. Jennifer said the relief was indescribable: 'it had been such a battle I hardly knew what to do or say.' She hugged defence barrister Carol Hawley.

The case confirmed the misrepresentation of the protest as a whole. In the Metropolitan Police briefing for the demonstration, gold commander Bob Broadhurst instructed officers that the event should be policed 'in a manner compatible with the Commissioner's five Ps, in particular, Pride, Professionalism and Presence'.[34] The briefing said that in response to any incidents of disorder, 'We have developed a cunning plan.'[35]

This phrase used in jest in association with Baldrick, an idiotic character in the television series *Blackadder*, was to prove unfortunate because as events panned out it was indeed as if Baldrick had been in charge. Through their actions the police appeared to contrive to cause antagonism. Philip Herd from the BBC recounted how the police 'were saying, "We're not kettling you, you are free to go, you can exit by the back of the square",' and that when the protesters took 'that opportunity' tensions escalated. Herd just got out of the way of a horse charge which took place after the Hilliards' arrest that made 'the protesters the most angry'.[36] He questioned the police tactic to push the crowd back into Parliament Square onto the original route: 'I honestly cannot see how that's going to happen.'

The result of these disastrous police tactics was reflected in the Metropolitan Police's own figures of the numbers injured: forty-three protesters as compared with only twelve officers.[37] One of the protesters injured was Alfie Meadows, who suffered a truncheon blow to his head that required life-saving brain surgery. Remarkably the authorities still pursued Meadows on a violent disorder charge for which he was subsequently acquitted with the help of his campaigning mother, Susan Matthews. Another person hospitalised was *Guardian* journalist Shiv Malik. Caught between the police and protesters on the exit to Victoria Street, he described how 'a baton strike came to the side of my face and then onto the top of my head. Directly onto the crown of my head. I felt a big whacking thud and I heard it reverberating inside my head.'[38]

This clear evidence that police were striking student protesters on the head contrasts with the development of the minimum standards for use of truncheons over the previous forty years. The 1983 manual, which formalised tactical options, included manoeuvres that allowed police to 'incapacitate' protesters with their truncheons. However, when truncheons were used, 'striking' should be in a 'controlled manner with batons about the arms and legs or torso so as not to cause serious injury'.[39]

After the Orgreave trial, the 1987 manual removed 'incapacitate' and introduced 'light blows' to the arms, legs or torso. Following the introduction of the Human Rights Act (1998), the subsequent 2004 manual included the concepts of 'minimum' and 'proportionate force' and a warning that 'individual officers can be held accountable for their actions.' In addition, the use of truncheons had to be 'purposeful to make arrests or prevent crime' and their use should not be 'punitive'. The 2018 training manual expressly states in a number of places that officers should 'avoid strikes to the head'.

The reason for the excessive number of injuries suffered by student protesters, including a number to the head, can be explained by the disproportionate police tactics through horse charges and batoning, combined with kettling, which often keeps protesters contained and in close proximity to police with truncheons. Kettling had apparently been invented in order to minimise violence but this was another protest that confirmed it did no such thing. As David Lammy MP asked in the debate after the protest, 'Is not the point of a kettle that it brings things to a boil?'[40] Peter Hallward, a professor of modern European philosophy at Kingston University, concluded that the great majority of the violence has been suffered rather than inflicted by the protesters … In reality, although police justify the use of 'containment' as a means of preventing violence, most of what violence there was during the 9 December rally began well after the vast kettling operation was set up.[41]

The anger was exacerbated by the use of kettling, with horse charges. The use of horses has remained controversial since Peterloo in 1819 when the cavalry charged into a crowd of 60,000 people seeking a voice in Parliament, leaving up to eighteen people dead. In 1829 the Metropolitan Police were introduced in part to avoid such blatant use of force by the authorities on their people. As we have seen, it did not stop the use of horses against miners, anti-racists and ravers. In 1988 and 2010, the Met Police used horse charges against children and young people.

Once again, the institution of the police was not held to account for failures at a protest.[42] Only one officer, PC Andrew Ott, was charged and convicted of an assault on a student, with the help of irrefutable evidence against him that was recorded on Ott's personal recording device. Following his conviction, Ott was dismissed from the Met.

With the exception of *Channel 4 News*, the majority of the media did not report on the Hilliard case. This failure of the media to investigate violent police action was obvious. No doubt this was a reflection of the 'frequency and extent' of meetings between Met Police officers and media which came to light during the Leveson inquiry.[43] They took as read the home secretary's early presumption that it was protesters, not the police, who were responsible.

After the protest, Commissioner Stephenson only offered his resignation to Prince Charles for failing to protect him.[44] Stephenson survived, but not for long. Seven months after the student protest he suddenly resigned, saying, 'my integrity is completely intact,' which raised the question, why resign from the top police job drawing a salary of £260,000? Some unfortunate facts taken together explain why. Commissioner Stephenson had stayed for five weeks at a luxury Champneys health farm for free (which on its own should have raised serious professional concerns). Champneys' public relations consultant was Neil Wallis, the same man who had been hired by Stephenson at a rate of a £1,000 a day to handle his public relations when he was Met commissioner. Wallis was a former *News of the World* executive, who had been arrested in the investigation into phone hacking.

The police had twice failed to investigate the *News of the World* for extensive unlawful hacking. Stephenson himself had attended more than a dozen meetings with representatives of the *News of the World* during the period the police failed to investigate them. Worse still, Stephenson had personally taken time out of his diary to attend a meeting with the *Guardian* in December 2009 to criticise their reporting of the hacking story two months after Wallis had been employed by the Met. Despite these facts, the mayor of London, Boris Johnson, felt 'great sadness and reluctance' to accept Stephenson's resignation, as 'there is absolutely no question about his own personal integrity.'[45]

Stephenson's resignation statement modestly referred to achievements under his tenure, including 'the professional and restrained approach to unexpected levels of violence in the student demonstrations' in 2010.[46] This description cannot withstand any detailed analysis of the protest. If the police had been candid about their failings at Parliament Square from the outset and politicians had not prejudged the issue, excessive charging of the student protesters could have been avoided. A steady stream of students turned up for trials at Kingston Crown Court facing the prospect of imprisonment, accompanied by their terrified parents.

Thankfully, with the campaigning and legal support of the organisations Defend the Right to Protest and the Legal Defence Monitoring Group, many were assisted through the exhausting trial process and acquitted. After a number of students were acquitted, the DPP, Keir Starmer QC, finally brought in guidelines for the CPS in an attempt to protect peaceful protesters. These guidelines were criticised for not protecting young people or appreciating that ' "violence" often flows from police "crowd-control" tactics at demonstrations, such as kettling, the use of batons, agents provocateurs and undercover policing, all of which have been deployed with increasing frequency in recent years.'[47]

The overcharging of protesters has also been allowed to continue. Twelve Asian men known as the 'Rotherham 12' were charged in 2015 with violent disorder after defending their community against the English Defence League. One was prosecuted on the basis that he may have been throwing chewing gum at the racists. They were acquitted by an all-white jury in Sheffield Crown Court but they never should have been charged.[48]

After Chris and Andrew Hilliard were acquitted they took out a civil action against the Metropolitan Police. Finally, on 31 March 2015 they received damages of £25,000 each and an apology from the Met for the 'distress and upset you suffered as a result of your arrest'. Ironically the apology was provided by a chief inspector, Ms Horsfall, who confirmed, 'you should not have been arrested.' Reflecting on their cases, Andrew says, 'I used to do judo with police officers. And I really got on with them, with the people. It seems that now I don't trust the uniform.' The Hilliards' lack of trust in the police mirrors the view of many other protesters, particularly those who have met brutal police tactics when protesting against racism, unfair job losses or draconian laws, or for environmental protection.

By the time of the student protests in 2010, the relationship between the police, government and media meant that statements blithely made would hardly be questioned. When the prime minister, David Cameron, stated that not just one but a number of police officers were 'dragged off police horses and beaten' his comments not only went unchallenged but enabled the police, once again, to denigrate protesters while the police were praised and able to continue to act with impunity.[49]

As Chris reflects, 'I do honestly believe that the only way to hold the police to account is for officers to be prosecuted for their wrongdoing. Unless there is an active response to misconduct, unless there is actual discipline following it, I don't believe that the police force in any way, shape or form is going to improve.' The Hilliards are still waiting for an apology from the former prime minister, David Cameron, for the lie he told the day after the protest.

When the rules governing the mounted police unit remain secret, having been introduced in a back room yards from where the student protests took place, hidden from Parliament, can we still justify the continued use of the mounted police against protesters?

12

State of Play

This government will always defend the right to protest. That right is a fundamental pillar of our democracy, but the hooliganism and thuggery we have seen is not. It is indefensible.

Home Secretary Priti Patel to virtual Conservative
Party Conference, 4 October 2020

There hasn't really been a lot of direct engagement between the government and a lot of the Black Lives Matter organisations in this country ... I feel like we are being ignored.

Amia, protest organiser, aged eighteen,
BBC *Newsbeat*, 25 August 2020

A clear pattern has emerged over the last forty years: policing of protest has been conducted in a routinely violent way. It is a systemic approach, condoned by a culture of tolerance that starts at the top of government. Politicians and police chiefs publicly laud this country's proud history of dissent as a fundamental democratic right. But this book has shown how the very same people have consistently sought to undermine it.

It is not just since 1983 that powerful dissent has faced violent policing. Back in 1887, the Met commissioner banned meetings in Trafalgar Square, where a protest was due to take place against unemployment. This did not deter protesters in their thousands. One man, Alfred Linnell, a legal clerk, was killed by a police horse stamping on his neck. His funeral was attended by 120,000 people, and the poet and textile designer William Morris gave a eulogy.[1] Morris's poem *A Death Song* was sold as a pamphlet to pay for the funeral costs and included the verse

> Not one, not one, nor thousands must they slay,
> But one and all if they would dusk the day.[2]

The movement won the right to protest at Trafalgar Square, which remains to this day. From 1910, hundreds of thousands of women were fighting for the right to vote. Initially they were patronised and ignored. On 18 November 1910, Prime Minster Herbert Asquith removed suffrage from the parliamentary agenda. Some 300 suffragettes immediately attended the House of Commons in protest. The police intercepted them; 'women were kicked, their arms were twisted, their noses were punched, their breasts were gripped, and knees were thrust between their legs. After six hours of struggle, 115 women and four men had been arrested. On the following day, the charges against most of those arrested were withdrawn.' It became known as Black Friday.[3] During the near decade-long movement a thousand suffragettes were imprisoned, but after the war, in 1918, the vote was finally extended to women.

What protests and movements have done, over time, is brought a sense of unity, pride and strength to individuals when they act collectively. During the miners' strike of 1984, many lesbian and gays supported the miners and after initially suffering some homophobia found solidarity in struggle. As portrayed in the film *Pride*, miners led the Pride march the following year. The protests covered in this book drew widespread praise for the policing and condemnation of protesters. By considering the public and private faces of the police and the government it is now evident that they have been willing to repeatedly act outside their powers in order to suppress protest. This was no accident. This abuse of power became possible, in the early 1980s, when the Home Office instigated and approved the creation of *Public Order Manual of Tactical Options and Related Matters*. This started a long clandestine relationship between the Home Office and police focused on protests. Throughout this book we have looked at the role of this manual with regard to protests of various kinds and the policing of them. Arguably a national police force was created for dealing with public order while at the same time the Thatcher government legislated to make it more difficult for people, through their trade unions or otherwise, to act collectively.

Throughout this time the public position of the state was that the police dealt with operational issues independently; however, behind the scenes a strong collaboration developed between home secretaries and chief police officers to manage protests and evade scrutiny. The use of internal police reviews following several protests, rather than public inquires, has allowed this trend to continue. The most prominent report was on the poll tax riot in 1990 – the full findings of which remain secret to this day. In every protest investigated in this book the police and senior officers were supported by the home secretary despite controversial policing.

ACPO benefited from their relationship with government. They grew from a membership organisation with revenue of approximately £200,000 in 1988 to one with nearly £20 million, mainly from government grants, working in 'partnership' with government.[4] Under the leadership of Peter Wright, 'the strongest President for many years', a new ACPO protocol was issued.[5] Concerned about 'mavericks or colleagues with personal agendas', ACPO decided to ensure that all senior officers fell into line.[6]

The 'Wright protocol' meant that ACPO central office policy was to be adopted by each police force across Britain unless prior notice was given in writing setting out objections.[7] Despite numerous successful civil actions against the police for their handling of mass protests since 1983, the police have obtained a vast array of powers against protesters through the Public Order Act 1986 and the Criminal Justice Act 1994.

Blair's Labour did not repeal any of these draconian powers; instead they brought in a criminal law for every day they were in office, including a law which outlawed unauthorised protests near Parliament. While ACPO was disbanded in 2014, the National Police Chiefs' Council (NPCC) that replaced it could be found at the same address with the same contributory members and chief police officers.

Chief officers have shown themselves to be self-serving. The policing of the Welling protest appears to have been more about protecting the police's reputation after the Stephen Lawrence murder than about a genuine need to maintain public order. Two ACPO police officers – Grundy and Imbert – directly involved in the Beanfield and poll tax protests should never have been in that position of power as they had previously been involved in the interrogations of the Guildford Four, one of the most notorious of all miscarriages of justice. Virtually all the individual chief officers who 'successfully' managed these protests were rewarded with medals and honours, despite often being personally discredited.

CR

What has also come to light is that this subterfuge of the police and government has only been possible with the support of others. Civil servants instigated the manual's creation, set up and hosted the meetings at the Home Office, chaired the secret meetings and wrote the minutes. Minutes reveal that the Home Office officials would contribute to the manual to ensure the home secretary's 'interests' were met.[8]

Throughout this book, we have seen how the civil service bolstered the power of the police. Years before the Wright protocol was conceived, permanent under-secretary Sir Brian Cubbon expressed concern, following the Brixton and UK-wide riots of 1981, that chief constables had drifted 'away from the Home Office and there was some need for us to pull [them] back'.[9] The idea was to move ACPO from a membership organisation akin to your local chess club, to one that the Home Office 'equipped' to speak in a 'clear and effective voice on major policy issues'.[10] This support was not offered to other staff associations. Concerns were raised that this could, 'however falsely', be seen as 'an emerging national police force under Home Office influence', which would also raise questions about the tri-party nature of government, local authorities and the police.[11]

Cubbon continued to establish the close relationship between government and ACPO. He was also integral to government influence over police operations during the miners' strike and the level of charges meted out. During the miners' strike, Cubbon stated 'the system' over the first eight months 'had worked'. Setting the tone for future protests he pondered, 'how does the Home Office relay to the police service the political influence on operational policy which was wanted in the early days of the dispute … without prejudice to the coherence and direction of the more strategic role' of the Home Office Police Department.[12]

Black Lives Matter protesters marching from Parliament
Square to the US Embassy, June 2020.

The media have supported the police to suppress protest
through biased reporting. The worst example of this is the BBC,
reversing the order of the footage in order to blame the miners
for causing the violence at Orgreave. In 1986, Rupert Murdoch's
business operations at Wapping were protected by the police – a
move which led to the decline of independent media voices. The
media maintained close relationships with the commissioners
and promoted the commissioners' negative views of protesters
in advance of organised and planned demonstrations.

May Day 2001 was a prime example of this. Years later, Commissioner Stevens was given his own column in the *News of the
World*. The controversial relationship between media and the
police was examined by Lord Justice Leveson in his inquiry. The
second part of his inquiry, which was due to further examine the
close relationship, was cancelled. So embroiled were Commissioners Stevens and Stephenson with the media that the Met twice
failed to investigate the phone hacking scandal, and Stephenson

tried to place pressure on the *Guardian* not to publish articles on phone hacking.

Wapping and Warrington confirmed how vast police resources from public funds were invested in supporting the private enterprises of anti-union businessmen Rupert Murdoch and Eddy Shah. After the *Messenger* dispute, Cheshire County Council proposed suing the NGA for £314,000 in policing costs despite the level of the operation resulting from pressure from the home secretary. By the time of the first Wapping anniversary demonstration on 24 January 1987, 1.2 million extra police hours had been worked at Wapping at an estimated cost of £5.3 million.

The judiciary too have consistently supported the police in their interpretation of laws relating to protest and have exonerated them of culpability for their brutal policing. A shocking example of this is the dismissal of cases against police officers after Wapping by a judge who had been a student at Cambridge University with a future home secretary. Other judges have been only too keen to order injunctions and sequestration during protest and have defined more than six pickets as 'intimidatory' even in the face of vast numbers of police officers.

The police, the government, the civil service, the media, corporations and the judiciary have combined to form an unofficial, and often undemocratic, state. The clandestine way they have operated together since the introduction of the secret manual confirms that they are institutionally opposed to protest. The police force have carried out indiscriminate violence, kettled children, repeatedly lied to the public and had sexual relations with women protesters, even fathering children. They have conducted themselves with impunity for behaviour no one could have imagined of a police officer. The impact on protesters' mental health through the decades is incalculable.

CR

To some extent it is arguable that following the student tuition fees demonstration of 2010 the state achieved its aim. Over the next decade there was no mass protest on the same scale that involved confrontation with the police. However, more recently, mass movements have grown around wider social issues challenging the devastation of the environment, racism and sexism. The response of the police and the state to these movements has been no less significant in suppressing dissent.

In February 2019, children unexpectedly left their classrooms to protest in city centres demanding that more be done about the climate emergency. In April 2019, Extinction Rebellion – a non-violent civil disobedience movement – arrived at Oxford Street in London with a pink boat escorted by hundreds of people. They were joined by the Oscar-winning actor Emma Thompson. They occupied the crossroads for up to ten days until the police carried out mass arrests. Commissioner Cressida Dick confirmed, 'I've been a police officer for 36 years. I have never known an operation, a single operation, in which over 700 people have been arrested.'[13] This spectacular and disruptive protest raised the profile of climate change across a swathe of young people and in the media.

When the Extinction Rebellion protesters returned in October 2019 for further peaceful sit-downs they were soon confronted with a blanket London-wide ban against any protest.[14] Home Secretary Priti Patel welcomed arrests against 'unlawful' protesters. Unfortunately, many of the arrests themselves were unlawful. In their rush to disperse peaceful protesters, the High Court found that the blanket police ban was in clear breach of the law. The lawyer who took up the case, Jules Carey, said the police 'grossly overstepped the mark' and 'a significant clean-up operation is now required in the criminal justice system to deal with hundreds of cases that should never have been brought.'[15]

© Guy Smallman

School walkout to stop climate change, 2019.

Over the years police and government have often justified robust policing on the basis they were dealing with a violent minority – but by 2019, peaceful protests had become the subject of large-scale police operations. The strategy of undermining dissent reached a new peak with the alliance between Home Secretary Priti Patel and Commissioner Cressida Dick. In 2019 Dick wrote to Patel suggesting, 'In light of the challenges posed by this year's Extinction Rebellion protests, there are opportunities for much-needed legislative change to update the Public Order Act 1986. My colleagues and I will continue to work constructively and positively with ministers and officials to take forward these changes.'[16] In response, Kate Allen, director of Amnesty International UK, commented, 'It's extremely worrying that the Metropolitan Police is apparently still seeking to curtail the right to peaceful protest.'[17]

History shows us that when governments try to silence issues and dissenting voices, or to remove basic rights, it can galvanise people into pushing back. On 25 May 2020 in Minnesota, USA, a police officer knelt on George Floyd's neck for nine minutes and twenty-nine seconds, until he died. Floyd was a forty-six-year-old black man. A teenager filmed the arrest and Floyd can be heard screaming, 'I can't breathe.' The reaction to his death led to immediate protests in America and across the world. In the UK there were 260 demonstrations. The scale of the protests reflected a wider discontent with racist policing. In Britain black people are more than twice as likely to die in police custody and nine times more likely to be stopped and searched than white people.[18] At the time of the Macpherson report in 1999 black people were five times more likely to be stopped.[19]

In 2020, Met Commissioner Dick denied that there was 'institutional racism' in the police.[20]

On 6 June 2020, people gathered at a Black Lives Matter (BLM) assembly. Police sent horses into the young crowd, unprovoked and without warning. Just as they had done, in the same area, a decade earlier against students.[21] A horse bolted and its officer fell off after colliding with a traffic light. A black student nurse was trampled by the horse; 'I was told I was unconscious for a few seconds, I could just see a whole crowd around me – my sister crying over my shoulder. She was shaking me, trying to get me up. I just screamed in pain. If I'd made one wrong move that horse would have killed me.'[22]

A Network for Police Monitoring (Netpol) report into the policing of the BLM protests found 'excessive use of force, including baton charges, horse charges, pepper spray and violent arrest'.[23] These aggressive tactics originated from the 1983 manual. The young black protesters were experiencing the same brutality meted out to printers at Warrington just six months after the manual had been approved. The complaints being made now are very similar to those made after mass protests over the last forty years involving miners, printers, travellers and anti-racists.

This is in sharp contrast with the growing resentment of how racists and the far right are policed.

After counterprotests by the far right to the Black Lives Matter protests of June 2020, barrister Michael Etienne argued that

> it is only superficially true that equivalent conditions were imposed on all sides. The only group specifically named for police attention in these conditions was Black Lives Matter – even after the official march had been cancelled due to concerns about people becoming targets for racist violence.
>
> Whilst the police referred to any march or assembly promoted by 'the right wing and associated groups', no specific group was identified. This rendered the already perilously vague conditions virtually unenforceable.[24]

Two years earlier, the far right gathered to protest for 'freedom of speech' in London. A female bus driver in a headscarf showed incredible poise and dignity when they surrounded her bus in Trafalgar Square. For thirty minutes she was subject to verbal abuse, gestures, far-right posters put on the windscreen and banging on the window before the police who were present decided to clear the area.

Since 1983, the recurring tactics authorised at protests have often included mounted charges, baton charges and the use of dogs. Police dogs bit at least two protesters at Orgreave, one at the G20 protest and more recently, in 2021, seven during protests in Bristol against the proposed Police, Crime, Sentencing and Courts Bill. ACPO and Home Office representatives responsible for the manual's content discussed the viability of these tactics before the 1983 manual was finalised. The discussions included mounted charges, which 'on the face of it' were 'highly dangerous', and baton charges that would lead to injuries, and the Police

Advisory Committee on Police Dogs also 'rejected the use of dogs in crowd control'.[25] Those who developed the manual knew that, when applied, these tactics would likely be unsafe.

The manual has gone through several revisions since 1983. After the poll tax protest in 1990 when Deputy Chief Commissioner Metcalfe carried out his internal review into the policing of the poll tax, his full report was sent to the Home Office. To this day this remains undisclosed. The Home Office were reviewing a report dealing with how police tactics were applied during a mass protest that turned into a riot, when they themselves had secretly authorised the manual that was used on the day. As the lawyer Gareth Peirce stated in 1985, they have 'rewritten the law' and secretly exhorted 'manoeuvres which break the law'.[26]

There was opportunity after the Orgreave trial and after the poll tax demonstration to tell Parliament what had gone on. Neither the police nor the government did so. Instead it appears that following Metcalfe's 1991 review, the police tactical operations manual was divided into at least two parts. It is likely that tactical operational detail went into a training manual while police procedural issues were moved into a more palatable public-facing document. This split is reflected in the response from the Home Office minister, Giles Shaw, to a request from Clive Soley MP for the release of the whole manual during the 1986 Wapping dispute. At that time Shaw said he would consider releasing the 'relevant standard force procedures' but not the manual itself, which he said was the preserve of ACPO.[27]

The secrecy continued around questionable tactics that had been approved privately. This could only be sustained in a culture where the police were afforded a special status which allowed their indiscriminate or excessively brutal tactics to be used with impunity. By 2010 the force procedures around public order were published online as a glossy document entitled *Keeping the Peace*;

there were no tactical options included within it. Years later it was modified again, and by 2018 more detail was available to the public online.[28] However, specific tactical operations of the kind approved by the Home Office in 1983 remain secret and have never been discussed in Parliament.

This remains pertinent for protesters today. In 2021 during protests in Bristol against the Police Bill, officers used the side of their shields to hit protesters. Kevin Blowe of Netpol pointed out that 'defensive shields' were 'apparently being used for offensive purposes'. The resulting head injuries left an 'off-duty NHS nurse traumatized ... "I saw shields in front of me lifted and chopped down on top of protesters['] heads in a peaceful crowd ... in excess of 5 cm lacerations to the top of the skull."'

Superintendent Mark Runacres, an officer of twenty-five years' standing, said it's an 'unfortunate reality that in public order policing the tactics that are used – the shield strikes' – are 'an absolutely legitimate and trained tactic that officers are coached on in their public order training ... approved by the College of Policing and if they can justify that act as a proportionate response then they are entitled to do it'.[29] No one in Parliament would have known these tactics were approved. The culture in the police is such that new violent methods can be introduced without any consideration of the elected representatives.

Another 'approved' tactic was applied against Katie McGoran, a protester against the Police Bill. Four male police officers tricked their way into her house saying they were postal workers. They did not identify themselves before handcuffing the entirely innocent, half-clad, twenty-one-year-old in her bedroom. Of the 'very traumatic' arrest she said, 'It was like a punishment because I had been on the protest. It was revenge policing.'[30]

CR

A paranoia about protest has developed and is reflected in the decision of the South East Counter Terrorism Police to categorise a number of protest groups as potential terrorists to be reported. They included the Campaign for Nuclear Disarmament, Stand Up to Racism, the Stop the War Coalition and Extinction Rebellion. The list had been shared with a number of police forces, Counter Terrorism Headquarters, schools, the NHS and the Home Office. It appears that after the *Guardian* revealed the existence of the list it was recalled.[31]

This state creep was followed by a move towards totalitarianism with the introduction in 2021 of the Police, Crime, Sentencing and Courts Bill, including sweeping provisions that can outlaw any assemblies and processions deemed 'noisy' or which might cause 'serious unease, alarm or distress'.[32]

The Police Bill's intent was to protect organisations and the community from serious disruption. Extending these discretionary powers further can only mean more draconian policing. Home Secretary Patel, while trying to force through her bill, claimed involvement of the Police Federation. FOI requests and the Police Federation later confirmed that they were not consulted on the protest measures, leading to accusations of Patel misleading Parliament. Sam Grant of Liberty commented, 'This bill has triggered mass protests and almost universal opposition – including from ex-police chiefs who say it threatens democracy. The fact that policing bodies weren't even consulted shows how determined those in power are to stifle dissent.'[33]

The government even tried to extend police powers further by unusually adding several amendments while the bill was being reviewed by the House of Lords. These were voted out by the Lords following a campaign. Just hours after the toppling of the statue of slave trader Edward Colston in Bristol on 7 June 2020, Home Secretary Priti Patel demanded the police 'make sure justice is taken'. She also called the local chief constable. Nazir Afzal, a former chief prosecutor for north-west England, commented, 'It may be that she has overstepped the boundaries … that we have had for nearly 200 years by getting involved in police operational decisions.' Four protesters were subsequently charged with criminal damage to the statue, but were acquitted by a jury at their trial in 2022.[34]

This conflict between how those at the top of society believe we should protest and how the common person responds to injustice was laid bare after the death of Sarah Everard. On 13 March 2021, hundreds of women congregated at Clapham Common to show their respect for Sarah Everard. Everard had been murdered after being abducted walking home ten days prior. Following her disappearance a serving Met Police officer was arrested and charged with her murder (he later pleaded guilty). There was a national reaction among women who felt unsafe on the streets. The police then used COVID-19 provisions to prohibit the vigil, but hundreds of women ignored them and attended to recognise Everard and the violence that women encounter.

The Metropolitan Police decided to clear the vigil. Male officers arrested women by manhandling them to the ground and handcuffing them. The images of these dignified women opposing male violence being accosted by male officers caused London mayor Sadiq Khan to immediately criticise the policing as 'neither appropriate nor proportionate'.[35] Home Secretary Priti Patel made mild criticism but two days later agreed the vigil had been 'hijacked' by protesters.[36] It then materialised that prior to the vigil she had told the police that she wanted them to stop the gathering.[37]

There were calls for the resignation of Met Police commissioner Dick, which were directed to a police review. The police inspectorate found that the police 'acted appropriately' and were not 'heavy-handed'.[38] Dick survived and received a damehood soon after.

Nevertheless, these events confirm that draconian policing can fortify dissent as a series of large angry protests followed in support of the arrested women. A similar reaction to the mere announcement of the Police Bill led to protests in cities and small towns across the UK. The long history of protest confirms that dissent always returns despite attempts by the state to suppress it.

BLM demonstrations have shown how protest has the capacity to bring dramatic change. After highlighting the one-sided presentation of history, this movement has achieved cultural change, including an unofficial rewrite of many educational curricula in the absence of government-authorised change. BLM achieved more over a few single days than the government-sponsored diversity programme had managed over years. Journalist George Monbiot places achievements such as this into context: 'All the genuine progress, all the moves towards justice that we've ever seen in our society has come about through protest. It doesn't happen by itself.'[39]

One of those leading the charge of a new generation of protesters against injustice was nineteen-year-old Venus Oghweh, a care home worker from London, who in 2020 organised her first protest, for BLM. Within three days her team had recruited over 200 organisers. She reflects, 'If that does not show you that a change needs to happen and that we all feel the same, I don't know what else could. If we did a month of steady work, imagine what we could do. We are so focused on bringing a change.'[40]

Acknowledgements

This book would not have been possible without the support and investment of a number of people. Principally we would like to thank witnesses to the protests who have provided testimony describing the full force of the law. This book is dedicated to all who have protested for progress.

Wider support in the formation of this book was provided by Jim Nichol, Tariq Ali, Laurie Flynn, Madeleine Corr, Georgia Garrett, Neil Lyndon, Gareth Peirce, Jonathan Churchill, Henry Blaxland, Gill Ingall, the Orgreave Truth and Justice Campaign, Nick Davies, Granville Williams and Sue Williams of the Campaign for Press and Broadcast Freedom (North), Nicholas Jones, Ray Goodspeed of Lesbians and Gays Support the Miners (LGSM), Ann Field, and Henrietta Hill QC.

We wish to thank a number of people who have assisted on chapters in this book, including: Tony Burke, Denise Sherriffs, Diane Allsop, Nigel Costley, Phil Turner, Jason Gold, Andrew Wiard, Neil Findlay, Bruce Shields, Andrew 'Watty' Watson, Iain Chalmers, Tony Bunyan, Solomon Hughes, Andrew French, Tyrone Steele, photographer Matt Smith, Barry Faulkner, Guy

Taylor, the Hilliard family, Kevin Blowe, Denise Sherriffs, Diane Allsop, Gavin Hawkton, and John Houston.

Jim Mowatt and Joan Francis for unfettered access to TUC and Unite the union archives. The staff at the British Library, specifically Karen Waddell; the Modern Records Centre at the University of Warwick; Trades Union Congress Library at the London Metropolitan University; Hull History Centre, specifically Sarah Pymer; Glasgow Caledonian University Archive, specifically Carole McCallum; Marx Memorial Library and Workers School; and the National Mining Museum Scotland Archive.

For financial support for expenses on this book – Unite the union: GPM&IT Sector, JLR Solihull WM7686, WM909, Jaguar WM7687, LE128 Trade Union Employees' Branch, WM6110 Stoke, SE/6235 Slough and Unison, Knowsley Branch. Additional funding: Society of Authors and the Authors' Foundation.

Thanks to Matt's children, Joe and Tash. Kath Edmundson, R. Maitland and Rona Livingstone, Eileen and Steve Hunter-Brooks, Alison and Scott Fair, Liane Groves, Henrik Andersen, Amanda Morrison, Graeme Mackay, Karen Livingstone, Jonathan Bennett and Cordelia, David Condliffe, Tracey Bent, Louisa Bull, Tanya Bolton and the Wardie Bay swimmers.

Matt would like to dedicate his work on this book to his dad, Paul who remains a constant inspiration from the grave, in Highgate Cemetery.

Special thanks to Michael Mansfield, who is central to this history, for his foreword, Tom Foot for his comments and support, and John Foot for his advice on the whole book while in the midst of writing his own book on Italian Fascism. We also thank John Gaunt, Mark Martin and all at Verso. Lastly but top of this list, Leo Hollis, our wonderful editor for his salient patient advice.

Notes

Introduction

Interviews by the authors are not separately referenced.

1 *Guardian*, 'Willie Whitelaw dies aged 81', 1 July 1999.
2 The National Archive (TNA), HO 325/524, speaking note.
3 TNA, HO 325/524, notation on letter from Humberside Police, 20 October 1982.
4 *Regina* v. *William Albert Greenway and Others*, Sheffield Crown Court, His Honour Judge Coles (Orgreave trial transcript), ACC Clement, cross-examination Evidence, 14 May 1985. Official documents and articles refer to ACC Clement as both Clement and Clements. In this book we have followed court and South Yorkshire Police documents.
5 Hansard, Tony Benn, Labour MP, 22 July 1985, Vol. 83, cc. 735–6.
6 Gareth Peirce, 'How they rewrote the law at Orgreave', *Guardian*, archive, 12 August 1985, reprinted 17 June 2014.
7 Nadine White, 'Brixton riots 40 years on: from policing to inequality, residents say "progress slipping away"', *Independent*, 11 April 2021.
8 BBC News, 'Margaret Thatcher's criticism of Brixton riot response revealed', 30 December 2014.
9 Oxford had ordered the use of CS gas on protesters, for the first time on the UK mainland, at the Toxteth riot in 1981.
10 TNA, HO 498/2, report of ACPO working group, Chapter 1.
11 Hansard, Willie Whitelaw MP, 3 May 1983, Constitution Of Police Authority, Vol. 42.
12 Gerry Northam, *Shooting in the Dark* (Faber and Faber, 1988), p. 40.

13 Ibid., p. 41.

14 TNA, HO 325/523, undated.

15 TNA, HO 325/523, Public Order Steering Group report.

16 HMIC, *Without Fear or Favour: A Review of Police Relationships*, December 2011, quoting from *The Policing Principles of the Metropolitan Police*, 1985.

17 TNA, HO 325/525, 17 January 1983.

18 TNA, HO 325/525, 6 May 1983.

19 TNA, HO 325/525, 17 January 1983.

20 TNA, HO 325/523, undated.

1. The Guinea Pig

1 Mark Dickinson, *To Break a Union* (Booklist, 1984), p. 141.

2 The 1983 manual includes a tactic for the use of vehicles to disperse crowds. The danger is discussed between the Home Office and ACPO and recorded in notes: TNA, HO 325/523–5. The text quoted is from the 1987 manual, not the 1983 one. From TNA files it is 'believed' that the tactic is the same, or very similar, in both versions.

3 Many in the media use the spelling 'Eddie' but we have used the spelling Mr Shah uses.

4 An independent boarding school in Moray, north Scotland. Prince Charles was also a pupil there – he is four years younger than Shah.

5 Now the *Evening News*.

6 LBC Radio, 'Court rules to seize NGA property', 25 November 1983.

7 LBC Radio, 'Violence at Messenger Group works picket', 30 November 1983.

8 Michael MacMillan, ITN *News at One*, Created: 1 December 1983, (source: Getty ref 804925328, not known if broadcast).

9 Home Office (HO), FOI 57133, report from DCC to Home Office, 29 November 1983.

10 Dickinson, *To Break a Union*, p. 125.

11 Author interview, Tony Burke, 2019.

12 'Warring-town by night', *Economist*, 3 December 1983.

13 Richard Dixon-Payne, private papers, statement to his solicitor, 1983.

14 '1,000 police in Shah battle', *Daily Telegraph*, 30 November 1983.

15 Dickinson, *To Break a Union*, p. 132. Grunwick was a two-year industrial dispute that started in 1976 after six Asian women walked out of the film

processing plant after fellow workers were sacked. Led by Jayaben Desai it became a much wider fight for human rights and a cause célèbre for the trade union movement. There were accusations of police brutality, with the Met Police's controversial Special Patrol Group deployed.

16 Ibid., p. 128.

17 Dickinson, *To Break a Union*, p. 133.

18 The 1 December 1983 edition of the *Sun* that Mr Royston refers to should have been deposited in the British Library Archive. On the date of search it was found to be missing from the microfilm archive.

19 James Wightman, 'Prepared for violence', *Daily Telegraph*, 1 December 1983.

20 Dixon-Payne, private papers, statement.

21 'Police "thuggery" not provoked says JP', *Chronicle and Echo*, 1 December 1983.

22 'Battered, bruised and bloody, MP horrified by violence', *Evening Chronicle*, 30 November 1983. Robert Clay, MP for Sunderland North, was at Warrington at the invitation of Sunderland NGA.

23 Dixon-Payne, private papers, statement.

24 Dickinson, *To Break a Union*, p. 139.

25 Dickinson, *To Break a Union*, p. 139. Jim Arnison, 'Protesters face barricaded plant', *Morning Star*, 30 November 1983.

26 Frank Walsh, *From Hulme to Eternity* (Self-Published, 2007). Police Complaints Authority letter to Mr. G Jerrom [NGA National Officer] 5 November 1985, pp. 362–3.

27 'How it looked in Warrington's front line', *Guardian*, 1 December 1983.

28 'Weekend brief: at the heart of things in Warrington', *Financial Times*, 3 December 1983.

29 Hansard, NGA (dispute), 30 November 1983, Vol. 49, c. 886.

30 Andrew Neil, *Full Disclosure* (Macmillan, 1996), 'A lesson from the north', p. 84.

31 Hansard, statement from the Secretary of State for the Home Department (Mr Leon Brittan), 30 November 1983, Vol. 49, c. 883, repeated in the House of Lords, Lord Elton, 30 November 1983, Vol. 445, c. 703.

32 Dickinson, *To Break a Union*, p. 143.

33 Hansard, National Graphical Association dispute, 30 November 1983, Vol. 49, c. 886. In 1983 Fergus Montgomery was the MP for Altrincham and Sale, where Shah distributed his newspapers.

34 'Police "thuggery" not provoked says JP'.

35 'A battle for Britain', *Sunday Times* editorial, 4 December 1983; Peter Gillman, Donald MacIntyre, Kim Fletcher and Phillip Knightley, 'Union at bay', *Sunday Times*, 4 December 1983.

36 HO, FOI 57133.

37 LBC Radio, 'Shah denies Kinnock allegations over Stockport Messenger dispute', 2 December 1983.

38 TNA, PREM 19/3038, High Court, 14 October 1983.

39 HO, FOI 57133.

40 Ibid.

41 Ibid., redaction per FOI response.

42 Neil, *Full Disclosure*, pp. 67–8.

43 HO, FOI 57133.

44 Ibid.

45 Ibid.

46 Ibid., p. 26.

47 Ibid.

48 Ibid.

49 Neil, *Full Disclosure*, p. 72.

50 Ibid., pp. 72–3.

51 TNA, PREM 19/3038, note for record ref. A083/3351, 30 November 1983.

52 Ibid.

53 Ibid., ref. A083/3350, 30 November 1983.

54 Hansard, NGA (dispute), 30 November 1983, c. 883.

55 David Goodhart, 'Police maintain heavy presence', *Financial Times*, 1 December 1983.

56 Michael MacMillan, ITN, *News at One*.

57 '72 charged over mass picket', *Daily Telegraph*, 1 December 1983; and '23 more face charges', *Daily Telegraph*, 2 December 1983.

58 Unite the union, Modern Records archive, Warwick University (hereafter UA), NGA minutes, July–September 1984.

59 The Guildford Four were wrongly convicted of bombings carried out by the IRA.

60 TNA, CAB 128/76/35.

61 UA, NGA minutes, July–September 1984.

62 Robert Taylor, 'New recipe for peace in print war', *Observer*, 4 December 1983.

63 Dickinson, *To Break a Union*, p. 24.

64 Neil, *Full Disclosure*, p. 72.

65 Ibid., p. 75.

66 HO, FOI 57133.

67 Ibid.

68 Ibid.

69 Ibid.

70 Walsh, *From Hulme to Eternity*, reproducing Police Complaints Authority letter, 5 November 1985, p. 363.

71 Walsh, *From Hulme to Eternity*. Cheshire County Council, 6 November 1985, p. 369.

72 John Weeks, 'Papers seized as 13 Kent police stations raided', *Daily Telegraph*, 12 August 1986.

73 *Made in Dagenham*, screenplay by William Ivory, directed by Nigel Cole (Audley Films, BBC Films, BMS Finance, HanWay Films, Lipsync Productions, Number 9 Films, UK Film Council, 2010).

2. Maggie's UK War

1 Peirce, 'How they rewrote the law at Orgreave'.

2 Orgreave Truth and Justice Campaign, submission to the home secretary, December 2015.

3 *Regina* v. *William Albert Greenway and Others*, evidence of ACC Clement, 10 May 1985, p. 20.

4 Affidavit of Rajendra Bhatt on behalf of the plaintiff (Arthur Chritchlow and thirty-eight others) in civil case against chief constable of South Yorkshire Police, exhibit RB2 (correspondence with the defendant's solicitor, Chapter 7), pp. 85–91, at otjc.org.uk.

5 *Regina* v. *William Albert Greenway and Others*, Clement, 10 May 1985.

6 Bernard Jackson with Tony Wardle, *The Battle for Orgreave* (Vanson Wardle Productions, 1986), p. 34.

7 Granville Williams, 'Orgreave: The Battle for Truth and Justice', in Allsop, Stephenson and Wray, eds, *Justice Denied* (Merlin Press, 2017), p. 165, quoting former miner Paul Winter.

8 Jackson with Wardle, *The Battle for Orgreave*, p. 35.

9 IPCC review of matters relating to the policing of events at Orgreave coking plant in 1984, May 2015.

10 TNA, HO 287/3604, newspaper, no reference.

11 Margaret Thatcher Archive (MTA), PREM 19/1329, pp. 241–3.

12 Hansard, Coal Industry Dispute, 19 June 1984, Vol. 62.

13 The Ridley plan focused on reducing trade union power in support of increased profitability and free market forces by taking on one industry at a time.

14 MTA, PREM 19/0514, various.

15 MTA, PREM 19/776, p. 54, and PREM 19/0541, pp. 201, 152.

16 MTA, PREM19/1329, pp. 8–10.

17 Ibid., pp. 32–49.

18 David Waddington, 'An Open and Shut Case? Reappraising "Conspiracy" and "Cock-Up" Theories of the Strike', in Allsop, Stephenson and Wray, eds, *Justice Denied*, pp. 97–117.

19 MTA, PREM 19/1329, pp. 117–18.

20 MTA, minutes of Ministerial Group on Coal – MISC101(84) 21st (Industrial Action in the Coal Industry), 20 June 1984.

21 MTA, PREM 19/1329, pp. 117–18.

22 Ibid., pp. 119–21.

23 Ibid.

24 Ibid.

25 Ibid.

26 Havers had previously prosecuted cases of miscarriage of justice – the Guildford Four and the Maguire Seven. MTA, PREM 19/1329, pp. 119–21.

27 Hansard, Police National Reporting Centre, HC Deb, 5 April 1984, Vol. 57, cc. 608–9W.

28 TNA, HO 325/624, secret memo, F4 division, 23 July 1984.

29 TNA, CAB 130/1268, Cabinet minutes, Tuesday, 8 May 1984.

30 '1984 Miners' Strike saw 300 arrests in one day at Ravenscraig', *Daily Record*, 13 May 2009.

31 'Miners v cops in the Battle of Hunterston', *Ardrossan and Saltcoats Herald*, 15 May 2014.

32 1983 manual pages, private source, Parliamentary Library.

33 TNA PREM 19/1331 p. 293.

34 Alex Callinicos and Mike Simons, *The Great Strike* (Socialist Worker, 1985), p. 91.

35 TNA PREM 19/1331 p. 293.

36 'Questionable tactics', *Glasgow Herald*, 10 May 1984.

37 Glasgow Caledonian University Archive Centre, records of the Scottish Trades Union Congress, General Council minutes and papers, April to June 1984, p. 007837, from a STUC report of a meeting to discuss police action during the miners' dispute, 11 May 1984.

38 TNA, HO 325/623, letter, 14 May 1984.

39 Affidavit of Rajendra Bhatt.

40 TUC Archive Library at London Metropolitan University (hereafter TUCA), Sheffield Police Watch report No. 4, 12 June 1984.

41 TNA, HO 325/623, various.

42 MTA, Cabinet: MISC101(84) 17th (Industrial Action in the Coal Industry), 30 May 1984. Interestingly the official minutes did not include this; it was found in an internal memo. TNA, HO 325/623, memo, 30 May 1984.

43 TNA, HO 498/20, minutes, 21 May 1984.

44 TNA, HO 325/623, memo from Sir Brian Cubbon, 31 May 1984.

45 MTA, PREM 19/1331, pp. 264–72.

46 Cited in Brown and Rees letter to Neil Kinnock MP, 9 May 1985, p. 35.

47 David Conn, 'The scandal of Orgreave', *Guardian*, 1 May 2017.

48 TNA, HO 325/623, various.

49 Jackson with Wardle, *The Battle for Orgreave*, p. 33.

50 *The Miner*, 2 June 1984, cited in David Hencke and Francis Beckett, *Marching to the Fault Line* (Constable, 2009), p. 98.

51 TNA, HO 287/3064, undated.

52 Orgreave Truth and Justice Campaign, legal submission to the home secretary, 11 December 2015, p. 12.

53 Len Masterman, 'The Battle of Orgreave', in Len Masterman, ed., *Television Mythologies: Stars, Shows and Signs* (Comedia/MK Media Press, 1984), p. 99, emphasis original.

54 TUCA, Campaign Group of Labour MPs' report, *Justice*, 1986.

55 MTA, PREM 19/541, p. 133.

56 MTA, PREM 19/1329, p. 81, and PREM 19/1330, p. 38.

57 Masterman, 'The Battle of Orgreave', p. 107.

58 Ibid., p.103.

59 Dan Johnson, 'Orgreave: The battle that's not over', BBC News, 10 October 2016, at bbc.co.uk/news.

60 Simon Pirani, editor, 'The miner', *Guardian* letters, 26 July 2007.

61 Masterman, 'The Battle of Orgreave', pp. 99, 105.

62 Williams, 'Orgreave the battle for truth and justice', *Justice Denied*, p. 158.

63 Ibid.

64 *Regina* v. *William Albert Greenway and Others*, Clement, 14 May 1985.

65 *Regina* v. *William Albert Greenway and Others*, questioning by Mr Mansfield QC, 14 May 1985, pp. 38–40.

66 Cathie Lloyd, 'Public Order: Political Policing', in Christina Dunhill, ed., *The Boys in Blue* (Virago Press, 1989), p. 271.

67 *Regina* v. *William Albert Greenway and Others*, Clement, 21 May 1985, p. 56. TNA, MEPO 8/95, Metropolitan Police notes of guidance for senior officers 1982, as amended June 1983; and HO 325/323–5, various.

68 TUCA, Sheffield Police Watch report No. 5, 19 July 1984.

69 *Regina* v. *William Albert Greenway and Others*, Clement, 15 May 1985.

70 TNA, HO 325/524, letter, 13 September 1982, and Home Office note in preparation for Public Order Liaison Group meeting, 13 October 1982.

71 TNA, HO 498/19/1, minutes, 2 March 1983.

72 *Regina* v. *William Albert Greenway and Others*, Clement, 15 May 1985, and PC Robert White, 6 June 1985.

73 TUCA, Sheffield Police Watch report No. 5, 19 July 1984.

74 TNA, HO 287/3598, ACPO report on policing arrangements of the National Union of Minerworkers dispute.

75 *Regina* v. *William Albert Greenway and Others*, ACC Clement, 14 May 1985, p. 45, and Chief Superintendent Povey, 24 May 1985, pp. 12–13 and 15.

76 *Regina* v. *William Albert Greenway and Others*, Clement, 15 May 1985.

77 Gareth Peirce, opening statement on behalf of National Union of Mineworkers to the Undercover Police Inquiry, 26 October 2020.

78 Newspapers were discovered to be hacking people's phones, including the phone of murdered child Milly Dowler. The scandal resulted in the closure of a Murdoch newspaper, the *News of the World*, and reached inside Downing Street when the prime minister's spokesperson was one of the former editors. Staff were charged with conspiracy to intercept voicemails.

79 IPCC review.

80 Hansard, Business of the House, Tony Benn MP, 20 June 1991, Vol. 193, para. 463.

81 TNA, HO287/3604, speaking note ref. 1016.

82 IPCC review, pp. 15, 33.

83 Mikey Smith, 'Top Tories blocked Orgreave inquiry "because it would tarnish Thatcher's memory"', *Mirror*, 4 October 2021.

84 Ibid., p. 25.

85 Ibid.

86 TNA, PREM 19/1331, pp. 123, 129.

87 Brown and Rees letter to Kinnock, p. 31.

88 NCCL, *Civil Liberties and the Miners' Dispute* (National Council for Civil Liberties, 1984), p. 11.

89 Peirce, opening statement.

90 TNA, HO 287/3598, ACPO report on policing arrangements.

91 Office of National Statistics, at ons.gov.uk; Orgreave Truth and Justice Campaign, legal submission.

92 Brown and Rees letter to Kinnock; Orgreave Truth and Justice Campaign, legal submission.

93 Orgreave Truth and Justice Campaign, legal submission, p. 4.

94 MTA, PREM 19/0541, pp. 208, 223.

95 Waddington, 'An Open and Shut Case?', p. 113.

96 TNA, HO 325/624, memo, 3 August 1984.

97 Ibid., report on management of information, 3 September 1984.

98 Ibid., draft minute from home secretary to the prime minister, 1 August 1984.

99 Ibid., secret memo to the prime minister from home secretary, 15 October 1984 (drafted by Sir Brian Cubbon, 9 October).

100 Ibid., memo, 7 September 1984.

101 Ibid., memo, October 1984.

102 Ibid., memo, 10 September 1984.

103 Ibid., secret memo, home secretary 15 October 1984.

104 Ibid., memo, 16 October 1984.

105 MTA, minute for Margaret Thatcher, March 1985.

106 Orgreave Truth and Justice Campaign, legal submission.

3. Boot Boys in the Beanfield

1 Nick Davies, 'Bad omens for next Stonehenge festival', *Observer*, 23 March 1986.

2 TNA, HO 325/568, Thames Valley Police report, 29 September 1983.

3 Davies, 'Bad omens for next Stonehenge festival'.

4   Nick Davies, 'The Battle of the Beanfield, where the police ran riot', *Observer*, 9 June 1985.

5   Andy Worthington, ed., *The Battle of the Beanfield* (Enabler, 2005), Interview with Nick Davies. Conducted by Neil Goodwin and Gareth Morris, p. 80.

6   NCCL, *Stonehenge* (National Council for Civil Liberties, 1986), p. 4; 'Barbed wire up at Stonehenge', *New York Times*, 10 June 1985.

7   Nick Davies and Ian Bailey, 'Neo Nazi "tried to sell guns" to Hippies', *Observer*, 9 June 1985.

8   'Stonehenge quiet after battle', *Press and Journal*, 3 June 1985.

9   NCCL, *Stonehenge*, p. 24.

10 Worthington, *The Battle of the Beanfield*, p. 80.

11 Ibid., p. 115.

12 Ibid., p. 117.

13 Alan Lodge, 'One eye on the road', at digitaljournalist.eu.

14 Worthington, *The Battle of the Beanfield*, p. 122; Neil Goodwin and Nick Davies, 'Bean and gone', *Observer*, 31 May 1985.

15 Lodge, 'One eye on the road'.

16 Worthington, *The Battle of the Beanfield*, p. 131.

17 Worthington, *The Battle of the Beanfield*, interview with Nick Davies, p. 87.

18 Nick Davies, 'Battle of Stonehenge', *Observer*, 2 June 1985.

19 Worthington, *The Battle of the Beanfield*, interview with Kim Sabido. Conducted by Neil Goodwin and Gareth Morris, p. 90.

20 Ibid., Worthington, *The Battle of the Beanfield*, interview with the Earl of Cardigan. Conducted by Neil Goodwin and Gareth Morris, pp. 104–5; excerpts from the police radio log, 1 June 1985, p.130.

21 Davies, 'Battle of Stonehenge'.

22 Ibid.

23 Ibid.

24 Neil Goodwin and Gareth Morris, *Operation Solstice* (Channel 4, Maya vision, 1991). For more information refer to Goodwin's account, 'The making of the "Operation Solstice" film' and 'Interview with Kim Sabido' – chapters in Worthington, *The Battle of the Beanfield*.

25 Goodwin and Morris, *Operation Solstice*.

26 Nick Davies, 'Remembering the Battle of Beanfield', *Guardian*, 31 May 1995 (published ten years after the battle).

27 Letters to the editor, *Listener*, 18 June 1987.

28 Lodge, 'One eye on the road'.

29 Goodwin and Morris, *Operation Solstice*.

30 Simon Green, 'Hop it, hippies!', *Sunday Mirror*, 2 June 1985.

31 Martin Wainright, 'Convoy poised to roll again', *Guardian*, 3 June 1985.

32 History of Wiltshire Police, at wiltshire-opc.org.uk.

33 'Hippies battle – 40 in court', *Journal*, 3 June 1986.

34 Worthington, *The Battle of the Beanfield*, interview with Deputy Chief Constable Ian Readhead. Conducted by Richard Hester, pp. 140–2.

35 Neil Goodwin, 'Jack Boot and the Beanfield', *New Statesman and Society*, 23 June 1985.

36 Nick Davies, 'Police attack convoy on way to Stonehenge' (2 June 1985), at nickdavies.net.

37 Davies, 'Remembering the Battle of Beanfield'.

38 'Photographers under pressure', *British Journal of Photography*, No. 45, 8 November 1985.

39 Don Aitkin and Alex Rosenberger, 'Beanfield "battle" trial', *Festival Eye*, Summer 1991.

40 Goodwin and Morris, *Operation Solstice*; Worthington, *The Battle of the Beanfield*, interview with Nick Davies, p. 83.

41 Worthington, *The Battle of the Beanfield*, interview with Lord Gifford QC. Conducted by Neil Goodwin and Gareth Morris, p. 158.

42 John Griffith, 'A watchdog with no bite', *Guardian*, 3 April 1987.

43 Worthington, *The Battle of the Beanfield*, interview with Nick Davies, p. 87.

44 Paul Keel, 'Police guilty of hippy attack', *Guardian*, 25 March 1987.

45 TNA, HO325/568, various.

46 Ibid., memo, 15 September 1983.

47 Ibid., memo, 12 October 1983.

48 Martin Turner, 'The wild bunch', *News of the World*, 30 October 1983.

49 TNA, HO325/568, message from ACC Hull to F3 division, undated.

50 TNA, HO 297/3525, memo, 9 January 1984.

51 TNA, HO 287/2977, various.

52 Ibid., letter to Rt Hon Nigel Lawson from Home Secretary Leon Britain, undated.

53 Worthington, *The Battle of the Beanfield*, interview with Deputy Chief Constable Ian Readhead, p.143.

54 Gerry Conlon, 'Was it like this for the Irish?', Marxism Festival, July 2010.

55 Charles Oulton and David Leppard, 'Guildford 4 officer faces interrogation', *Sunday Times*, 22 October 1989.

56 Jonathon Seed, 'Senior Wiltshire politician and police officer endorses Jonathon', blog, at jonathonseed.com.

57 TNA, HO 287/3959, memo, 23 June 1986.

58 *Independent*, 'Battle of Stonehenge charges dropped', 2 December 1986.

59 Nick Davies, 'Stonehenge battle police in retreat', *Observer*, 17 November 1985.

60 *The Times*, 'Festival charges dropped', 2 December 1986.

61 Goodwin and Morris, *Operation Solstice*.

62 Worthington, *The Battle of the Beanfield*, interview with Lord Gifford QC, p. 161.

63 Worthington, *The Battle of the Beanfield*, interview with Deputy Chief Constable Ian Readhead, p. 145.

4. Murdoch's Paper Boys

1 Nick Davies and Amelia Hill, 'Missing Milly Dowler's voicemail was hacked by News of the World', *Guardian*, 4 July 2011.

2 Rupert Murdoch Leveson inquiry evidence live reporting, 26 April 2012, at itv.com.

3 'As unions went out the door, ethical reporting followed them', *Wapping Post*, twenty-fifth anniversary special edition, 6 September 2011.

4 Graham Ruddick, 'Ken Clarke: Tories had deal with Rupert Murdoch for 2010 election', *Guardian*, 23 November 2017.

5 The Right Honourable Lord Justice Leveson, *An Inquiry into the Culture, Practices and Ethics of the Press* (November 2012), Vol. 2, p. 613.

6 Brian Cathcart, 'Piers Morgan & phone hacking: what even he can't deny' (21 January 2020), at Bylinetimes.com.

7 In the 1980s the job of a compositor was to manually arrange words onto the pages of books or newspapers ready for printing. It was a highly skilled job that required mirror image typesetting of the letters.

8 John Bailey, 'How sackings opened the door to abuse', *Wapping Post*, 6 September 2011. A proofreader was someone who looked for errors, including grammar, punctuation, spelling, capitalisation and formatting, in the newspaper.

9 Ibid.

10 Ibid.

11 TUCA, Tony Dubbins NGA, 'One year on: a Wapping victory?', *Marketing*, 29 January 1987.

12 Letter, Farrer & Co. Originally published by, *Morning Star*, 21 February 1986. With thanks to Ann Field of the Wapping Dispute Archive.

13 William Shawcross, *Murdoch* (Chatto & Windus, 1992), p. 343.

14 UA, ref Mss126_tg_1313_9_1, unsigned copy of statement made to a solicitor in evidence dated 31 January 1986, referencing a meeting at the Tower Hotel on or around 22 January 1986.

15 Murdoch had invested £7 million in TNT, which enabled the purchase of 800 vehicles and enabled 2,000 new employees to deliver Murdoch's papers. Shawcross, *Murdoch*, p. 342.

16 UA, ref Mss126_tg_1313_9_1.

17 Woodrow Wyatt, *The Journals of Woodrow Wyatt*, ed., Sarah Curtis (Pan Books, 1999), Vol. 1, pp. 59, 63.

18 TNA, HO 317/97, note of morning meeting, 22 January 1986.

19 Johan Lang and Graham Dodkins, *Bad News* (Spokesman, 2011), p. 71.

20 Barry Clement, 'A refusenik with no regrets', *Journalist*, April–May 2011.

21 HO response to 2016 FOI request.

22 Ibid.

23 TNA, HO 498/58, note for the record, meeting with commissioner, 14 May 1986. DAC Jones had previously been in charge at Greenham Common, a peace camp predominantly made up of women against cruise missiles who were forcibly removed and manhandled by police.

24 HO response to 2016 FOI request. The Haldane Society of Socialist Lawyers, 'A case to answer', September 1987, p. 5.

25 Hansard, Tony Benn, Crime Prevention, 8 May 1986, Vol. 97, c. 306.

26 'I showed my press card to the police inspector. He told me to F... off', *Wapping Post*, 18 May 1986.

27 'Freedom of the press, 1986 style', *Wapping Post*, 18 May 1986.

28 HO response to 2016 FOI request.

29 'PC's off-the-shoulder look raises eyebrows', *Wapping Post*, 7 June 1986.

30 HO response to 2016 FOI request.

31 Ibid.

32 Ibid, emphasis in original.

33 UA, Mss126_tg_1313_9_3.

34 HO response to 2016 FOI request.

35 Ibid.

36 UA, Mss126_tg_1313_9_1.

37 UA, Mss126_tg_1313_9_3; Mike Power, 'Wapping one year on', *Free Press*, February 1987.

38 'Shock verdict on lorry youth' newspaper clipping, missing reference likely *Wapping Post*, source: UA, Mss126_tg_1313_9_1.

39 *Financial Times*, 26 January 1987 quoted by Jean Sargent, *Liberation Christianity on the Wapping Picket Line* (Jubilee Group, 1992) sourced from TUCA. Note: the number of protesters quoted in various reports and articles sits between 12,000 and 25,000. Over 12,500 is generally quoted.

40 HO response to 2016 FOI request. Haldane Society, 'A case to answer'.

41 TNA, HO 325/776, meeting notes, 20 May 1986.

42 HO response to 2016 FOI request. 'Durty at Fortress Wapping', *Police Review*, December 1986.

43 Stephen Davis and Ian Bailey, 'The war on Wapping', *Sunday Times*, 1 February 1987; Haldane Society, 'A case to answer'.

44 Davis and Bailey, 'The war on Wapping'.

45 Haldane Society, 'A case to answer'.

46 Walter Ellis, '60 police hurt as mob besiege Murdoch plant', *Sunday Telegraph*, 25 January 1987.

47 TNA, HO 325/777; Wyn Jones, 'Wapping: an open letter', *Police Review*, 6 January 1989.

48 HO response to 2016 FOI request, PCA report.

49 Haldane Society, 'A case to answer', p. 9.

50 HO response to 2016 FOI request, PCA report.

51 Haldane Society, 'A case to answer', p. 11.

52 Ibid., p. 23.

53 HO response to 2016 FOI request, PCA report.

54 Haldane Society, 'A case to answer', p. 23.

55 1983 manual pages.

56 Haldane Society, 'A case to answer', p. 12; Davis and Bailey, 'The war on Wapping'.

57 Terry Kirby, 'Police "violence" at Wapping demo', *Independent*, 25 January 1990.

58 Andy Petter, 'London's Mounted Police 1960 to 2000' (2017), at lulu.com, p. 8.

59 HO response to 2016 FOI request, PCA report.

60 Heather Mills, 'Wapping's anniversary of violence', *Independent*, 26 January 1987.

61 Terry Smith interview with Morag Livingstone, *Belonging: The Truth Behind the Headlines* (Livingstone Media, 2017).

62 Davis and Bailey, 'The war on Wapping'.

63 Haldane Society, 'A case to answer', p. 25.

64 TUCA, Sargent, quoting *Financial Times*, 26 January 1987.

65 TUCA, Sargent.

66 HO response to 2016 FOI request.

67 TUCA, Sargent, quoting *Guardian*, 26 January 1987.

68 Haldane Society, 'A case to answer', p. 31.

69 LBC Radio, *Wapping Dispute Violence*, interview with Kenneth Newman, Commissioner of the Metropolitan Police (January 1987), sourced from BUFVC.

70 HO response to 2016 FOI request. Note that the PCA later increased this figure substantially, confirming in their report that the true number of civilian injuries would never be known.

71 Stewart Tendler, 'Police defend use of horses', *The Times*, 27 January 1987.

72 HO response to 2016 FOI request, PCA report.

73 Heather Mills, 'Hurd to enter bitter row over Wapping riot', *Independent*, 26 January 1987.

74 Heather Mills, 'Wapping anniversary of violence', *Independent*, 26 January 1987.

75 HO response to 2016 FOI request, PCA report.

76 TNA, HO 325/777; Jones, 'Wapping: an open letter'.

77 Tendler, 'Police defend use of horses'; Guy Rais, '"Spears" found after Wapping clashes', *Daily Telegraph*, 26 January 1987.

78 TUCA, *Labour Research*, 'The Wapping police force', October 1986.

79 David Graves, 'Wapping trio win £87,000 damages', *Daily Telegraph*, 25 June 1993.

80 HO response to 2016 FOI request, underlining original.

81 Stephen Goodwin, 'Hurd defends police tactics', *Independent*, 27 January 1987.

82 HO response to 2016 FOI request; Ben Emmerson and Quentin McDermott, 'Wapping police in court at last', *City Limits*, 16–23 February 1989.

83 HO response to 2016 FOI request.
84 Haldane Society, 'A case to answer', p. 28.
85 HO response to 2016 FOI request.
86 HO response to 2016 FOI request, PCA report.
87 HO response to 2016 FOI request.
88 Ibid.
89 UA, Mss126_tg_1313_9_3. Heather Mills, 'Photographers "target for police violence"', *Independent*, 26 January 1987.
90 'Police criticised in report', *Courier and Advertiser*, 25 January 1990.
91 Chris Mair, obituary of Sir Cecil Clothier, *Scotsman*, 8 June 2010.
92 HO response to 2016 FOI request.
93 TNA, HO 287/4233, handwritten note to Waddington (only last page available).
94 Haldane Society, 'A case to answer', p. 32.
95 Rob Evans and Paul Lewis, *Undercover* (Guardian Books, 2014), p. 31.
96 Haldane Society, 'A case to answer', p. 31.
97 Steve Peak, *Troops in Strikes* (Cobden Trust, 1984), p. 11.
98 TNA, HO325/452.
99 TNA, HO 325/452, memo, 6 August 1981.
100 Wyatt, *The Journals*, p. 54.
101 Shawcross, *Murdoch*, p. 345.
102 MTA, THCR 3/2/182 f14.
103 TUCA, 'The press conference with Andrew Neil', *Press Gazette*, 20 January 2006.
104 Linda Melvern, *The End of the Street* (Methuen, 1986), p. 117.
105 Ann Field 'Wapping: The workers' story', *Wapping Post*, 6 September 2011.
106 Bailey, 'How sackings opened the door to abuse'.
107 'Murdoch denies using power to sway politics', Al Jazeera, 25 April 2012.
108 Andrew Neil, witness statement to the Leveson inquiry, 8 May 2012, p. 12.
109 Nicholas Comfort, 'Tempers frayed as Hurd refuses Wapping inquiry', *Daily Telegraph*, 27 January 1987.
110 TUCA, 'Don't blame me, says Barbara Dean', *Police Magazine Letters*, April 1987.
111 Hansard, Metropolitan Police, 25 July 1986, Vol. 102, c. 911.
112 Keir Starmer, 'Wapping: end of the street', *Socialist Alternatives*, April–May 1987.

113   Duncan Campbell, 'Last police cleared of Wapping charges,' *Guardian*, 1 November 1991. Note: it is generally reported that twenty-four officers were charged. In total there were twenty-six officers charged but two had left the Met. HO response to 2016 FOI request.

114   HO response to 2016 FOI request.

115   Ronald Bartle, *Bow Street Beak* (Barry Rose Law Publishers, 2000), p. 82.

5. The Tinderbox

1   BBC News website, 'On This Day', 31 March 1990.

2   Simon Hannah, *Can't Pay Won't Pay: The Fight to Stop the Poll Tax* (Pluto Press, 2020), p. 82.

3   Nicholas Comfort, 'Thatcher woos and wins back party faithful', *Independent on Sunday*, 1 April 1990.

4   Danny Burns, *Poll Tax Rebellion* (AK Press, 1992), citing the *Guardian*, no specific reference, p. 10.

5   P. A. J. Waddington, 'Coercion and accommodation: policing public order after the Public Order Act', *British Journal of Sociology*, Vol. 45, No. 3 (Sept. 1994), p. 370.

6   Senior police officer Richard Cullen speaking on *I Predict a Riot: The Battle of Trafalgar Square* (Bravo Productions, 1990).

7   Solomon Hughes, FOI papers, pp. –22, at specialbranchfiles.uk/polltax-story, pp. 311–22.

8   Hansard, London March (Disorder), 2 April 1990, c. 894.

9   Tony Benn, *The End of an Era Diaries 1980–90* (Hutchinson, 1992), p. 589.

10   TNA, PREM 19/3021, meeting with Sir Peter Imbert, 3 April 1990.

11   Burns, *Poll Tax Rebellion*, p. 101.

12   Hughes, FOI papers, p. 134, letter from home secretary, 11 April 1990, believed to be to R. Auld QC.

13   Hughes, FOI papers, p. 122, letter to home secretary, 10 May 1990.

14   *Independent* magazine, letters, 14 April 1990, emphasis in original.

15   Hughes, FOI papers, p. 122.

16   Hughes, FOI papers, p. 140. Letter 3 April 1990 to the prime minister from a man from Clifton, Bristol who attended the poll tax protest.

17   Ibid. Hughes, FOI papers, p. 142.

18   Solomon Hughes, 'Confidential police log', *Vice Blog*, 31 March 2015, at vice.com.

19 Hughes, FOI papers, p. 104, letter dated 14 June 1990 to home secretary from councillor on behalf of Westminster Council.

20 Hughes, FOI papers, p. 97.

21 Ibid., p. 101.

22 Ibid., p. 97.

23 Operation Carnaby report, Sgt Ramm, para. 3.124.

24 Ibid., paras 1.1, 1.2.

25 There was a long-standing campaign to disband the Special Patrol Group after Blair Peach died in 1979. The Cass report, an internal police report, found that Peach had 'almost certainly' been killed by one of six SPG officers.

26 David Rose, *In the Name of the Law* (Jonathan Cape, 1996), p. 283.

27 'Alistair Mitchell, 61: lawyer whose calling knocked him at a riot', *The Times*, 2 March 2019.

28 *London Gazette*, Supplement 53282, p. 26.

29 P. A. J. Waddington, *Liberty and Order: Public Order Policing in a Capital City* (UCL Press, 1994), p. 54.

30 Statewatch bulletin, May–June 1991, No. 2.

31 Burns, *Poll Tax Rebellion*, p. 99.

32 *Observer*, 1 April 1990.

33 Hughes, FOI papers, p. 332.

34 Hansard, Dave Nellist MP, House of Commons, 2 April 1990, c. 900; and House of Lords, Vol. 517, Lord Hatch of Lusby.

35 Burns, *Poll Tax Rebellion*, p. 100.

36 Trafalgar Square Defendants' Campaign (TSDC) leaflet, *Drop All the Charges Now*.

37 Burns, *Poll Tax Rebellion*, p. 90.

38 The footage clearly shows the police vans travelling at speed. Numerous witnesses said they accelerated into the crowd. Ian Hernon, *Riot* (Pluto Press, 2006), p. 242. See also Burns, *Poll Tax Rebellion*, p. 90.

39 The advert was published in 1987. See think.gov.uk.

40 HO, FOI ref. 54986, October 2019, and FOI ref. 60048, September 2020, 1987 manual, pp. 147–8.

41 Hughes, FOI papers, pp. 15–72.

42 Burns, *Poll Tax Rebellion*, p. 98.

43 Hughes, FOI papers, p. 28.

44 Linda Smith obituary, *Independent*, 1 March 2006.

45 TNA, HO 287/3604, letter from HO to leader of the House, June 1991 on early day motion on policing of Orgreave.
46 Statewatch bulletin, May–June 1991, No. 2.
47 Hughes, FOI papers, p. 100.
48 Hannah, *Can't Pay Won't Pay*, p. 91.
49 David Butler, Andrew Adonis and Tony Travers, *Failure in British Government: The Politics of the Poll Tax* (Oxford University Press, 1994).
50 Robert Chesshyre, 'Thatcher's "boot boys": when the unholy trinity of police, press and government took root', *Independent*, 15 September 2012.
51 MTA, Harvey Thomas VHS: OUP transcript, 12 October 1990.

6. The Trap

1 Representing Newham Monitoring Project, a community project in east London.
2 Seventeen reported attacks on the Isle of Dogs in January 1993 compared to fifty-seven for January 1994. Human Rights Watch report, *Racist Violence in the United Kingdom*, April 1997; 'Racist wave sweeps East End', *Observer*, 13 February 1994.
3 Human Rights Watch, *Racist Violence in the United Kingdom*, footnote 31. Nigel Copsey, *Contemporary British Fascism: The British National Party and the Quest for Legitimacy* (Palgrave Macmillan, 2008), p. 47. Between August 1990 and May 1991, 863 incidents of racist attacks and harassment were reported to the Greenwich Action Committee Against Racist Attacks, and between 1991 and 1992, in the Plumstead area, there was a 61 per cent increase in the number of reported cases of racist violence.
4 Duncan Campbell, *Guardian*, 20 February 1993.
5 *CARF: Campaign Against Racism and Fascism*, No. 15, July–August 1993, p. 16.
6 Roger Huddle and Red Saunders, eds, *Reminiscences of RAR: Rocking Against Racism 1976–1982* (Redwords, 2016).
7 Listed 156 of the highest-attended concerts of all time.
8 Duncan Campbell and Vivek Chaudrey, 'Armies clash blindly in racism's surburban battleground', *Guardian*, 18 October 1993.
9 Kit Wharton and Andrew Mourant, '60 hurt in race march violence', *Sunday Telegraph*, 17 October 1993.
10 Neil Derbyshire, Richard Spencer, Ben Fenton and David Millward,

'Phone calls that rang alarm bells for Condon', *Daily Telegraph*, 18 October 1993.

11 Ibid.

12 Steve Platt, 'Or was it a police riot?', *New Statesman and Society*, 22 October 1993.

13 Ibid.

14 Commander H. N. L. Blenkin, 'Selecting a route for the anti-racist march', *Independent*, 23 October 1993.

15 Section 12 of the Public Order Act gives power to the senior officer to impose conditions on processions, which he reasonably believes are necessary to prevent serious public disorder, serious criminal damage or serious disruption to the life of the community. A breach of such an order can carry a three-month maximum sentence.

16 Duncan Campbell, 'Condon amends anti-race demo', *Guardian*, 15 October 1993.

17 *Fighting the Naʐi Threat Today*, an educational pamphlet written and produced by anti-nazi teachers, May 1994, p. 15. 'Unity demonstration 60,000 fight back'.

18 See Chapter 5, endnote 45 above for FOI detail.

19 Northam, *Shooting in the Dark*, pp. 191–2.

20 1987 manual.

21 Jason Bennetto and David Connett, 'Race march explodes into riot: policeman paralysed, fighting and arrests as 25,000 head for headquarters of British National Party', *Independent on Sunday*, 17 October 1993.

22 Hansard, government statement made in the Lords by minister of state for Home Office Earl Ferrers, 18 October 1993.

23 'London police battle anti-fascist protesters', *New York Times*, 17 October 1993.

24 For more on the Mangrove story see Darcus Howe, *From Bobby to Babylon: Blacks and the British Police* (Bookmarks, 2020), 'Cause for concern', pp. 35–59; also Steve McQueen's Small Axe BBC production *Mangrove*, November 2020.

25 'One dark secret to another: can the Met go any lower?', *Independent*, 30 June 2013.

26 Rupert Morris, 'Club class', *Daily Telegraph*, 25 February 1989.

27 'Officer admits "omissions" in murder review"', *Independent*, 5 June 1998.

28 Sir William Macpherson, Stephen Lawrence inquiry report (hereafter SLIR), 24 February 1999, paras. 28.40 and 28.46.

29 Michael Gillard and Laurie Flynn, *The Untouchables* (Cutting Edge, 2004), p. 163.

30 SLIR, paras 28.41, 28.61, 28.44.

31 Ibid., para. 28.49.

32 Ibid., para. 28.42.

33 Richard Stone, *Hidden Stories of the Stephen Lawrence Inquiry: Personal Reflections* (Policy Press, 2013), p. 16.

34 'Lawrence parents urge police chief to quit', BBC News, 20 July 1998, at bbc.co.uk.

35 SLIR, para. 29.39.

36 Kathy Marks, 'Detectives "should have sued Lawrence family"', *Independent*, 10 June 1998.

37 Paul Foot, 'Racism, incompetence, collusion or corruption?', *Socialist Review*, No. 221, July 1998.

38 Marks, 'Detectives "should have sued Lawrence family"'.

39 SLIR, para. 28.54.

40 Ibid., para. 29.18.

41 Ibid., para. 28.60.

42 Hansard, Lords Chamber, Welling: Disturbances, 18 October 1993, Vol. 549.

43 'Hairies' was a term used by the spy cops at this time to describe themselves, reflecting the police stereotype of a left-winger.

44 Chris Salewicz, *Redemption Song: The Definitive Biography of Joe Strummer* (Harper, 2012), p. 218.

45 'Chief steward awarded £5,000 damages', *The Firefighter*, Vol. 28, No. 2, March–April 2000, p. 25.

7. A Succession of Repetitive Beats

1 Simon Reynolds, *Energy Flash* (Macmillan Publishers, 1998), pp. 135–7.

2 Ibid, pp. 139–40.

3 Jerry Chester, 'Castlemorton Common: the rave that changed the law', BBC News, 28 May 2017, at bbc.co.uk/news.

4 Section 63(1)(b) Criminal Justice and Public Order Act 1994.

5 Ian Dunt, 'What's the worst British law of all time?', 12 June 2015, at politics.co.uk.

6 Criminal Justice and Public Order Bill, HL Deb. 24 May 1994, Vol. 555, cc. 609–85.

7   Barry Faulkner provided information on how the CD was produced as support for the campaign against the bill, with a cover by Jamie Reid, who did album art for the Sex Pistols.

8   Roger Leng, 'The right to silence reformed', *Journal of Criminal Law*, Vol. 6, No. 107, 2001, p. 112: 'It is my thesis that the Commission's treatment of the topic contained the seeds of the arguments which would ultimately be employed to overcome the Commission's objections and change the law.'

9   Ibid., p. 117.

10   *Defend Diversity, Defend Dissent*, NCCL pamphlet, January 1995, 3rd edn.

11   Pass notes, *Guardian*, 26 July 1994.

12   *Defend Diversity, Defend Dissent*, NCCL.

13   'Way of the world', *Daily Telegraph*, 12 October 1992.

14   See discussion with Jonathan Dimbleby and Tony Blair, *On the Record* (BBC2), 4 July 1993, at bbc.co.uk.

15   Hansard, Criminal Justice and Public Order Bill, 11 January 1994, Vol. 235, c. 21.

16   Francesca Klug, Keir Starmer and Stuart Weir, 'Civil liberties and the parliamentary watchdog: the passage of the Criminal Justice and Public Order Act 1994', *Parliamentary Affairs*, Vol. 49, No. 4, October 1996, p. 542.

17   Ibid., pp. 544–5.

18   Hansard, Criminal Justice and Public Order Bill, 11 January 1994, Vol. 235, c. 21.

19   Alan Travis, 'Has posture killed protest?', *Guardian*, 8 October 1994.

20   Matthew Collin, *Altered State: The Story of Ecstasy Culture and Acid House* (Five Star, 1998), p. 245.

21   Liberty were founded in the 1930s. In 1932, 100,000 people had gathered at Hyde Park to greet the National Hunger March, who had travelled from Glasgow. When the organisers attempted to deliver a petition with a million signatures to Parliament, 'The petition was blocked ... thousands of police were mobilised ... Serious violence erupted in the park, and spread throughout Central London, leaving many seriously injured. In Trafalgar Square, Kidd [co-founder of Liberty] witnessed police agent provocateurs disguised as workers attempting to incite violence among the peaceful protestors.' See 'How Liberty was founded', at liberty humanrights.org.uk.

22   In the McLibel case, McDonalds sued David Morris and Helen Steel for libel for a campaign leaflet they put out about the company. The case

became the longest libel case in history, as after being defeated the two took their case to the European Court, who found they had not had a fair hearing without legal aid. They were assisted by Keir Starmer.

23 'Council arranged bill rally outing', *The Times*, 14 October 1994.

24 HO FOI No. 54986, 1987 manual, Section 24, 'Truncheon charge'.

25 Ibid., Section 12, 'Artificial lighting systems'.

26 Frankie Mullin, 'How UK ravers raged against the ban', 15 July 2014, at vice.com.

27 Duncan Campbell, 'Blame disputed after demo violence', *Guardian*, 10 October 1994.

28 Danny Penman, 'The Park Lane riot: how Park Lane was turned into a battlefield', *Independent*, 11 October 1994.

29 Letter from Mr Jeremy Corbyn MP, Tony Benn MP, Paul May and Weyman Bennett, *Independent*, 12 October 1994.

30 Penman, 'The Park Lane riot'.

31 'What do they know? "Kendrick report" into policing of 1994 Hyde Park demonstration', FOI reference No. 2013100000946, 11 October 2013.

32 Kendrick fails to mention anywhere in his report that a 'sweep' means serials of riot police running and brandishing their truncheons on the crowd; while in the description of the events of the day, the Kendrick report records every minor alleged incident of violence by protesters. Another example of the actual police violence being brushed over in the report is a complaint about the 'wide divergence in standards of those officers completing' the Form 3166, and where these forms were sent. He fails to mention that Form 3166 relates to the use of CS gas (p. 41, paras 4.3.8–4.3.10).

33 Kendrick report, p. 2, para. 1.1.9.

34 Ibid., para. 1.2.3.

35 The gold–silver–bronze command structure was introduced into the police after failures in command at the death of PC Blakelock at the Broadwater Farm riot in Tottenham, London (1985). Gold has overall command and sets the strategy; silver coordinates individual strategies developed by public order strategic commanders, bronze, who are also in charge of implementation. See app.college.police.uk.

36 Kendrick report, p. 12, paras 3.1.10–3.1.13.

37 Ibid., p. 19, para. 3.6.7.

38 Ibid., p. 21, para. 3.8.2.

39 Tony Gallagher and David Connett, 'The ravers who called the tune', *Daily Mail*, 11 October 1994.

40 Kendrick report, p. 22, para. 3.8.7.

41 'Level I' and 'Level II' reflect the amount of public order training a police officer has had.

42 Kendrick report, p. 23, paras 3.8.13, 3.8.14.

43 Ibid., p. 25, para. 3.10.4.

44 Ibid., p. 30, paras. 3.16.3–3.16.5.

45 Ibid., pp. 31–2, paras 3.16.6–3.17.2.

46 Ibid., p. 23, para. 3.8.14.

47 Ibid., p. 46, paras 4.6.4–4.6.5.

48 Ibid.

49 Ibid., p. 20, para. 3.7.3.

50 George McKay, *DiY Culture: Party and Protest in Nineties Britain* (Verso, 1998), p. 27.

51 Edited by Rob I. Mawby and Richard Yarwood, *Rural Policing and Policing the Rural: A Constable Countryside* (Ashgate, 2010), relying on T. Bucke and Z. James, *Trespass and Protest: Policing under the Criminal Justice and Public Order Act 1994* (Home Office, 1998).

52 Mawby and Yarwood, *Rural Policing and Policing the Rural*.

53 Home Office Research Study 190, 'Trespass and protest: Criminal Justice And Public Order Act 1994', pp. xi, 11.

54 Danny Penman, 'Trespass law used against road protest', *Independent*, 13 January 1996.

55 Ally Fogg, 'The prophecy of 1994', *Guardian*, 21 July 2009.

56 'Criminal justice and innocent fans caught in the Act', *Guardian*, 8 April 1995.

57 David Ward, 'Party atmosphere at arrest-free demonstration', *Guardian*, 17 October 1994.

58 Chester, 'Castlemorton Common'.

8. The Commissioner's Kettle

1 Alan Travis, 'Has posture killed protest? Tomorrow is a national day of action', *Guardian*, 8 October 1994.

2 Michael White, 'Things can only get better: Tony Blair's landslide election victory', *Guardian*, 2 May 1997.

3 Nigel Morris, 'Blair's "frenzied law making": a new offence for every day spent in office', *Independent*, 16 August 2006.

4 'Stop and search under the Terrorism Act 2000', at justice.org.uk.

5 'Blair's Britain in 2005 – where peaceful protest can be costly', *Independent*, 10 December 2005.

6 George Monbiot, *Captive State: The Corporate Takeover of Britain* (Macmillan 2000), p. 7, quoting Peter Mandelson, Secretary of State for Trade and Industry, speech to the Confederation of British Industry's annual conference, 2 November 1998.

7 Hannah Kuchler, 'Blair denies striking deal with Murdoch', *Financial Times*, 28 May 2012.

8 P. Joyce, *The Politics of Protest: Extra-parliamentary Politics in Britain since 1970* (Palgrave, 2002), p. 39.

9 John Vidal, 'Blair attacks "spurious" May Day protests', *Guardian*, 1 May 2001.

10 'NoW man admits advising two candidates who became Met boss', *Channel 4 News*, 2 April 2012.

11 Suzanna Andrews, 'Untangling Rebekah Brooks', *Vanity Fair*, February 2012.

12 James Cusick and Cahal Milmo, 'Met loses diary that may have proven former chief's links to Rupert Murdoch', *Independent*, 6 October 2011.

13 Statement to Leveson inquiry, 22 February 2012, paras 81 and 82. The Leveson inquiry report into the culture, practices and ethics of the press was published in November 2012.

14 Paul Harris, Nick Paton Walsh and Tony Thompson, 'For one day only...', *Observer*, 29 April 2001.

15 Hansard Demonstrations (London and Manchester), 2 May 2000, Vol. 349, cc. 21–35.

16 This section draws on an extremely helpful analysis of the press coverage in the run-up to the protest carried out by Ian Atkinson (University of Sheffield) in his article 'Profile: May Day 2001, the news media, and public order', *Environmental Politics*, Vol. 10, No. 3, 8 September 2010, pp. 145–50.

17 D. Bamber, 'Police mobilise for May Day mayhem', *Sunday Telegraph*, 29 April 2001; N. Rosser, 'Anarchists to loot Oxford Street', *London Evening Standard*, 19 April 2001.

18 Bamber, 'Police mobilise for May Day mayhem'.

19 M. Bright and F. Kane, 'Armed police on May Day riot alert', *Observer*, 22 April 2001.

20 M. Tempest, 'May Day protest propaganda', *Guardian Unlimited*, 24 April 2001.

21 'Blair backs May Day police', BBC News, 30 April 2001, at news.bbc. co.uk; Vidal, 'Blair attacks "spurious" May Day protests'.

22 Statement to Leveson inquiry dated 22 February 2012, para. 67; 'The London May Day protests at a glance', *Guardian*, 1 May 2001.

23 J. Vidal, 'Confusion reigns as police brace for mayhem', *Guardian*, 1 May 2001.

24 Atkinson, 'Profile: May Day 2001', p. 147.

25 'The London May Day protests at a glance', *Guardian*, 1 May 2001.

26 Andrea Perry, 'May Day violence flashpoint in London's shopping heartland', 1 May 2001, at *femail.co.uk*.

27 Bill Stackpole and Eric Oksendahl, *Security Strategy: From Requirements to Reality* (CRC Press, 2010), p. 113.

28 'Thousands hold May Day protests', 1 May 2001, CNN World, at cnn. com.

29 'Kettling campaigners lose legal battle', *London Tonight* (ITN), 15 March 2012.

30 Gettyimages.co.uk, ref. 812606484.

31 Steve Boggan, Jason Bennetto, Cahal Milmo and Matthew Beard, 'May Day protests: violence mars May Day protest: London brought to a standstill as clashes between police and anti-capitalist demonstrators leave 50 injured', *Independent*, 2 May 2001.

32 'Peter Waddington, academic behind police "kettling" – obituary', *Daily Telegraph*, 14 May 2018.

33 *Austin (FC) and Another* v. *Commissioner of Police of the Metropolis* [2009] UKHL 5; *ECHR Austin and Others* v. *The United Kingdom*, 15 March 2012. Saxby was the original co-claimant in the UK proceedings.

34 Boggan et al., 'May Day protests'.

35 Ibid.

36 'Kettling campaigners lose legal battle', *London Tonight*.

37 Gillard and Flynn, *The Untouchables*, p. 23.

38 Jason Bennetto, 'Police sued over May Day protests', *Independent*, 29 April 2002.

9. Barriers to Protest

1 Katherine Casey-Sawicki, 'Seattle WTO protests of 1999', *Encyclopedia Britannica*, 21 November 2020 update.

2   Kit Oldham and David Wilma, Essay 2142, posted 20 October 2009, at historylink.org.

3   Don McIntosh, 'Looking back on the Battle in Seattle', *NWLaborPress*, 15 November 2019.

4   Chloe Hadjimatheou 'Ex-Seattle chief: "Occupy" police use "failed" tactics', *Witness* (BBC World Service), 28 November 2011, at bbc.co.uk/news.

5   The G8 comprises leaders from Canada, France, Germany, Italy, Japan, Russia, the UK and the United States of America. They meet annually in a private room to discuss global issues.

6   'If a mob overruns Gleneagles, G8 delegates will take refuge in castle', *The Times*, 30 June 2005. The Scottish Parliament was established in 1999 as an administration devolved from Westminster to make laws for Scotland. It is made up of 129 elected representatives, who are known as Members of the Scottish Parliament or MSPs.

7   'Police recalled from G8 duty', *Guardian*, 7 July 2005.

8   The Police Act (1996), Section 98, 'Cross-border aid of one police force by another'.

9   Chief Constable's annual performance report, 2004–5.

10 Tayside Joint Police Board, report by the chief constable, No. PB 54/ 2005, 'Policing and security at the 2005 G8 summit', 22 August 2005.

11 The Scottish Parliament, Official Report, G8 and Council of the European Union Presidencies inquiry, 8 March 2005.

12 Ibid.

13 Dr Eveline Lubbers, *Political Undercover Policing in Scotland* (SCOPS, January 2019).

14 H. Gorringe and M. Rosie, 'It's a long way to Auchterarder! "Negotiated management" and mismanagement in the policing of G8 protests', *British Journal of Sociology*, Vol. 59, No. 2, 2008, p. 187.

15 Ibid., citing D. Waddington and M. King, 'The Disorderly Crowd: From Classical Psychological Reductionism to Socio-Contextual Theory – The Impact on Public Order Policing Strategies', *Howard Journal*, Vol. 44, No. 5, 2005, pp. 490–503.

16 Angus Macleod, 'Protesters will be in with a shout', *The Times*, 2 July 2005.

17 Tayside Joint Police Board, 'Policing and security at the 2005 G8 summit'.

18 H. Gorringe and M. Rosie, 'The polis of global protest: protest and policing during the G8 in Scotland' (2007), interview with policeman identified as 'Tayside 2', April 2007, p. 7.

19 Address by Nelson Mandela for the Make Poverty History campaign, London, 3 February 2005.

20 John Pilger, 'The ghost at Gleneagles', 11 July 2005, at Johnpilger.com.

21 David Lister, 'The revolution begins on Platform 18', *The Times*, 2 July 2005.

22 Pilger, 'The ghost at Gleneagles'. Fallujah and Abu Ghraib are two US-run prisons synonymous with prisoner abuse, rape and systematic torture during the Iraq War that came to light after the publication of photographs by CBS News in April 2004.

23 ACPO, *Keeping the Peace: Manual of Guidance, Pubic Order, Standards, Tactics and Training*, 2004. Released under FOI to Mr Richard Taylor by the National Policing Improvement Agency, ref. FOI 148/11, 6 October 2011.

24 Gorringe and Rosie, 'The polis of global protest', p.10.

25 Hanae Baruchel and Steve Dasilva, 'Global civil society action at the 2005 G8 Gleneagles summit', G8 Research Group, Civil Society and Expanded Dialogue Unit, August 2005.

26 Bruno Vincent, photograph ref. 53184172, at Make Poverty History march, Getty Images, 2 July 2005.

27 Gorringe and Rosie, 'The polis of global protest', interview with policeman identified as 'Tayside 3' p. 7.

28 Jo Harvie, 'Mass protests send a message to the G8', *Socialist Worker*, 8 July 2005.

29 Ibid., quoting Frances Curran, Scottish Socialist Party MSP.

30 Scottish Cabinet papers are generally released after fifteen years. Scott Macnab, 'Scots ministers feared "hardcore" G8 protesters would bring havoc to Scotland', *Scotsman*, 1 January 2021, quoting Scottish Cabinet meetings from National Records of Scotland.

31 Lubbers, *Political Undercover Policing in Scotland*, p. 42.

32 Ibid.

33 Legal Support Group, 'Statement on the policing of the G8 Protests – UK', *Indymedia*, 13 July 2005.

34 Lubbers, *Political Undercover Policing in Scotland*, p. 39.

35 Paul Hutcheon, 'Demands for Scottish Government to set up inquiry into undercover police operations amid allegations over secret Met cop Mark Kennedy', *The Herald*, 22 November 2015.

36 Kara N. Tina, 'This is how we do it', in David Harvie, Keir Milburn, Ben

Trott and David Watts, eds, *Shut Them Down* (Dissent! Autonomedia, 2005), pp. 27–37.

37   Gorringe and Rosie, 'It's a long way to Auchterarder!', p. 10.

38   'G8 leaders gather at Gleneagles, amid protests, celebrations', 6 July 2005, *ENS Newswire*, at ens-newswire.com.

39   Many of those left behind in Edinburgh were arrested after an unofficial protest turned violent. Peter Wilson, chief constable of Fife, who was in charge of the Police Information Centre, described the protesters that day as 'an abomination causing serious alarm to members of the public'. Auslan Cramb, 'Protesters breach Gleneagles security fence', *Daily Telegraph*, 7 July 2005. However, a Tayside Police review of G8 policing stated that the force had predicted that protesters would block the roads, and 'effective intelligence-led policing tactics helped minimise disruption. Few delays were experienced anywhere on the roads'. Scottish Government, *Review of Tayside Police Primary Inspection of 2002*, May 2006, p. 6.

40   Paul Keeble, Johnathan Brown and Oliver Duff, 'Army flies in extra police for Battle of Gleneagles', *Independent*, 7 July 2005.

41   Gorringe and Rosie, 'The polis of global protest', p. 11.

42   Ibid., Officer LBP1.

43   ACPO 2004.

44   Police Scotland, FOI response, ref. IM-FOI-2020-2210, 17 December 2020.

45   Police Scotland, FOI response, ref. IM-FOI-2021-1216.

46   Tayside Joint Police Board, 'Policing and security at the 2005 G8 summit'.

47   Baruchel and Dasilva, 'Global Civil Action Society', citing 'Legal Support Group statement on the Policing of the G8 Protests', 13 July 2005, at indymedia.org.uk.

48   CounterSpin Collective, 'Media, movement(s) and public images(s): counterpinning in Scotland', in Harvie et al., *Shut Them Down*, pp. 321–31.

49   George Monbiot, 'No way to run a revolution', 10 May 2000, at monbiot. com.

50   Meaning that ACPO members were only responsible for any liabilities of the company up to the value of their membership fee.

51   Lubbers, *Political Undercover Policing in Scotland*.

52   'Victims of police spying accuse May of cover-up', *Scotsman*, 30 July 2016.

10. The MP's Kettle

1 Mark Hughes, 'Met chief praises "astonishing" G20 police work', *Independent*, 23 April 2009.
2 Ian Dunt, 'Boris establishes G20 liberty review', at politics.co.uk.
3 'Tom Brake MP reports from inside the police cordon', 3 April 2009, at youtube.com.
4 Home Affairs Committee, Policing of the G20 Protests, 23 June 2009, evidence, Ev. 55, paras 26–33.
5 Ibid., Ev. 24, Q228.
6 Ibid., Ev. 22–5, paras 239–40.
7 Ibid., Ev. 25, Q246–8.
8 There has been some useful commentary to suggest that the police have used kettling in the past, such as against the suffragettes. While such instances amounted to restriction of free movement by the police, they were not on the scale or length of containment applied in the kettling introduced by Peter Waddington.
9 'Obituary: Professor Peter Waddington', *The Times*, 1 May 2018.
10 Ibid.
11 *ACPO Manual of Guidance on Keeping the Peace, 2001*, p. 70; *ACPO Manual 2004*, p. 117. The 2001 manual was released to the authors in December 2020 following an inquiry to the College of Policing.
12 Peter Waddington, 'At boiling point: policing and crowd control expert, Professor Peter Waddington, assesses the controversial "kettling" technique employed at the G20 conference', *Birmingham Post*, 21 April 2009.
13 Home Affairs Committee, Policing of the G20 Protests, Ev. 57, para. 42.
14 Ibid., para. 43.
15 HMIC, *Adapting to Protest: Nurturing the British Model of Policing*, 25 November 2009, p. 77.
16 Home Affairs Committee, Policing of the G20 Protests, paras 44–5.
17 Greg Foxsmith, 'Opinion: 6 lessons to be learned from the G20 policing', *Liberal Democrat Voice*, 23 April 2009.
18 Tom Whipple, 'Why did the police punish bystanders?', *The Times*, 3 April 2009.
19 Waddington, 'At boiling point'.
20 'Key people: death of Ian Tomlinson during G20 protests', BBC News, 3 May 2011, at bbc.co.uk/news.
21 Inquest: briefing on the death of Ian Tomlinson, June 2009, p. 4, para. 12.

22 Andrew Pugh, 'New claims over Tomlinson death media "cover-up"', *Press Gazette*, 9 May 2011.

23 Billy Kenber, 'Man who filmed G20 officer saw baton strike news vendor', *The Times*, 1 April 2011.

24 Paul Lewis, 'Ian Tomlinson death: *Guardian* video reveals police attack on man who died at G20 protest', *Guardian*, 7 April 2009.

25 HMIC, *Adapting to Protest*, p. 23.

26 Two years later the High Court found that the kettle at the Climate Camp was unlawful. The judgment said that the police operation to push back Climate Camp protesters was 'not necessary or proportionate ... There never was a reasonable apprehension of imminent breaches of the peace at the Climate Camp.' Vikram Dodd and Paul Lewis, 'Kettling of G20 protesters by police was illegal, high court rules', *Guardian*, 14 April 2011.

27 David Renton, 'The killing of Blair Peach', *London Review of Books*, Vol. 36, No. 10, 22 May 2014; Paul Lewis, 'Blair Peach killed by police at 1979 protest, Met report finds', *Guardian*, 27 April 2010.

28 Paul Lewis and Matthew Taylor, 'Scotland Yard riot squad faces calls to end "culture of impunity"', *Guardian*, 6 November 2009.

29 Inquest: briefing on the death of Ian Tomlinson, p. 6, para. 21.

30 Mark Sweney, 'Police apologise for obstructing photographers at G20 protest', *Guardian*, 8 April 2009.

31 Marc Vallée, 'Journalists on the G20 front line', *Guardian*, 17 April 2009.

32 *ACPO Manual of Guidance on Keeping the Peace, 2001*, p. 89.

33 'Man left needing emergency dentistry by police awarded damages', at pearldentalclinic.co.uk.

34 'Police pay £30k to photographer injured at G20', *London Evening Standard*, 8 December 2010.

35 See phnat.org.

36 Michael Savage, 'Police chief condemns G20 officers for removing ID tags', *Independent*, 22 April 2009.

37 Hansard, House of Lords, Police: Identification, 29 April 2009, Vol. 710.

38 London Assembly, MQT, ref. 2009/1752, G20 policing, 15 July 2009.

39 HMIC, *Adapting to Protest*, p. 58.

40 Home Affairs Committee, Policing of the G20 Protests, Evidence, Ev. 43.

41 Paul Lewis, 'G20 police chief accused of misleading MPs about undercover mission', *Guardian*, 24 November 2009.

42 *The Times*, 'Senior commander misled MPs about G20 undercover officers', 20 January 2011.

43 Rob Evans, 'Met bosses knew of relationship deception by spy Mark Kennedy', *Guardian*, 21 September 2018.

44 Home Affairs Committee, Policing of the G20 Protests, p. 14, para. 41.

45 *Austin and Another* v. *Commissioner of Police of the Metropolis* [2009] UKHL 5.

46 *Austin (FC) (Appellant) and Another* v. *Commissioner of Police of the Metropolis (Respondent)* [2009] UKHL 5, para. 38.

47 'European Court says "kettling" tactics in 2001 lawful', BBC News, 15 March 2012, at bbc.co.uk/news.

48 Vikram Dodd and Paul Lewis, 'Kettling of G20 protesters by police was illegal, high court rules', *Guardian*, 14 April 2011.

49 Laurie Penny, 'It was no cup of tea inside the Whitehall police kettle', *New Statesman*, 25 November 2010.

50 Ben Charlie Smoke, 'Police accused of unlawful tactics at London BLM protest', *Vice News*, 9 June 2000.

51 Companies House, ACPO Limited, accounts, 1 April 1997 to 31 March 1998, and accounts, to March 2007.

52 Rob Evans and Paul Lewis, *Undercover* (Guardian Books with Faber and Faber, 2013).

53 Joanna Gilmore, 'Policing protest: an authoritarian consensus', *Centre for Crime and Justice Studies*, 2010.

54 ACPO, memorandum of association, 2006.

55 Martin Bentham and Kiran Randhawa, 'Family fury as police escape charges over Ian Tomlinson's G20 death', *Evening Standard*, 22 July 2010.

56 Clare Dyer, 'G20 pathologist is suspended and has limits put on his future practice', *BMJ*, 6 September 2010, p. 341, col. 4869.

57 'CPS "not altering" decision over Ian Tomlinson death', BBC News, 14 October 2010, at bbc.co.uk/news.

58 Benedict Birnberg, 'Unlawful killing of Ian Tomlinson', letter, *The Times*, 6 May 2011.

59 Home Affairs Committee, Policing of the G20 Protests, Evidence, Ev. 23, p. 61.

60 'Miliband says Mandelson was wrong about the "filthy rich"', *The Times*, 28 February 2011.

61 Annie Brown, 'Rupert Murdoch's political power games exposed as documentary charts rise of media empire', *Daily Record*, 14 July 2020.

62 'Tony Blair "godfather to Rupert Murdoch's daughter"', BBC News, 28 February 2012, at bbc.co.uk/news.

63 Youssef El-Gingihy, 'The great PFI heist: the real story of how Britain's economy has been left high and dry by a doomed economic philosophy', *Independent*, 16 February 2018. For more information, see George Monbiot's *Captive State: The Corporate Takeover of Britain* (Macmillan, 2000), an excellent exposé of Labour's promotion of the PFI.

64 'Tony Blair: my job was to build on some Thatcher policies', BBC News, 8 April 2013, at bbc.co.uk/news.

65 Nigel Morris, 'Blair's "frenzied law making": a new offence for every day spent in office', *Independent*, 16 August 2006.

66 Nigel Morris and Ben Russell, 'More than 1,000 children jailed for breaching Asbos', *Independent*, 23 October 2011.

11. Charged

1 Matt Myers, *Student Revolt* (Pluto Press, 2017), p. 170, referencing YovGov, 'The student vote', 30 November 2010.

2 John Rees, 'Student revolts then and now', in Michael Bailey and Des Freedman, eds, *The Assault on Universities: A Manifesto for Resistance* (Pluto Press, 2011), p. 118.

3 Gettyimages.co.uk, Sky News/Film Image Partner, ref. 107510167.

4 Myers, *Student Revolt*, p. 68.

5 'Student protest: footage reveals storming of Millbank', *Channel 4 News*, 11 November 2010.

6 'Student protest over fees turns violent', *Guardian*, 10 November 2010.

7 Adam Gabbatt, Paul Lewis, Matthew Taylor and Rachel Williams, 'Student protests: Met under fire for charging at demonstrators', *Guardian*, 26 November 2010. Video footage on YouTube shows mounted police riding at speed into a crowd of around 1,000 protesters in London.

8 Ibid.

9 'Met deny "horse charge" at London student fees protest', BBC News, 27 November 2010, at bbc.co.uk/news.

10 Graeme Wilson, 'Police use public order law', *Student*, 1 December 1988.

11 Ibid.

12 Graeme Wilson, 'MPs condemn police action', *Student*, 1 December 1988.

13 Petter, 'London's Mounted Police', pp. 86–7.

14 TNA, HO 287/3604, Independent Police Complaints Authority news release.

15 1987 manual, Section 21, Option 10, obtained on FOI request.

16 Section 134, Serious Organised Crime and Police Act 2005.

17 Prosecutions were taken, however, against Maya Evans and Milan Rai for undertaking an unauthorised protest in October 2005, after they read aloud the names of British soldiers and Iraqi civilians killed during the conflict in Iraq, at the Cenotaph.

18 Charlie Cooper, 'He can afford fees now ... student leader gets job on £125 an hour', *Independent*, 8 September 2011.

19 Feyzi Ismail, 'The politics of occupation', in Bailey and Freedman, *The Assault on Universities*, p. 129.

20 Clare Solomon and Tania Palmieri, eds, *Springtime: The New Student Rebellions* (Verso, 2011) p. 16.

21 Peter Walker and Jonathan Paige, 'Newsblog: student protests as they happened', *Guardian*, 9 December 2010.

22 Ibid.

23 Hansard, Public Order Policing, debated Monday 13 December, Vol. 520.

24 Ibid., c. 677.

25 Prime Minister David Cameron, BBC News, 14:00, 10 December 2010.

26 Nick Carbone, 'How Time Warner profits from the "anonymous" hackers', *Time*, 29 August 2011.

27 Chris Hilliard, *The Terrace Star*, 30 November 2009, p. 6.

28 Letter to the chair from Assistant Commissioner Allison, Metropolitan Police Service, 24 January 2011, para. 119, in House of Lords, House of Commons Joint Committee on Human Rights, 'Facilitating peaceful protest', Tenth Report of Session 2010–11, HL Paper 123, HC 684, 25 March 2011, p. 33.

29 'Facilitating peaceful protest', p. 33, para. 122.

30 Sky, Rushes A4N7K86Z – N20 Student Protest Horse Charge 160835 161617.

31 'Facilitating peaceful protest', p. 19.

32 Letter to the chair from Assistant Commissioner Allison, 24 January 2011.

33 Phillip Herd, BBC News 24, 9 December 2010, 15:35.

34 BBC FOIA request, reproduced in Metropolitan Police Authority Civil Liberties Panel, *Policing Public Protest: An Update Report on the Recommendations from the CLP Review 'Responding to G20'*, January 2012, p. 46.

35 Ibid., p. 47.

36 Herd, BBC News 24, 9 December 2010.

37 Metropolitan Police response on 19 November 2011 to request of journalist Sian Ruddick.

38 Walker and Paige, 'Newsblog', *Guardian*, Caroline Davies reporting at 4:31 p.m.

39 1983 manual pages.

40 Hansard, Public Order Policing, debated Monday, 13 December 2010, Vol. 520, c. 675.

41 Peter Hallward, 'A new strategy is needed for a brutal new era', in Solomon and Palmieri, *Springtime*, p. 37.

42 Simon Israel, 'Policeman found guilty of tuition fee protest assault', *Channel 4 News*, 19 May 2015.

43 'Leveson inquiry: police and press "were too close"' (quoting Met commissioner Bernard Hogan-Howe), BBC News, 20 March 2012, at bbc.co.uk/news.

44 'Sir Paul Stephenson offered to resign over attack on Charles and Camilla', *The Times*, 12 December 2010.

45 Simon Alford, 'Met commissioner Sir Paul Stephenson resigns: Britain's most senior police officer stands down after being drawn into phone hacking scandal', *The Sunday Times*, 17 July 2011.

46 Andy Davies, 'Metropolitan Police chief Sir Paul Stephenson quits', *Channel 4 News*, 17 July 2011.

47 Nadine El-Enany, 'Keir Starmer's troubling guidelines on protester prosecution', *Guardian*, 7 March 2012.

48 Muhbeen Hussain, 'The 12 Pakistani men from Rotherham you probably haven't heard about', *Independent*, 14 February 2018.

49 Prime Minister David Cameron, BBC News, 14:00, 10 December 2010.

12. State of Play

1 Hassan Mahamdallie, *Crossing the 'River of Fire': The Socialism of William Morris* (Redwords, 2008), pp. 59–60.

2 William Morris, *Poems of Protest* (Redwords, 2013), p. 47.

3 Andrew Rosen, *Rise Up Women* (Routledge & Kegan Paul Ltd, 1974), pp. 138–40.

4 TNA, HO 325/3375; and Companies House, the Association of Chief Police Officers of England, Wales and Northern Ireland, Memorandum of Association, 2006. Financial Statements for the year ended 31 March 2007.

5   TNA, HO 287/4572/2, memo from J. A. Chilcott, 4 November 1988.

6   Obituary, Peter Wright, *Guardian*, 27 September 2011.

7   Obituary, Peter Wright, *Daily Telegraph*, 14 October 2011.

8   TNA, HO 325/523, meeting note, 21 April 1982.

9   TNA, HO 325/452, meeting note, 4 August 1981.

10 TNA, HO 287/3375, draft letter from Sir Brian Cubbon, 17 April 1986.

11 Ibid.

12 TNA, HO 325/902, memo, 16 November 1984.

13 Jacob Jarvis, 'Extinction Rebellion protests: police "determined" to move activists as Oxford Circus is reopened and arrests top 750', *London Evening Standard*, 20 April 2019.

14 Andrea Germanos, '"Vindication" for climate activists as UK court rules London ban on Extinction Rebellion protests unlawful', *Common Dreams*, 6 November 2019, at commondreams.org.

15 'Lawyer in the news: Jules Carey, Bindmans', *Law Society Gazette*, 25 November 2019; Owen Bowcott, 'Charges dropped against more than 100 Extinction Rebellion protesters', *Guardian*, 27 November 2019.

16 Peter Geoghegan and Jenna Corderoy, 'Exclusive: police chief urged Priti Patel to use Extinction Rebellion "opportunity" to curb protest rights', *openDemocracy*, 4 June 2020, at opendemocracy.net.

17 Ibid.

18 Vikram Dodd, 'Black people nine times more likely to face stop and search than white', *Guardian*, 27 October 2020.

19 Vikram Dodd, 'How Stephen Lawrence and his family jolted a nation's conscience', *Guardian*, 3 January 2012.

20 Krishnan Guru-Murthy, 'Met Police commissioner Cressida Dick responds to institutional racism claims', *Channel 4 News*, 13 August 2020.

21 Netpol, *Britain Is Not Innocent*, 2020, p. 20.

22 Ibid., p. 21.

23 Ibid., p. 3.

24 Michael Etienne, 'Policing during the pandemic: an insight into racism in the UK', *OpenDemocracy*, at opendemocracy.net.

25 TNA, HO 325/324, briefing note for Public Order Liaison Group meeting, 13 October 1982.

26 Peirce, 'How they rewrote the law at Orgreave'.

27 HO response to 2016 FOI request.

28 College of Policing, at app.college.police.uk.

29 Tom Wall and Damian Gayle, 'Police accused of using shields as weapons at Bristol "kill the bill" protests', *Guardian*, 30 March 2021.

30 Tom Wall, '"It was humiliating": police apologise for handcuffing undressed student in raid', *Guardian*, 17 July 2021.

31 Vikram Dodd and Jamie Grierson, 'Terrorism police list Extinction Rebellion as extremist ideology', *Guardian*, 10 January 2020; Vikram Dodd and Jamie Grierson, 'Greenpeace included with neo-Nazis on UK counter-terror list', *Guardian*, 17 January 2020.

32 Jennifer Brown and Sally Lipscombe, House of Commons Library, 'Briefing paper: Police, Crime, Sentencing and Courts Bill: Part 3 and 4, Public Order and Unauthorised Encampments', 12 March 2021, p. 3.

33 Mark Towsend, 'Priti Patel "misled" MPs over plans for protest crackdown', *Observer*, 18 July 2021.

34 Rajeev Syal, 'Did Patel step over the line in urging pursuit of defendants?', *Guardian*, 6 January 2022.

35 Suyin Haynes, 'London police's treatment of women at a vigil prompted fury. Campaigners say a reckoning is overdue', *Time Magazine*, 16 March 2021; Sadiq Khan, Twitter account, 13 March 2021.

36 Peter Walker, Jessica Elgot and Vikram Dodd, 'Priti Patel spoke to Met chief before Sarah Everard vigil broken up', *Guardian*, 15 March 2021.

37 Vikram Dodd and Jamie Grierson, 'Priti Patel wanted Police to stop people gathering at Sarah Everard vigil', *Guardian*, 19 March 2021.

38 Jack Peat, 'Met Police officers "acted appropriately" at Clapham Common vigil', *London Economic*, 30 March 2021.

39 George Monbiot video, Twitter Extinction Rebellion UK, 6 November 2019.

40 Harry Shukman, 'Stay away from big Black Lives Matter rallies, Matt Hancock urges', *The Times*, 6 June 2020.

Index

Adams, Rolan 133
Adams, Nathan 133
Adie, Kate 94, 96
Allen, Kate 263
Armstrong, Frank 223
Asquith, Herbert 256
Auld, Richard 113
Austin, Lois 132, 140, 143, 156

Bailey, John 83, 102
Balls, Ed 241
Barker, John 149–51, 153, 154
Bartle, Ronald 104–5
Beackon, Derek 132, 156
Bell, Steve 148
Benn, Tony 3–4, 58, 81, 83, 87, 112, 169–70
Bennett, Weyman 163, 164–5, 168
Bent, Tracey 122–3
Biggs, John 235
Bishop, Jason 199
Black, George 187
Blair, Ian 175
Blair, Tony 161–2, 179, 180–1, 192, 196, 200, 206, 227, 229
Blakey, David 176
Blenkin, Hugh 136–7, 138, 141, 143–4, 145, 147, 148, 149–50, 153–4
Blowe, Kevin 267

Bolton, Tanya 202–4
Bourne, Colin 13–14, 16, 18, 19, 24, 32
Bowden, John 94
Bragg, Billy 144
Brake, Tom 212–13, 216–17, 222–3
Brittan, Leon 25, 28, 31, 42, 45, 59, 63, 76
Broadhurst, Bob 222–4, 249
Brockway, Fenner (Lord) xii
Brooks, Duwayne 133
Brooks, Rebekah 182
Broomhead, Russell 54
Brown, Gordon 50, 211, 229
Buck, Karen 214–15
Burke, Michael 169
Burke, Tony 15, 28, 36

Cameron, David 81, 82, 242, 254
Campbell, Duncan 132
Carey, Jules 262
Caulfield, Bernard 34
Chambers, Douglas 89
Clarke, Kenneth 82, 133
Clay, Robert 22–3
Clegg, Nick 229, 234
Clement, Anthony 3, 40, 41, 51–2, 55–8, 64
Clothier, Cecil 98

Clwyd, Ann 236
Coleman, Clive 225–6
Condon, Paul 96, 136–8, 142, 144, 147–8, 151–2, 153, 154, 155, 181
Conlon, Gerry 77
Conn, David 50–1
Corbyn, Jeremy 112, 157, 168–70, 174
Corrigan, Harry 47
Cotton, Chez 184, 188–9, 213
Coulson, Andy 82
Cowling, Jeffrey 247–8
Crichlow, Frank 147
Critchlow, Arthur 64–5
Cubbon, Brian 31, 49–50, 64, 259
Cullen, Richard 169–70, 171, 174
Curran, Frances 198
Curtis, Polly 239–40

Davies, Nick 68–9, 72, 73–5
Dean, Brenda 95
Delaney, Michael 88–90
Dennis, Mark xi
Devlin, Bernadette xii
Dias, Dexter 117–18
Dick, Cressida 262–4, 269
Dixon-Payne, Richard 19, 22, 23, 32
Dobson, Gary 154
Donaldson, John 33
Douglas, Brian 147
Douglas, Wayne 147
Dowler, Milly 81, 280 n. 78
Dubbins, Tony 18, 98
Duggal, Rohit 133
Dunt, Ian 159

Edmunds, Richard 132
Elton, Rodney (Lord) 8, 25, 76
Etienne, Michael 265
Evans, Dave 199
Evans, Maya 306 n. 17
Evans, Rob 224
Everard, Sarah ix, 269

Fenn, George 28–9, 31–2, 35
Ferres, Robert Shirley (Earl) 159

Field, Ann 101–2
Floyd, George 226, 264
Foot, Michael 161
Foot, Paul 152
Fox, Colin 202
Foxsmith, Greg 217
Francis, Peter 146, 155
Franklin, Maria 237
Friedman, Rhona 237

Gardner, Joy 147
Gately, Kevin xi, 145
Geldof, Bob 196
George, Malcolm 176
Gifford, Tony (Lord) 79, 99
Godwin, Tim 223
Goldsmith, Walter 34
Gordon, Mick 185
Granfield, Owen 22, 26
Grant, Sam 268
Greene, Tim 75, 78
Greenman, Leon 139
Greenwood, Ernie 94
Grundy, Lionel 68–71, 73, 76, 77, 258

Hall, David 61
Hallward, Peter 250–1
Halpin, Harry 208
Hanney, Roy 117–18
Harris, Toby (Lord of Haringey) 160, 183, 188
Harris, John (Lord of Greenwich) 160
Harwood, Andrew 228
Hatfield, Richard P. 30
Havers, Michael 39, 45, 278 n. 26
Haw, Brian 238
Hawley, Carol 249
Herd, Phillip 248–9
Heseltine, Michael 108, 128
Hicks, Mike 90
Hilliard, Andrew 242–8, 253
Hilliard, Chris 242–8, 253
Hilliard, Jennifer 245–8
Hoffman, David 220–1

Hope, David (Lord Hope of Craighead) 225
Horsfall, Jill 253
Howard, Michael 160–2, 180
Hudson, Derek 94
Hurd, Douglas 75, 76, 85, 87, 96, 98, 102, 104

Ibbotson, Johnny 20
Imbert, Peter 97, 104, 105, 110, 112, 258

Jackson, Bernard 41–2, 51
Jackson, Mike xiii
Jerrom, George 18
Johnson, Boris 212, 221, 238, 252
Johnson, Michael 246
Jones, Jenny 188
Jones, Wyn 86–8, 91, 92, 95, 98, 100, 285 n. 23
Jordan, Frank 35

Kamlish, Stephen 152–3
Kendrick, David 170–4, 295 n. 32
Kennedy, Mark (alias Mark 'Flash' Stone) 200, 208, 224
Key, Robert 73
Khan, Imran 148, 153
Khan, Sadiq 156, 189, 269
King, Paul 94, 96
Kinnock, Neil 27, 127
Kitson, Frank xii–xii

La Jaunie, Christopher 219
Lambert, Bob 99
Lammy, David 250
Lapite, Shiji 147
Lawrence, Doreen xiv, 148–55
Lawrence, Neville xiv, 148–55
Lawrence, Stephen xiv, 148–55, 258
Leighton, Ron 103
Lewis, Paul 224
Linnell, Alfred 256
Livingstone, Ken 183
Lodge, Alan (Tash) 69, 70

MacGregor, Ian 44
MacKenzie, Kelvin 82, 83
Macpherson, William 148–55, 264
Major, John 128, 157, 158–9
Malik, Shiv 249
Mandela, Nelson 148, 196
Mansfield, Michael 3, 55, 57–8, 150, 162, 179
Matthews, Susan 233, 249
May, Theresa xiv, 208, 224, 240–2
Masterman, Len 53, 55
McCarroll, Patrick 46–8, 52–3
McCarthy, Kerry 241–2
McCluskey, John (Lord) 48–9
McConnell, Jack 198
McGahey, Mick 49
McGoran, Katie 267
McLaughlin, Benny 236
Meadows, Alfie viii, 233, 249
Metcalfe, John 116, 118–21, 125–6, 266
Meynell, David 107, 109–12, 117, 119, 120–1, 123–4
Mitchell, Alistair 118
Monbiot, George 207, 270
Montgomery, Fergus 26–7, 275 n. 33
Moore, Andrew 87
Morgan, Piers 82
Morris, David 294 n. 22
Morris, William 256
Mullin, Chris 105
Murdoch, Rupert 31, 81–105, 180–1, 182, 229, 260, 261, 280 n. 78

Neil, Andrew 25, 28, 30–1, 34, 37, 101, 102
Neillist, Dave 112
Newman, Kenneth 6–7, 37, 85, 96, 100
Norris, David 154
Northam, Gerry 5–6

O'Connor, John 211
O'Driscoll, Dónal 191
Oghweh, Venus 270

Osland, David 141–2, 144–5, 147–50,
152–3, 154
Ott, Andrew 251
Oxford, Kenneth 4–5

Paddick, Brian 235
Pascall, David 43
Patel, Freddy 218, 228
Patel, Priti 255, 262, 263, 269
Patten, Chris 120
Peach, Blair xi, 145, 219, 290 n. 24
Peirce, Gareth 4, 40–1, 58, 61, 266
Penman, Danny 165–6
Petter, Andy 93
Pilger, John 196–7
Platt, Stephen 139–42, 146
Porter, Aaron 238
Primarolo, Dawn 121
Puddephatt, Andrew 161

Rai, Milan 306 n. 17
Ramm, Ray 117
Readhead, Ian 73, 77, 79
Rees, Merlyn 43–4, 50
Rehman, Asad 166
Reynolds, Simon 157–8
Ridley, Nicholas 43, 127, 278 n. 13
Roberts, Fiona 116
Rollin, Joe 168
Rose, David 118
Rosenberg, Chanie 196
Royston, Alan 13, 14, 15, 18, 20, 21,
36, 275 n. 18
Runacres, Mark 267

Sabido, Kim 70–3, 74
Saxby, Geoffrey 187, 298 n. 32
Scargill, Arthur 49, 50, 51, 54, 60, 83
Scarman, Leslie (Lord) xi, 4–7, 56,
57, 113
Sey, Ibrahima 147
Shah, Eddy 13–37, 182, 261, 274 n. 3
Shaw, Giles 81, 87, 266
Siblon, John 134, 143

Sim, Sue 214, 228
Smith, Donald 69
Smith, Linda 124–5
Smith, Terry 82–3, 93, 94
Soley, Clive 87–8, 266
Solomon, Clare 239
Speed, Tony 170, 236
Stamper, Norman ('Norm') 192
Starmer, Keir 103, 162, 189, 225, 228,
244, 253, 294 n. 22
Steel, Helen 294 n. 22
Stephenson, Mary-Ann 164, 167–8
Stephenson, Paul 211, 212, 221, 222,
233, 234, 235, 251–2, 260–1
Stevens, John 181–2, 183, 260
Stone, Richard 151
Straw, Jack 148, 183, 187, 188, 227
Sylvester, Roger 147

Taylor, Frank 62
Tebbit, Norman 108
Thatcher, Margaret xiii, 2, 19, 27, 30,
37, 39, 42–6, 49, 50, 60–1, 62–4,
78, 85, 99–101, 102, 107–9, 112,
115–16, 127–8, 158–9, 229, 257
Thompson, Emma 262
Thompson, Peter 133
Thorne, John 54
Tomalin, Claire 101
Tomlinson, Ian xi, 217–20, 228, 235
Travis, Alan 179–80
Turnbull, Andrew 60–1, 112

Vaughan, Les 68
Vaz, Keith 228
Vine, John 192, 193–4, 198–9, 206

Waddington, David 98–9, 111, 113
Waddington, Peter 186–7, 215–17,
220, 226–7, 302 n. 8
Wallis, Neil 181–2, 252
Waterson, Julie 131, 138, 156
Watson, Lynn 199
Waugh, Auberon 161

Weedon, Brian 149–50
West, Alan (Lord West of Spithead) 221
Whitehead, Bruce 196
Whitelaw, William 2–8, 25, 43, 59, 100, 155
Williams, Shirley 211
Windsor, Charles (Prince) 240, 251

Windsor, Camilla (Duchess) 240
Woodward, Shaun 181
Wright, Barry 203
Wright, Peter 49–50, 64, 258
Wyatt, Woodrow 85, 101
Wyrko, David 96, 100–1

Zahir, Hossein 131–2, 139